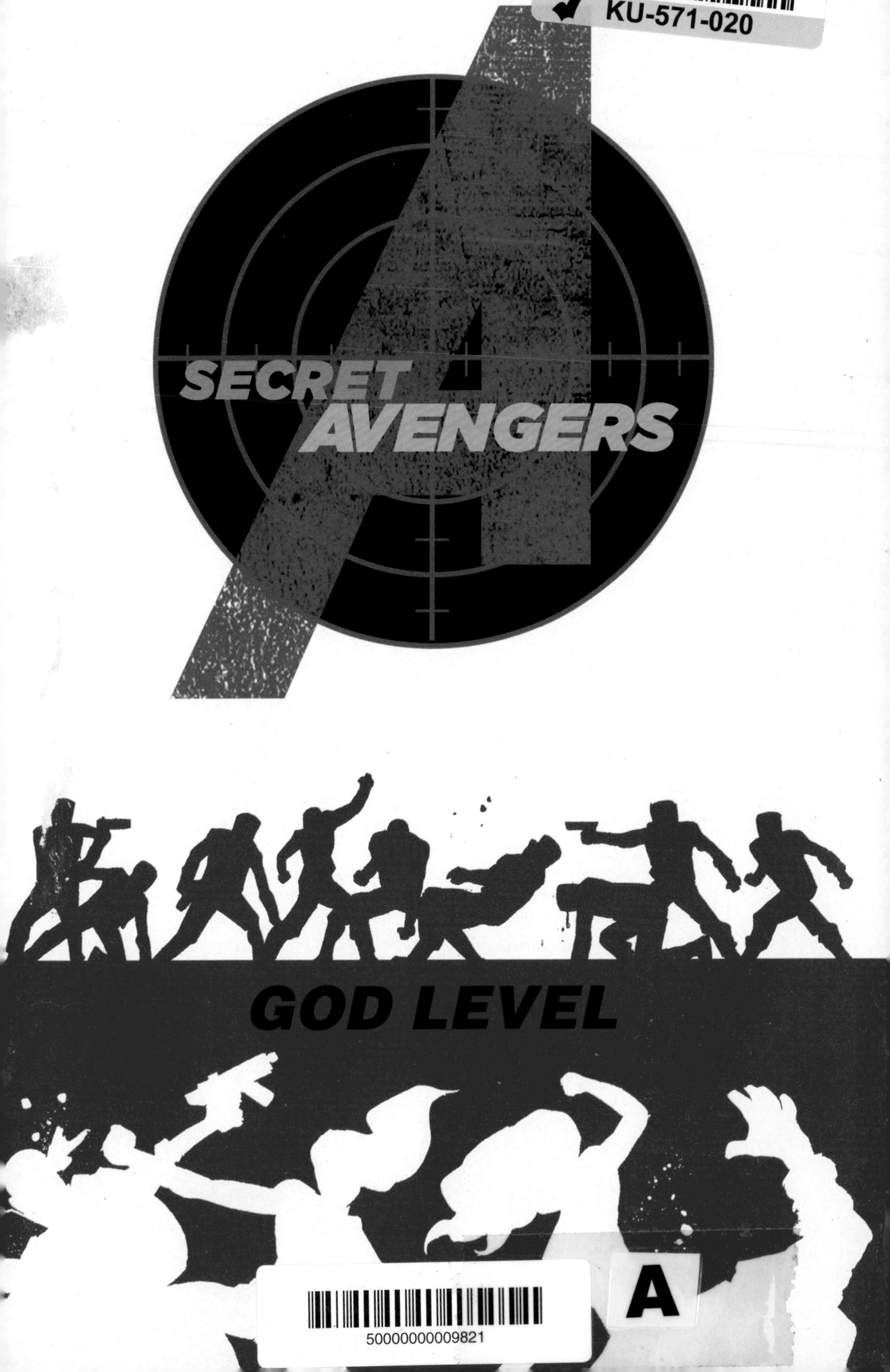
SECRET
AVENGERS
GOD LEVEL

COLLECTION EDITOR: **JENNIFER GRÜNWALD**
ASSISTANT EDITOR: **SARAH BRUNSTAD**
ASSOCIATE MANAGING EDITOR: **ALEX STARBUCK**
EDITOR, SPECIAL PROJECTS: **MARK D. BEAZLEY**
SENIOR EDITOR, SPECIAL PROJECTS: **JEFF YOUNGQUIST**
SVP PRINT, SALES & MARKETING: **DAVID GABRIEL**
BOOK DESIGNER: **RODOLFO MURAGUCHI**

EDITOR IN CHIEF: **AXEL ALONSO**
CHIEF CREATIVE OFFICER: **JOE QUESADA**
PUBLISHER: **DAN BUCKLEY**
EXECUTIVE PRODUCER: **ALAN FINE**

SECRET AVENGERS VOL. 3: GOD LEVEL. Contains material originally published in magazine form as SECRET AVENGERS #11-15. First printing 2015. ISBN# 978-0-7851-9710-2. Published by MARVEL WORLDWIDE INC., a subsidiary of MARVEL ENTERTAINMENT, LLC. OFFICE OF PUBLICATION: 135 West 50th Street, New York, NY 10020. Copyright © 2015 MARVEL No similarity between any of the names, characters, persons and/or institutions in this magazine with those of any living or dead person or institution is intended, and any such similarity which may exist is purely coincidental. **Printed in Canada.** ALAN FINE, President, Marvel Entertainment; DAN BUCKLEY, President, TV, Publishing and Brand Management; JOE QUESADA, Chief Creative Officer; TOM BREVOORT, SVP of Publishing; DAVID BOGART, SVP of Operations & Procurement, Publishing; C.B. CEBULSKI, VP of International Development & Brand Management; DAVID GABRIEL, SVP Print, Sales & Marketing; JIM O'KEEFE, VP of Operations & Logistics; DAN CARR, Executive Director of Publishing Technology; SUSAN CRESPI, Editorial Operations Manager; ALEX MORALES, Publishing Operations Manager; STAN LEE, Chairman Emeritus. For information regarding advertising in Marvel Comics or on Marvel.com, please contact Jonathan Rheingold, VP of Custom Solutions & Ad Sales, at jrheingold@marvel.com. For Marvel subscription inquiries, please call 800-217-9158. **Manufactured between 5/1/2015 and 6/8/2015 by SOLISCO PRINTERS, SCOTT, QC, CANADA.**

10 9 8 7 6 5 4 3 2 1

RUN THE MISSION. DON'T GET SEEN.
SAVE THE WORLD.

S.H.I.E.L.D. Director Maria Hill has assembled a covert squad of heroes she calls the Secret Avengers — Black Widow, Spider-Woman, Hawkeye, S.H.I.E.L.D. agents Nick Fury and Phil Coulson, and M.O.D.O.K., a (former?) terrorist Hill hired to create new technologies for S.H.I.E.L.D.

And now everything is falling apart. After realizing that M.O.D.O.K. had betrayed her, Director Hill brought his assistant Snapper in for interrogation...only for him to reveal that a covert team of terrorists had infiltrated the Helicarrier.

And how exactly were they able to sneak aboard? It probably had something to do with the fact that Nick Fury has been in the hospital after a near-fatal acid attack that was meant for Agent Coulson. And Agent Coulson? He's been M.I.A. That is, until Hawkeye managed to find him and confront him. To further complicate things, M.O.D.O.K. appeared to tell them both that he had the answer to all their problems. And answer that almost assuredly involved the mysterious world of Tlön...

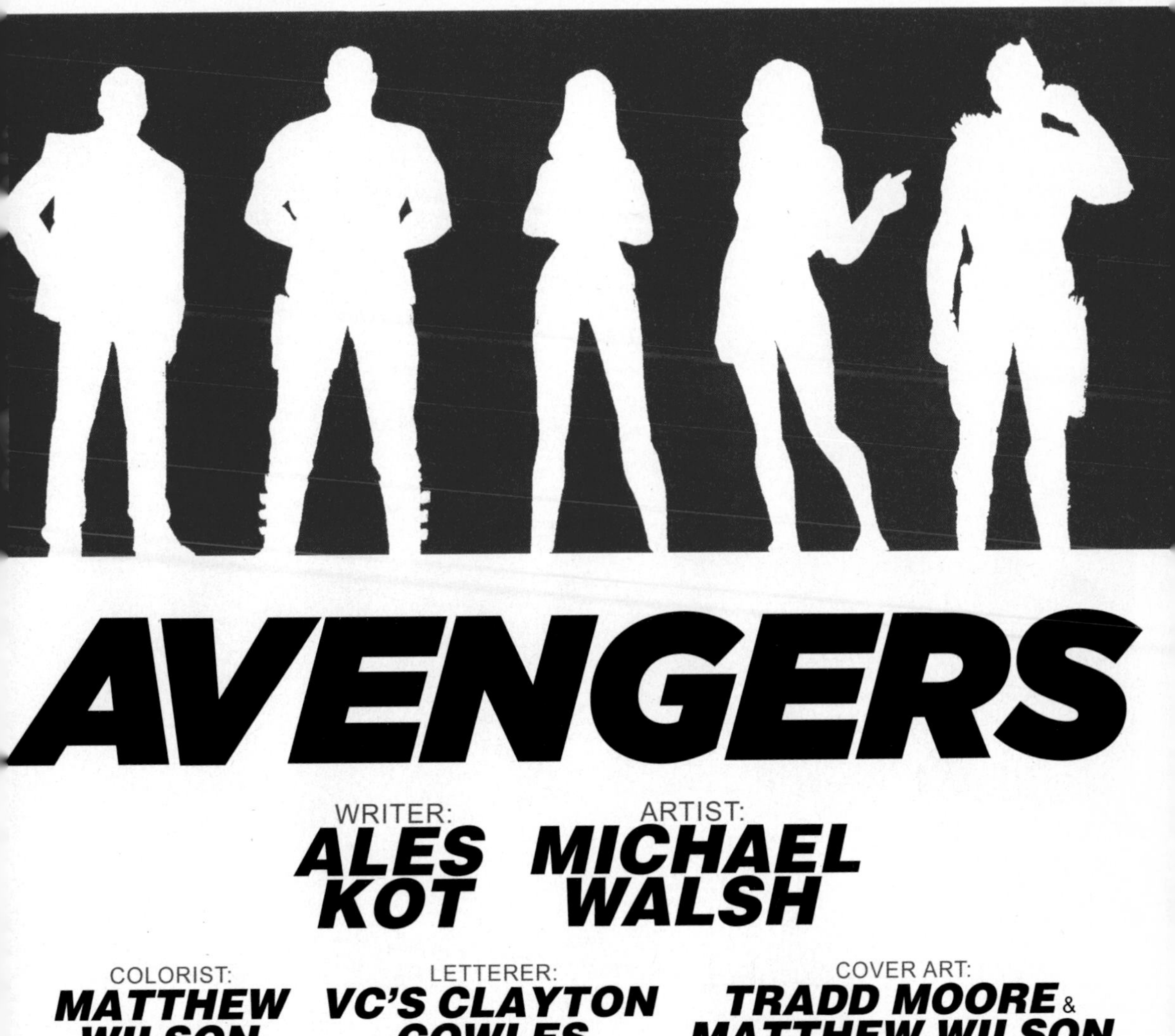

AVENGERS

WRITER:
ALES KOT

ARTIST:
MICHAEL WALSH

COLORIST:
MATTHEW WILSON

LETTERER:
VC'S CLAYTON COWLES

COVER ART:
TRADD MOORE & MATTHEW WILSON

ASSISTANT EDITOR:
JON MOISAN

EDITOR:
WIL MOSS

EXECUTIVE EDITOR:
TOM BREVOORT

AVENGERS CREATED BY STAN LEE & JACK KIRBY

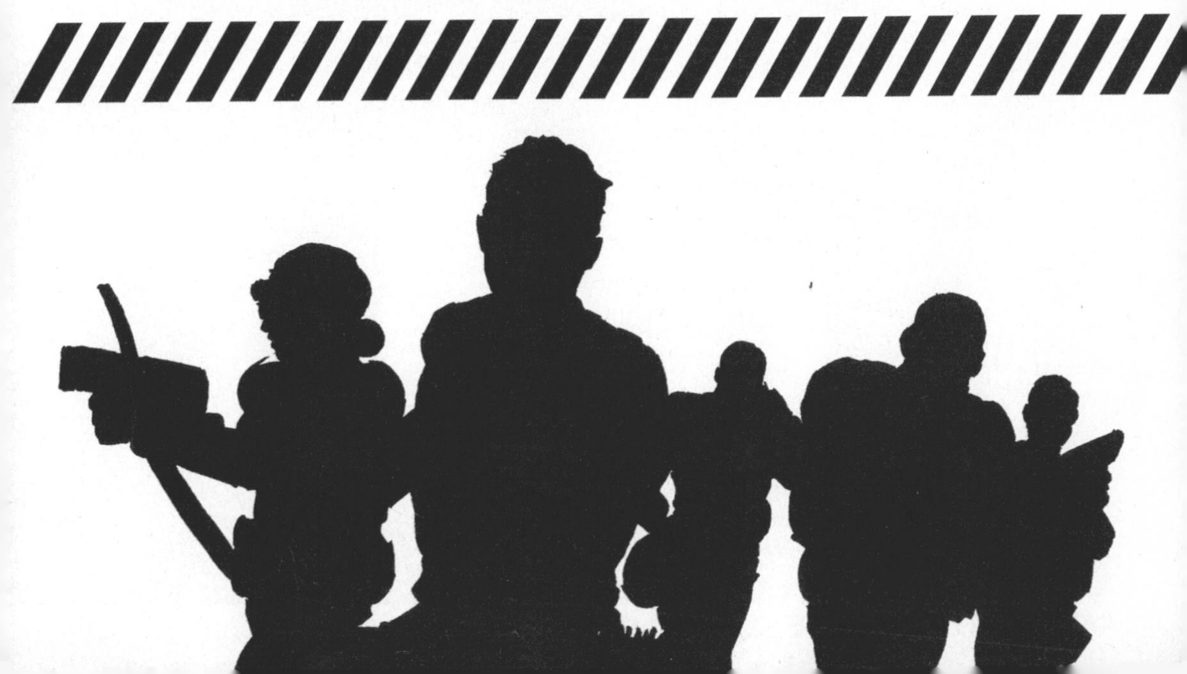

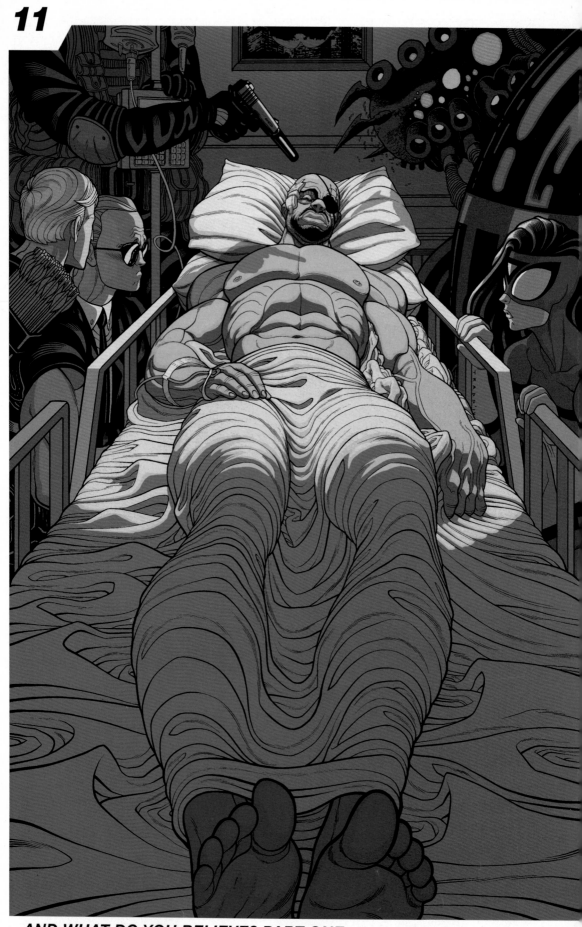

...AND WHAT DO YOU BELIEVE? PART ONE

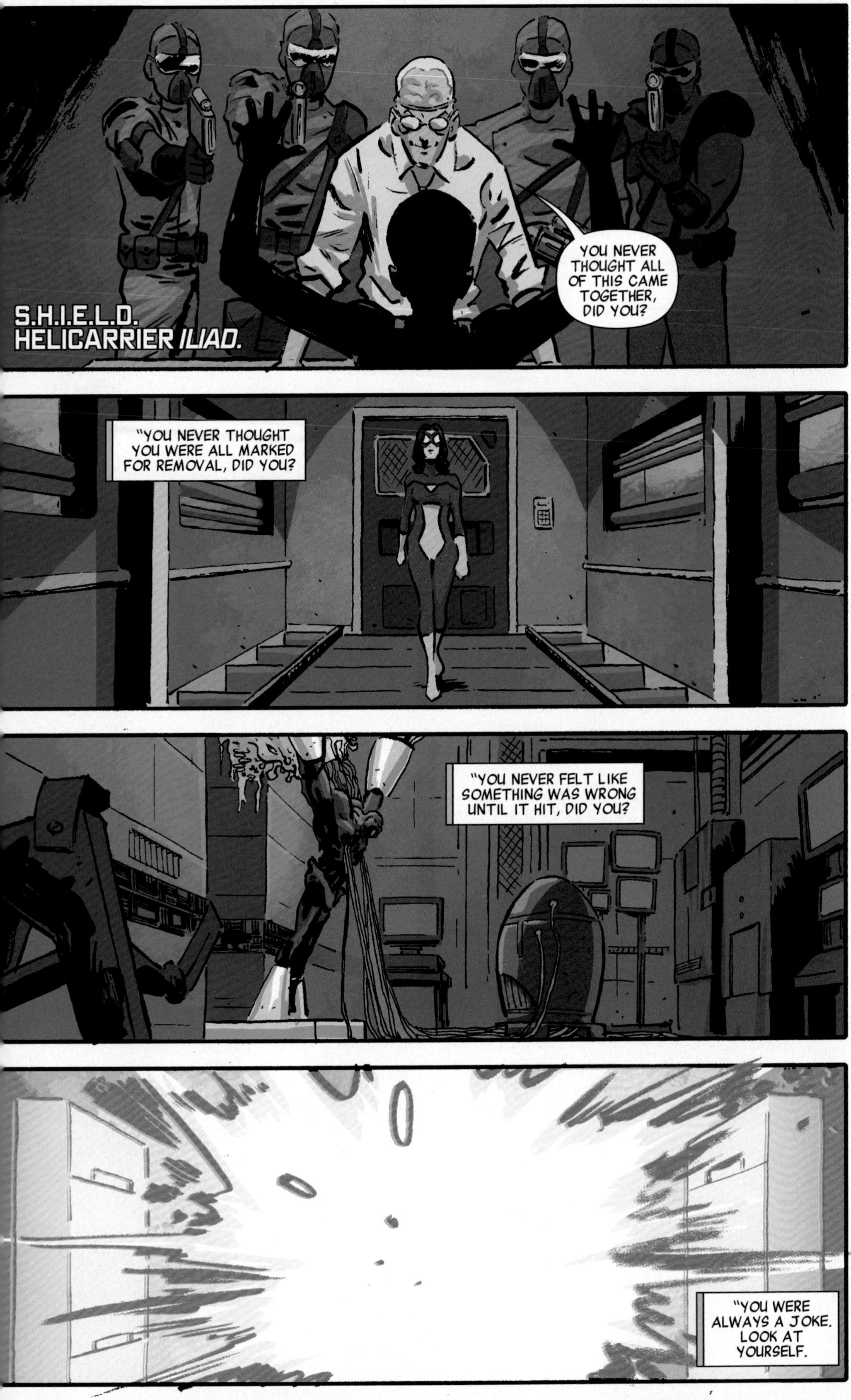
S.H.I.E.L.D. HELICARRIER ILIAD.
YOU NEVER THOUGHT ALL OF THIS CAME TOGETHER, DID YOU?
"YOU NEVER THOUGHT YOU WERE ALL MARKED FOR REMOVAL, DID YOU?
"YOU NEVER FELT LIKE SOMETHING WAS WRONG UNTIL IT HIT, DID YOU?
"YOU WERE ALWAYS A JOKE. LOOK AT YOURSELF.

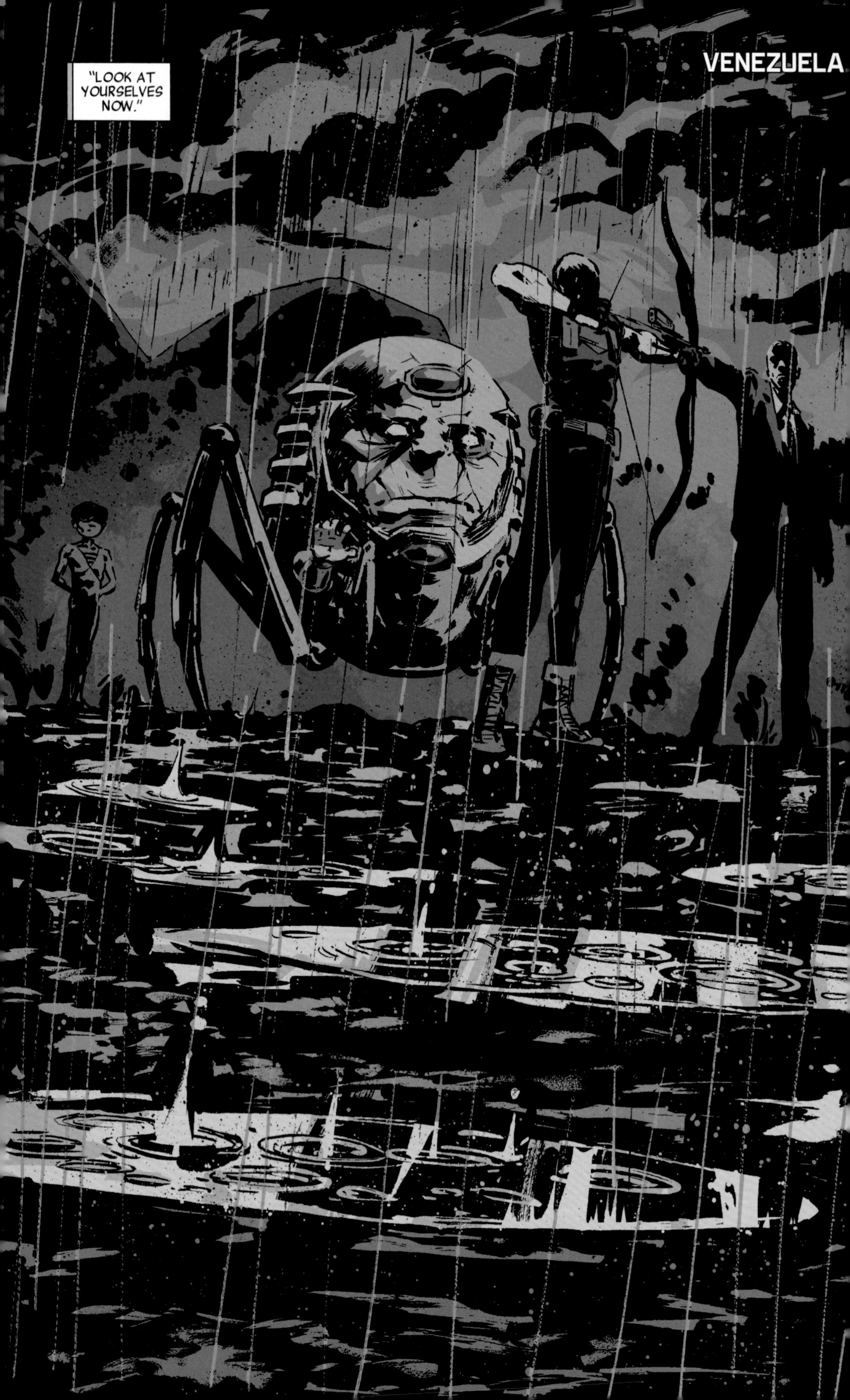
"LOOK AT YOURSELVES NOW."
VENEZUELA

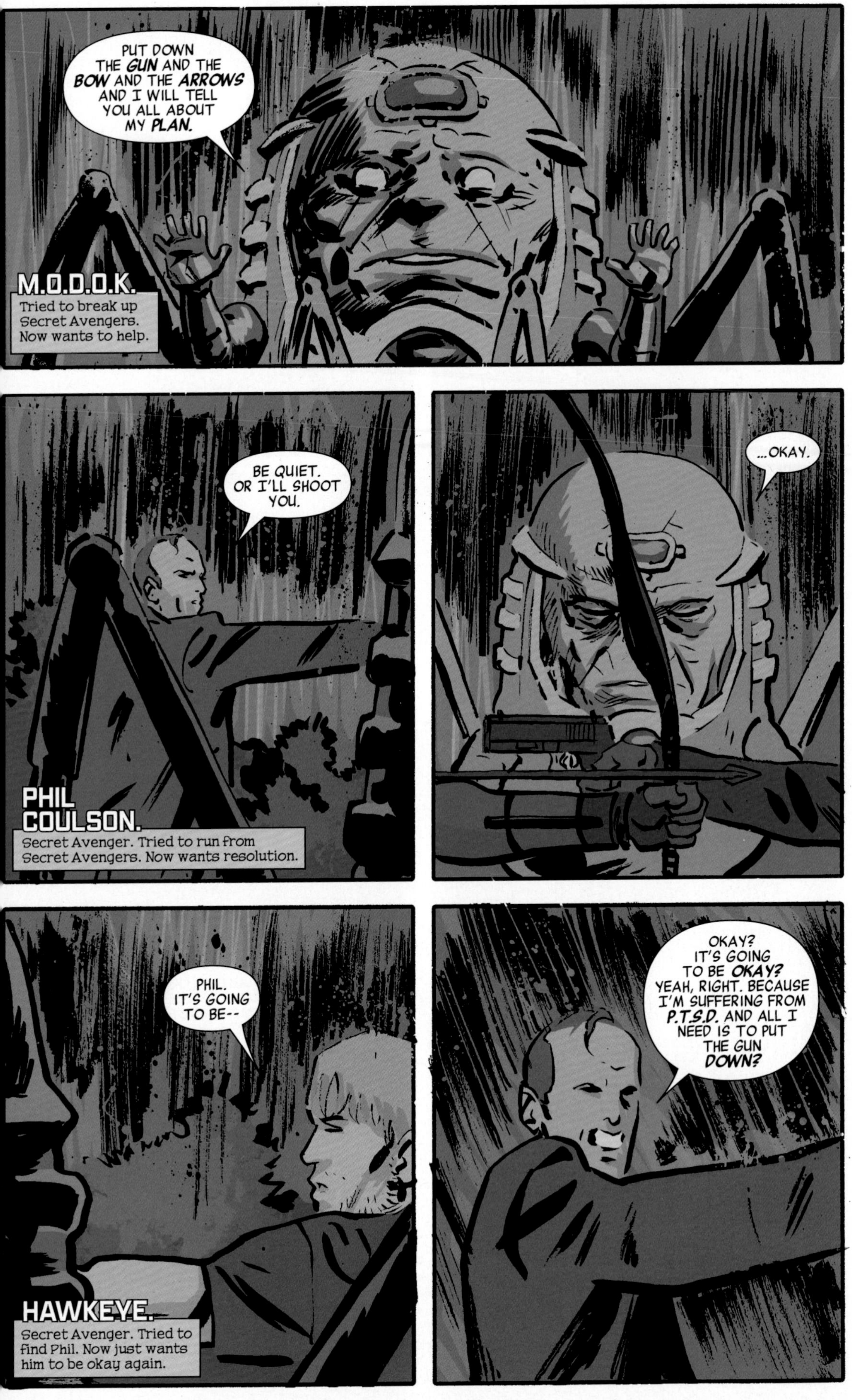
PUT DOWN THE GUN AND THE BOW AND THE ARROWS AND I WILL TELL YOU ALL ABOUT MY PLAN.
M.O.D.O.K.
Tried to break up Secret Avengers. Now wants to help.
BE QUIET. OR I'LL SHOOT YOU.
PHIL COULSON.
Secret Avenger. Tried to run from Secret Avengers. Now wants resolution.
...OKAY.
PHIL. IT'S GOING TO BE--
HAWKEYE.
Secret Avenger. Tried to find Phil. Now just wants him to be okay again.
OKAY? IT'S GOING TO BE OKAY? YEAH, RIGHT. BECAUSE I'M SUFFERING FROM P.T.S.D. AND ALL I NEED IS TO PUT THE GUN DOWN?

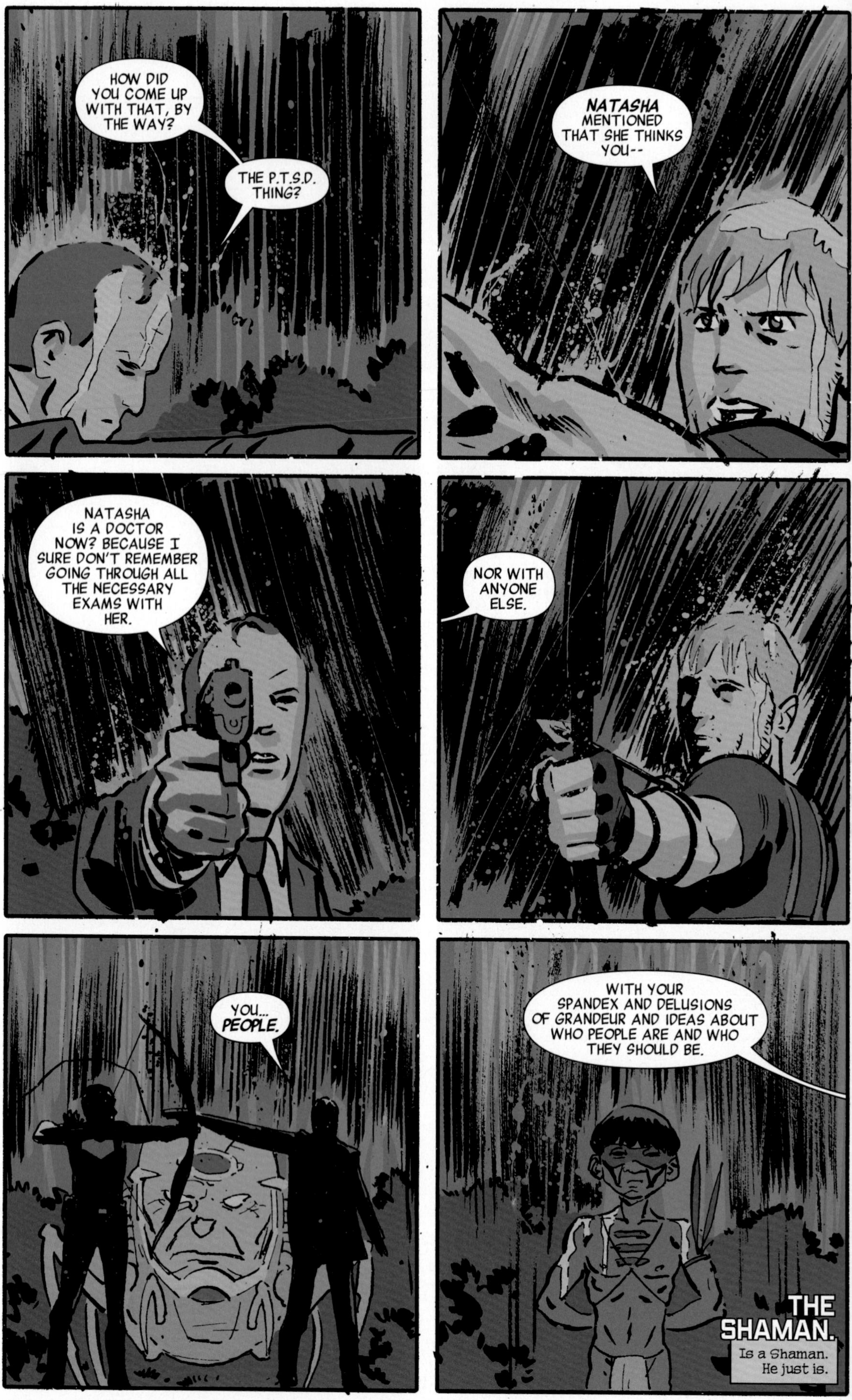
HOW DID YOU COME UP WITH THAT, BY THE WAY?
THE P.T.S.D. THING?
NATASHA MENTIONED THAT SHE THINKS YOU--
NATASHA IS A DOCTOR NOW? BECAUSE I SURE DON'T REMEMBER GOING THROUGH ALL THE NECESSARY EXAMS WITH HER.
NOR WITH ANYONE ELSE.
YOU... PEOPLE.
WITH YOUR SPANDEX AND DELUSIONS OF GRANDEUR AND IDEAS ABOUT WHO PEOPLE ARE AND WHO THEY SHOULD BE.
THE SHAMAN.
Is a Shaman. He just is.

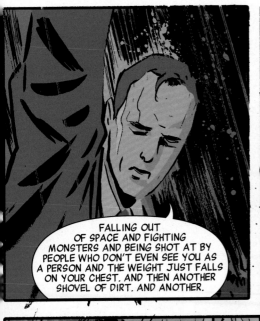

NO ONE PREPARES YOU FOR THIS. *NO ONE.* I TRIED TO TAKE IT EASY AND MAKE FUN OF IT AND DO MY JOB AND BE GOOD TO PEOPLE AND I DON'T EVEN KNOW WHAT I'M SUPPOSED TO DO BECAUSE *THIS #$%£ STICKS.*

IT *STICKS* TO US.

FALLING OUT OF SPACE AND FIGHTING MONSTERS AND BEING SHOT AT BY PEOPLE WHO DON'T EVEN SEE YOU AS A PERSON AND THE WEIGHT JUST FALLS ON YOUR CHEST. AND THEN ANOTHER SHOVEL OF DIRT. AND ANOTHER.

PHIL. YOU ARE RIGHT. WE DON'T KNOW WHAT HAPPENED.

BUT YOU CAN SEE THAT YOU ARE AT LEAST DISTURBED. YOU CAN SEE THAT, CAN'T YOU?

WHAT IF HILL TOLD YOU TO KILL ME?

WHAT?

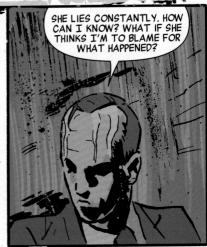

SHE LIES CONSTANTLY. HOW CAN I KNOW? WHAT IF SHE THINKS I'M TO BLAME FOR WHAT HAPPENED?

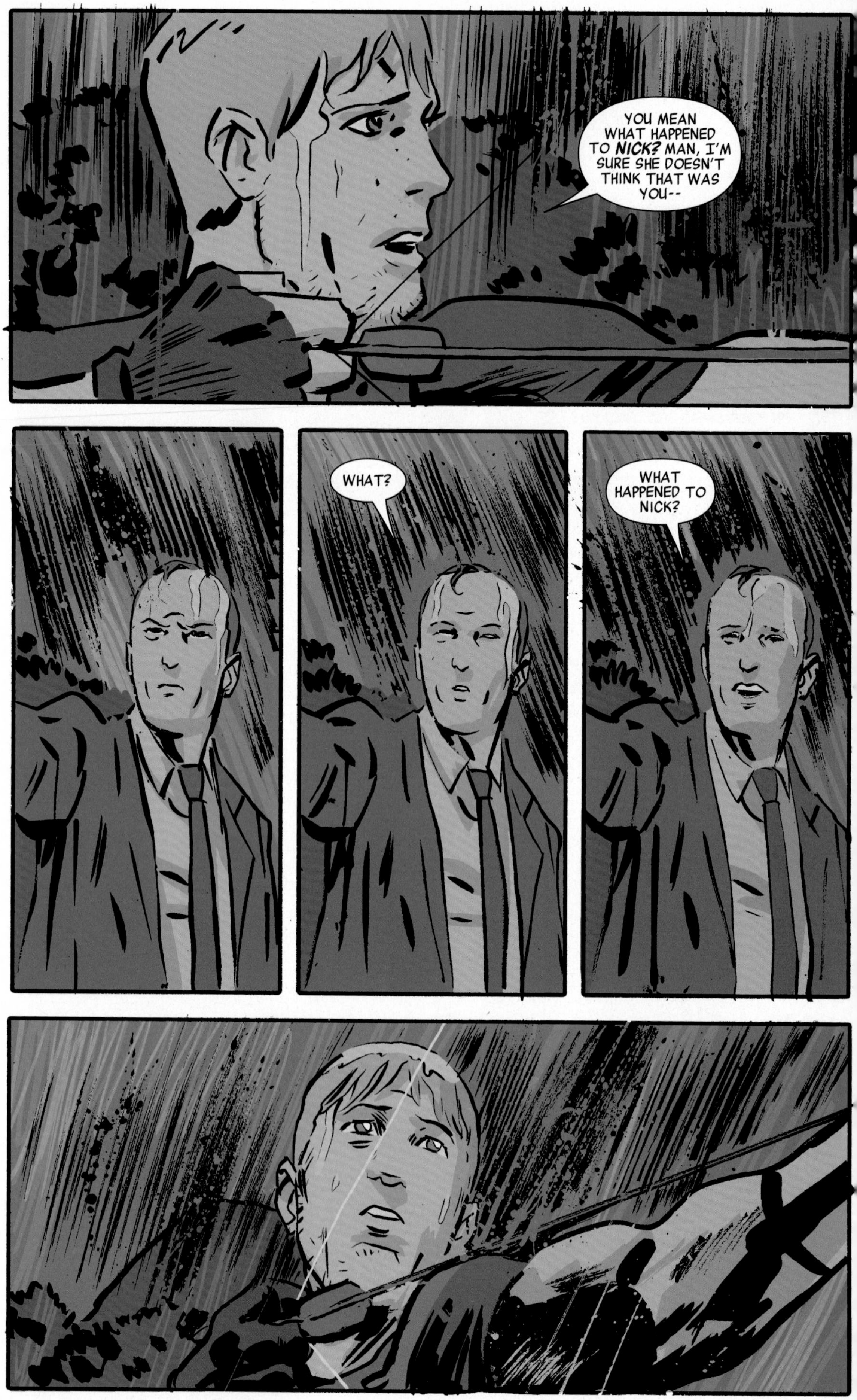
YOU MEAN WHAT HAPPENED TO NICK? MAN, I'M SURE SHE DOESN'T THINK THAT WAS YOU--
WHAT?
WHAT HAPPENED TO NICK?

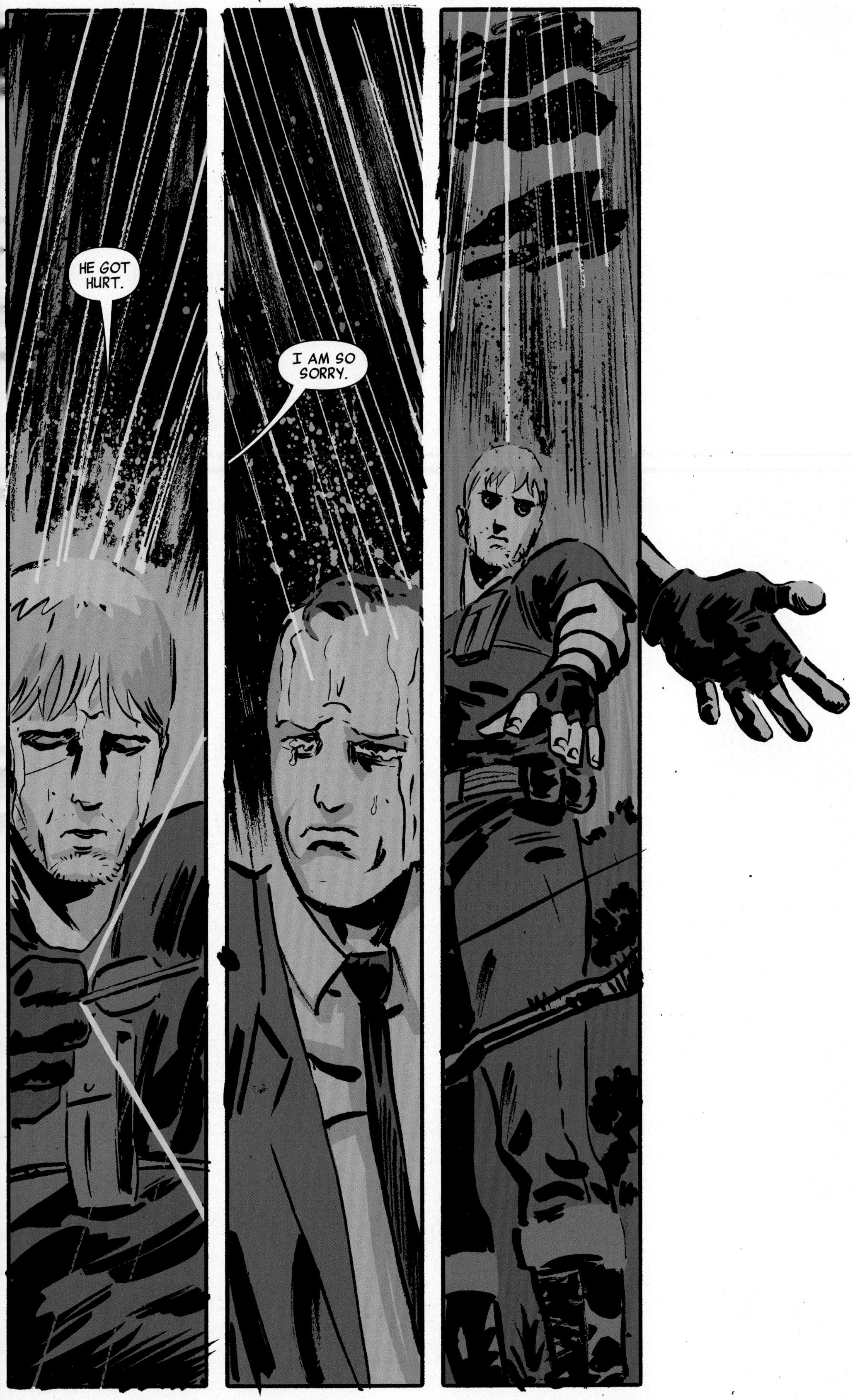
HE GOT HURT.
I AM SO SORRY.

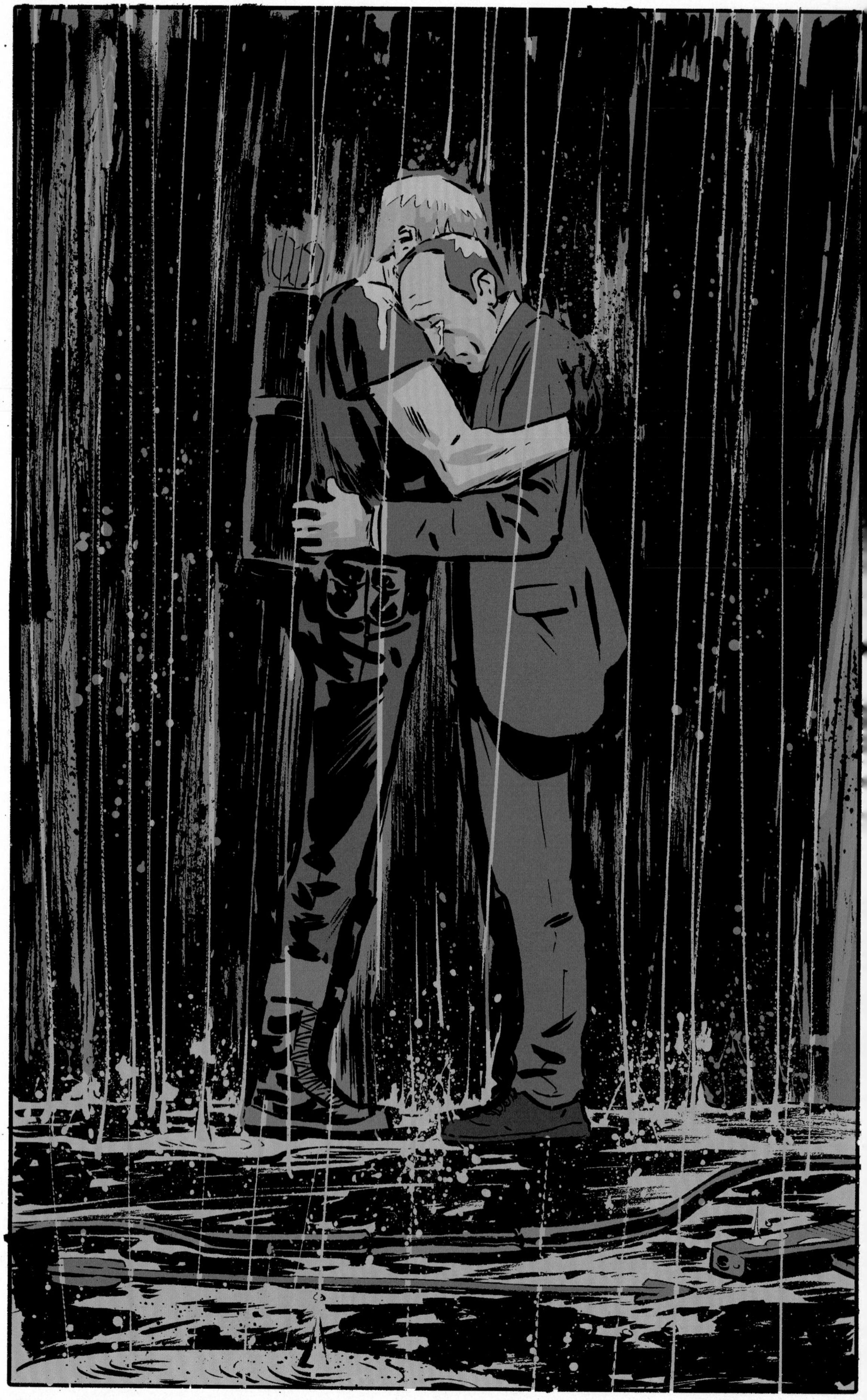

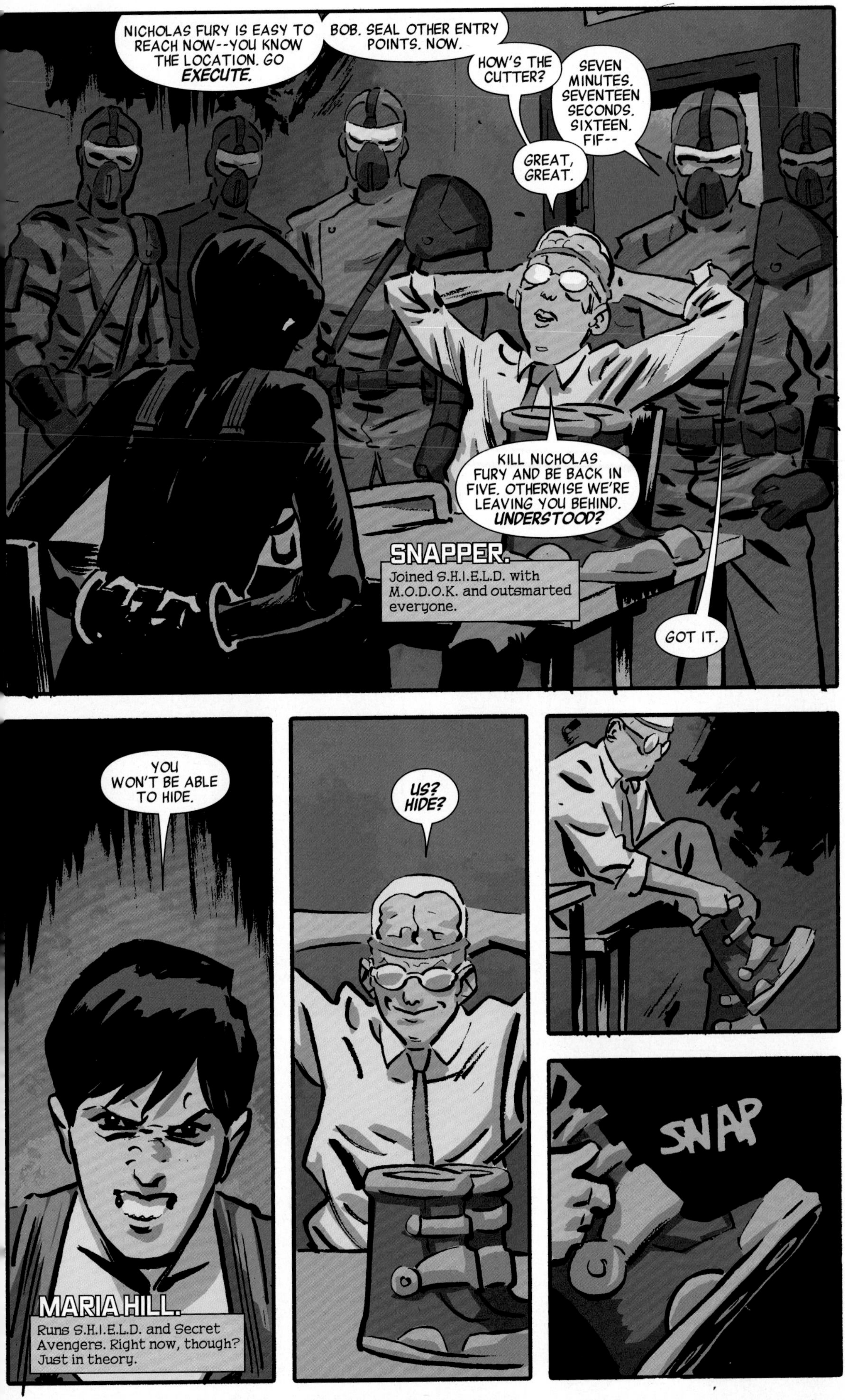

NICHOLAS FURY IS EASY TO REACH NOW--YOU KNOW THE LOCATION. GO **EXECUTE.**
BOB. SEAL OTHER ENTRY POINTS. NOW.
HOW'S THE CUTTER?
SEVEN MINUTES. SEVENTEEN SECONDS. SIXTEEN. FIF--
GREAT, GREAT.
KILL NICHOLAS FURY AND BE BACK IN FIVE. OTHERWISE WE'RE LEAVING YOU BEHIND. **UNDERSTOOD?**
SNAPPER.
Joined S.H.I.E.L.D. with M.O.D.O.K. and outsmarted everyone.
GOT IT.
YOU WON'T BE ABLE TO HIDE.
MARIA HILL.
Runs S.H.I.E.L.D. and Secret Avengers. Right now, though? Just in theory.
US? HIDE?
SNAP

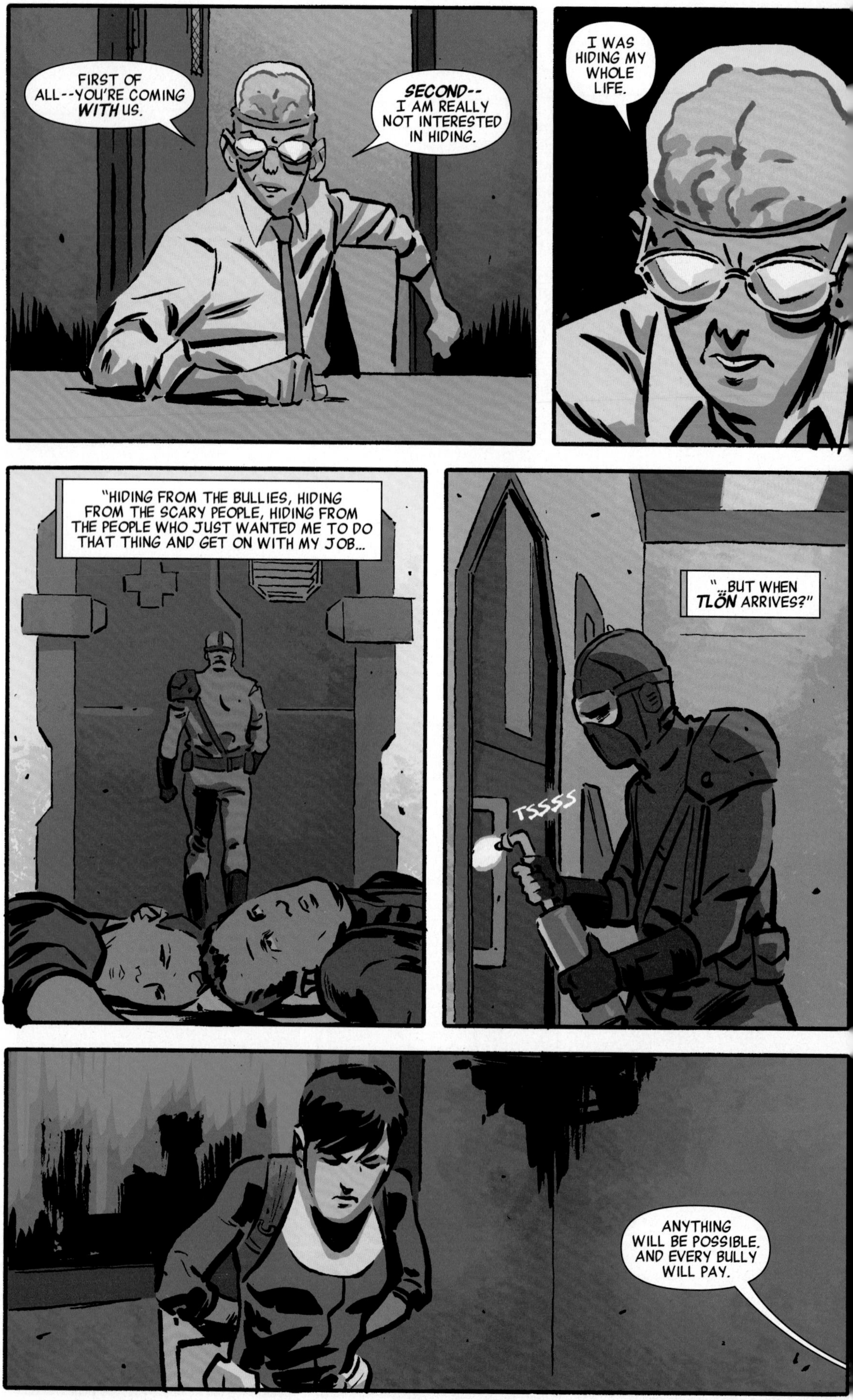
FIRST OF ALL--YOU'RE COMING WITH US.
SECOND-- I AM REALLY NOT INTERESTED IN HIDING.
I WAS HIDING MY WHOLE LIFE.
"HIDING FROM THE BULLIES, HIDING FROM THE SCARY PEOPLE, HIDING FROM THE PEOPLE WHO JUST WANTED ME TO DO THAT THING AND GET ON WITH MY JOB...
"...BUT WHEN TLÖN ARRIVES?"
TSSSS
ANYTHING WILL BE POSSIBLE. AND EVERY BULLY WILL PAY.

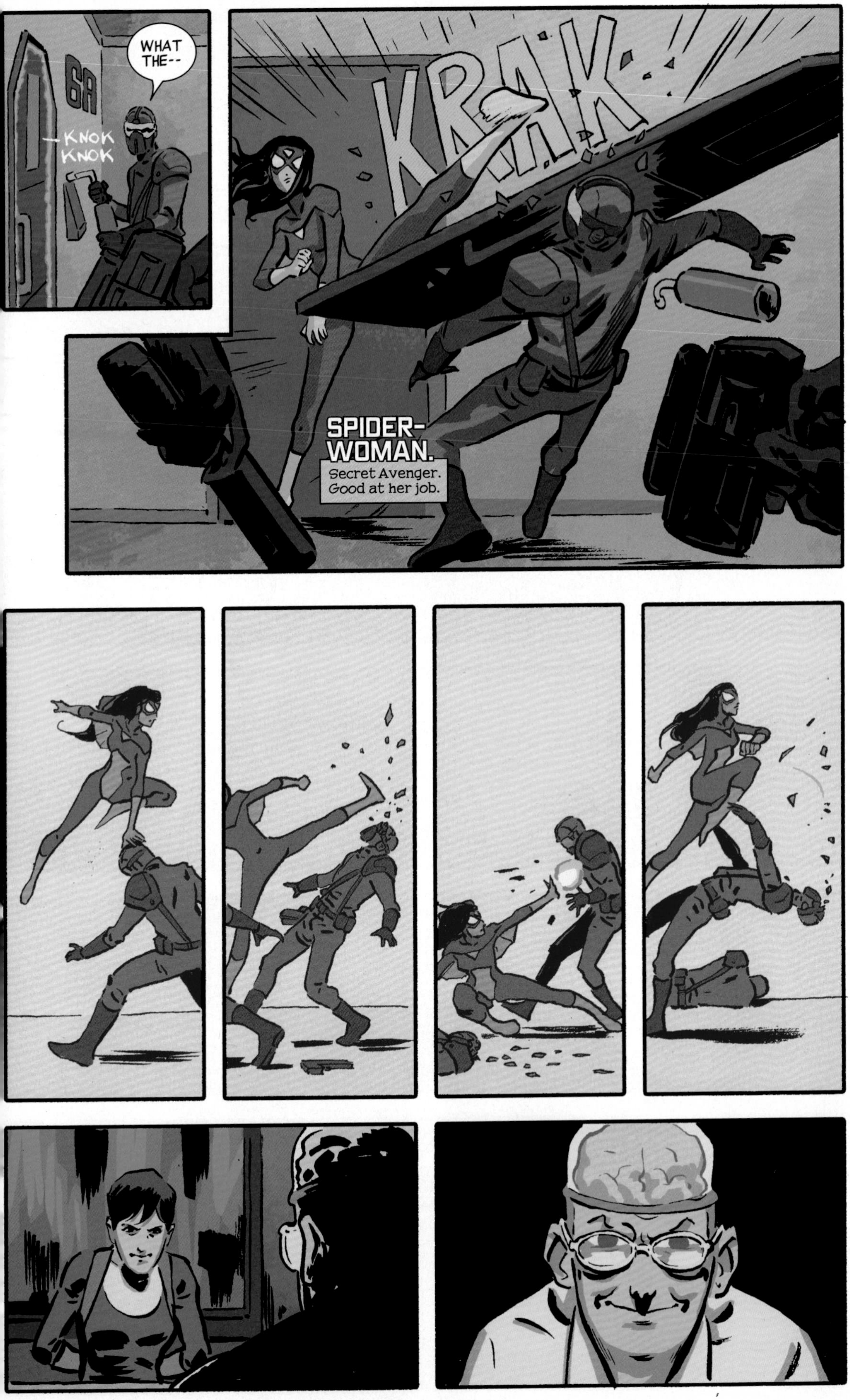

WHAT THE--
—KNOK KNOK
KRAK
SPIDER-WOMAN.
Secret Avenger. Good at her job.

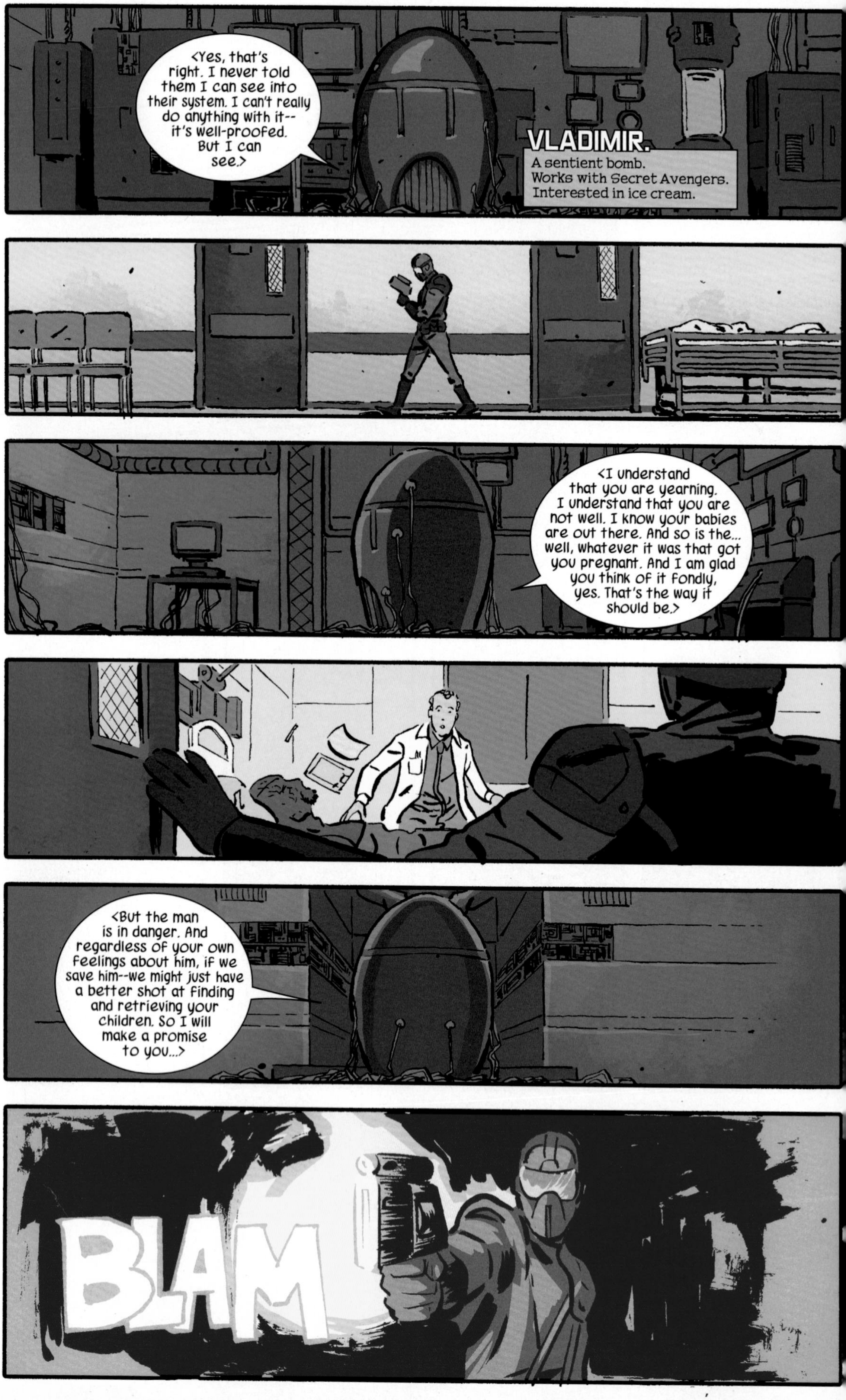
<Yes, that's right. I never told them I can see into their system. I can't really do anything with it-- it's well-proofed. But I can see.>
VLADIMIR.
A sentient bomb.
Works with Secret Avengers.
Interested in ice cream.
<I understand that you are yearning. I understand that you are not well. I know your babies are out there. And so is the... well, whatever it was that got you pregnant. And I am glad you think of it fondly, yes. That's the way it should be.>
<But the man is in danger. And regardless of your own feelings about him, if we save him--we might just have a better shot at finding and retrieving your children. So I will make a promise to you...>
BLAM

<Save Nick Fury and I will help you escape.>

FURY.
Not Nick Fury. *The* Fury. A killer cybiote without a trace of mercy. Or so some people say.

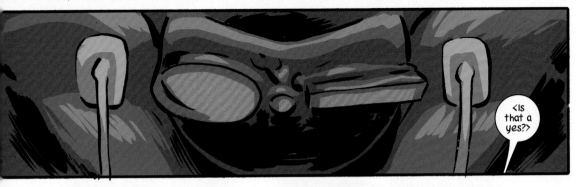

<Is that a yes?>

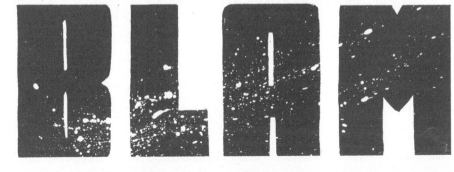

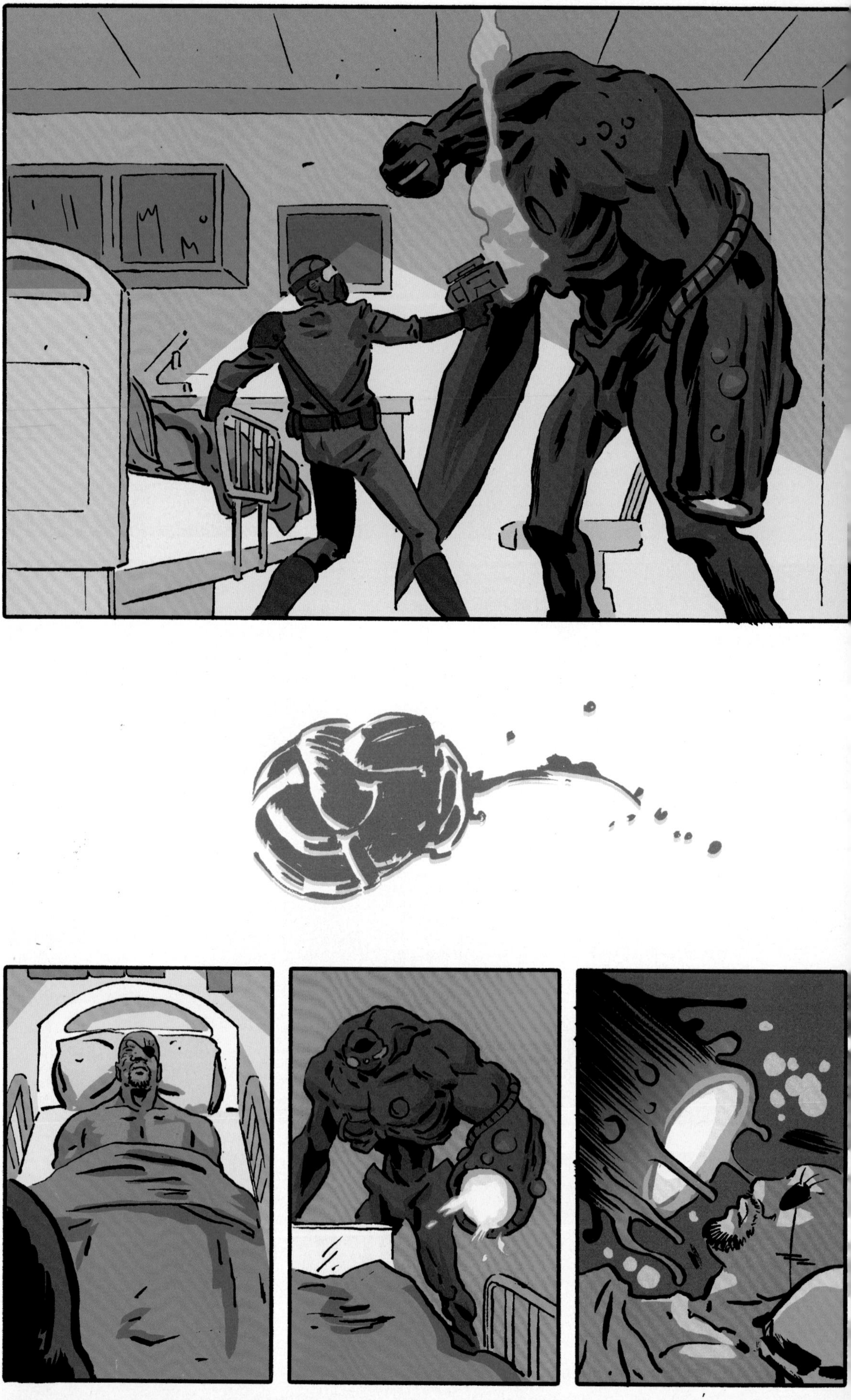

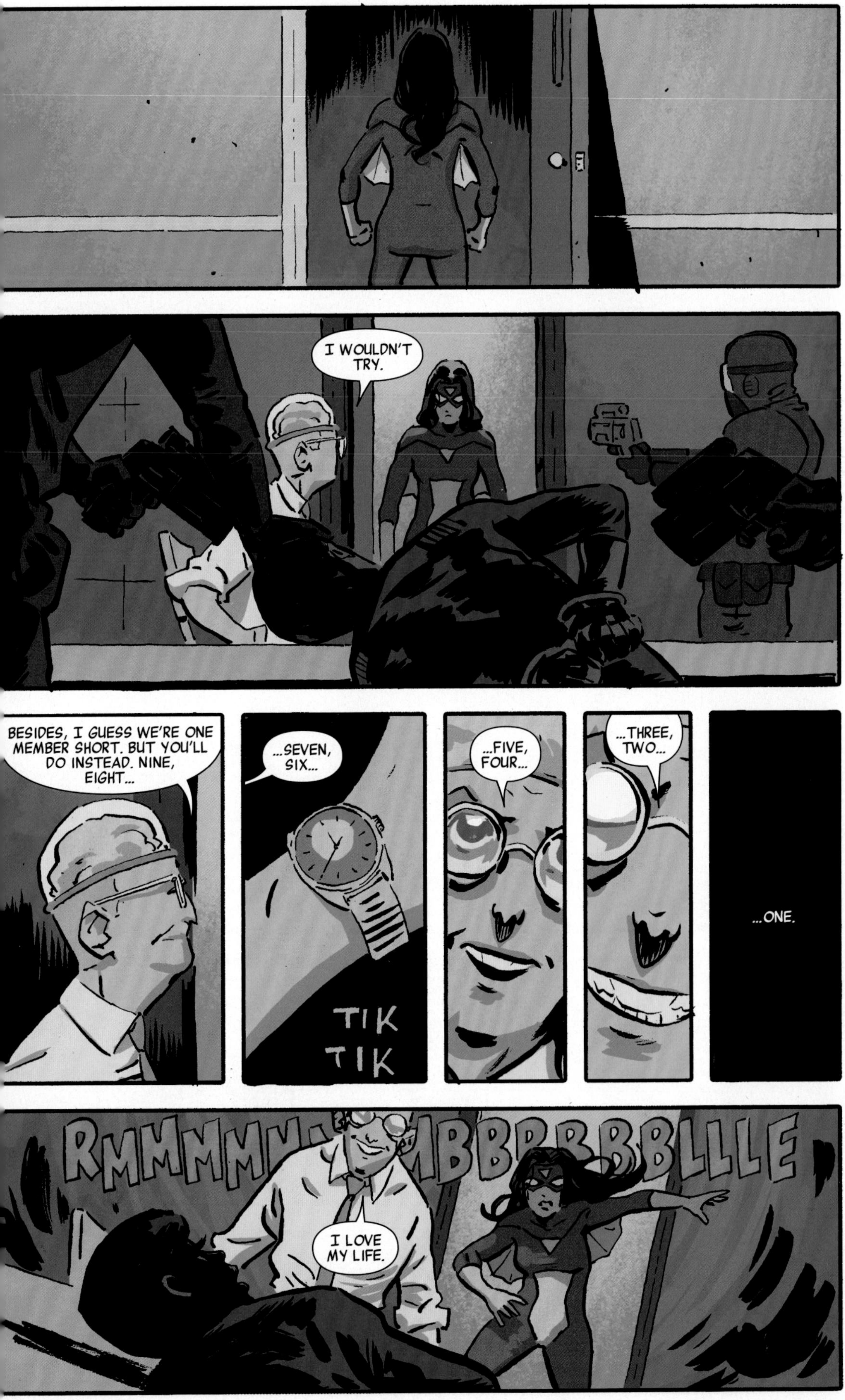
I WOULDN'T TRY.
BESIDES, I GUESS WE'RE ONE MEMBER SHORT. BUT YOU'LL DO INSTEAD. NINE, EIGHT...
...SEVEN, SIX...
TIK TIK
...FIVE, FOUR...
...THREE, TWO...
...ONE.
RMMMMM-MBBRRBBBLLLE
I LOVE MY LIFE.

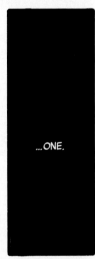

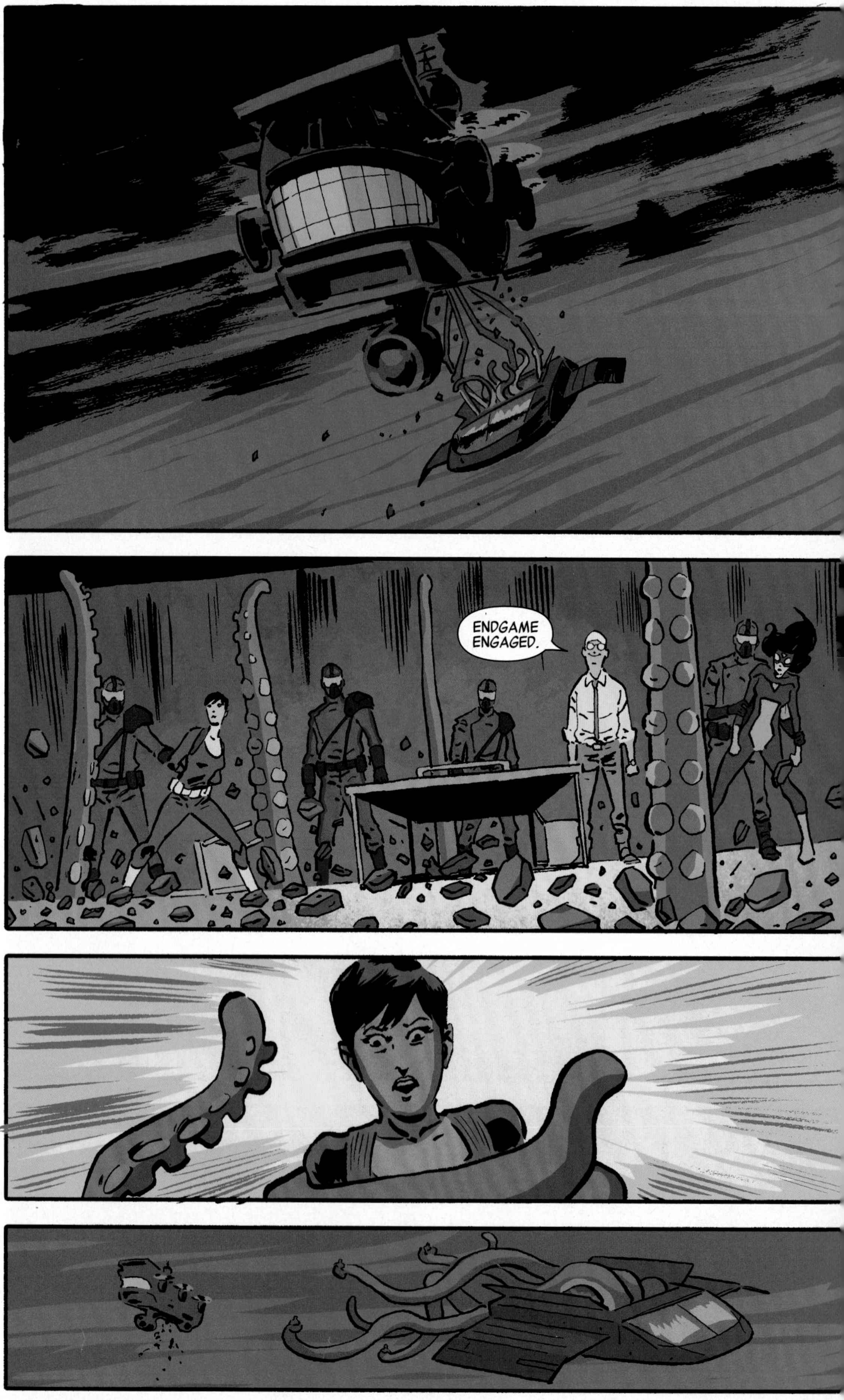
ENDGAME ENGAGED.

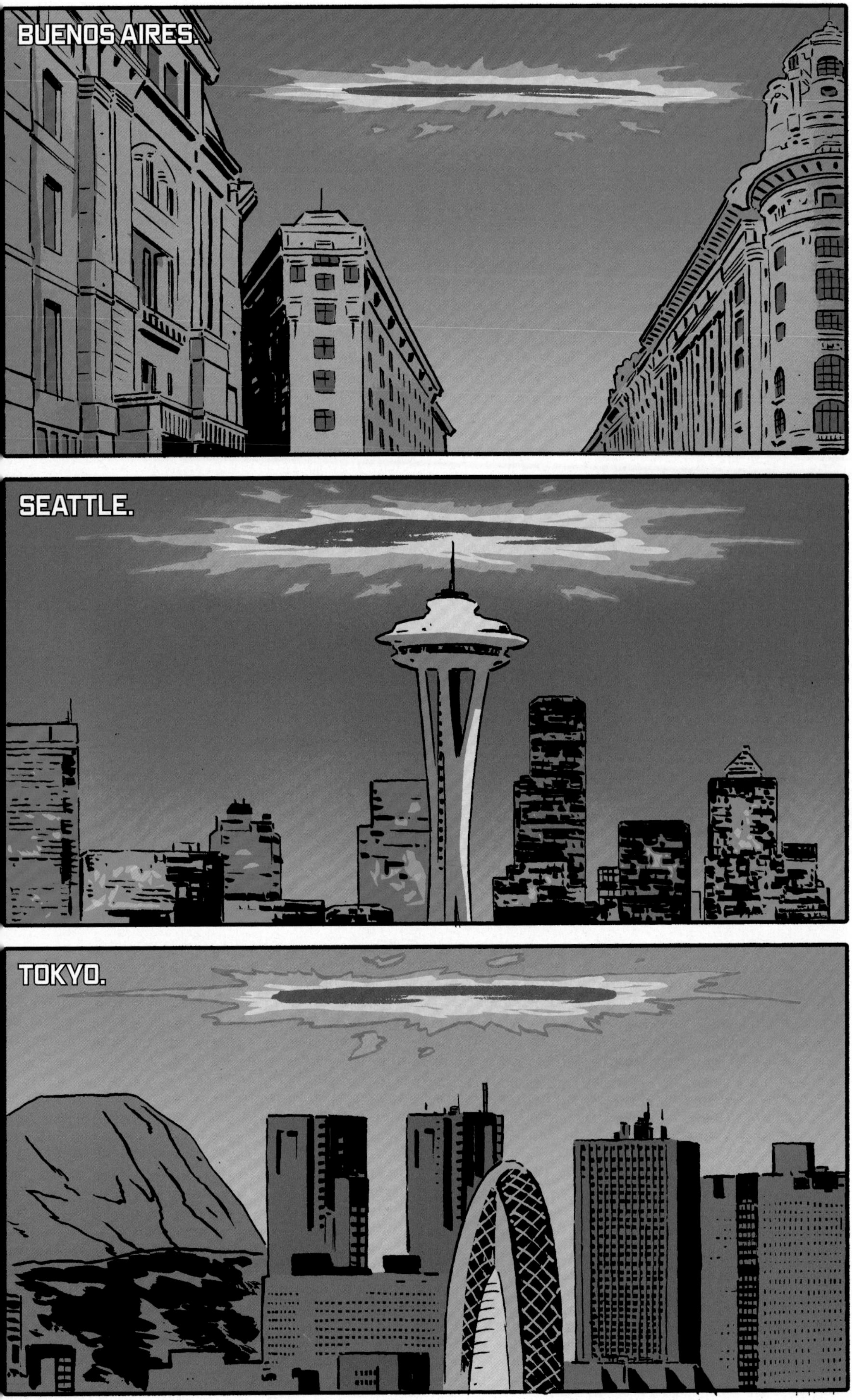
BUENOS AIRES.
SEATTLE.
TOKYO.

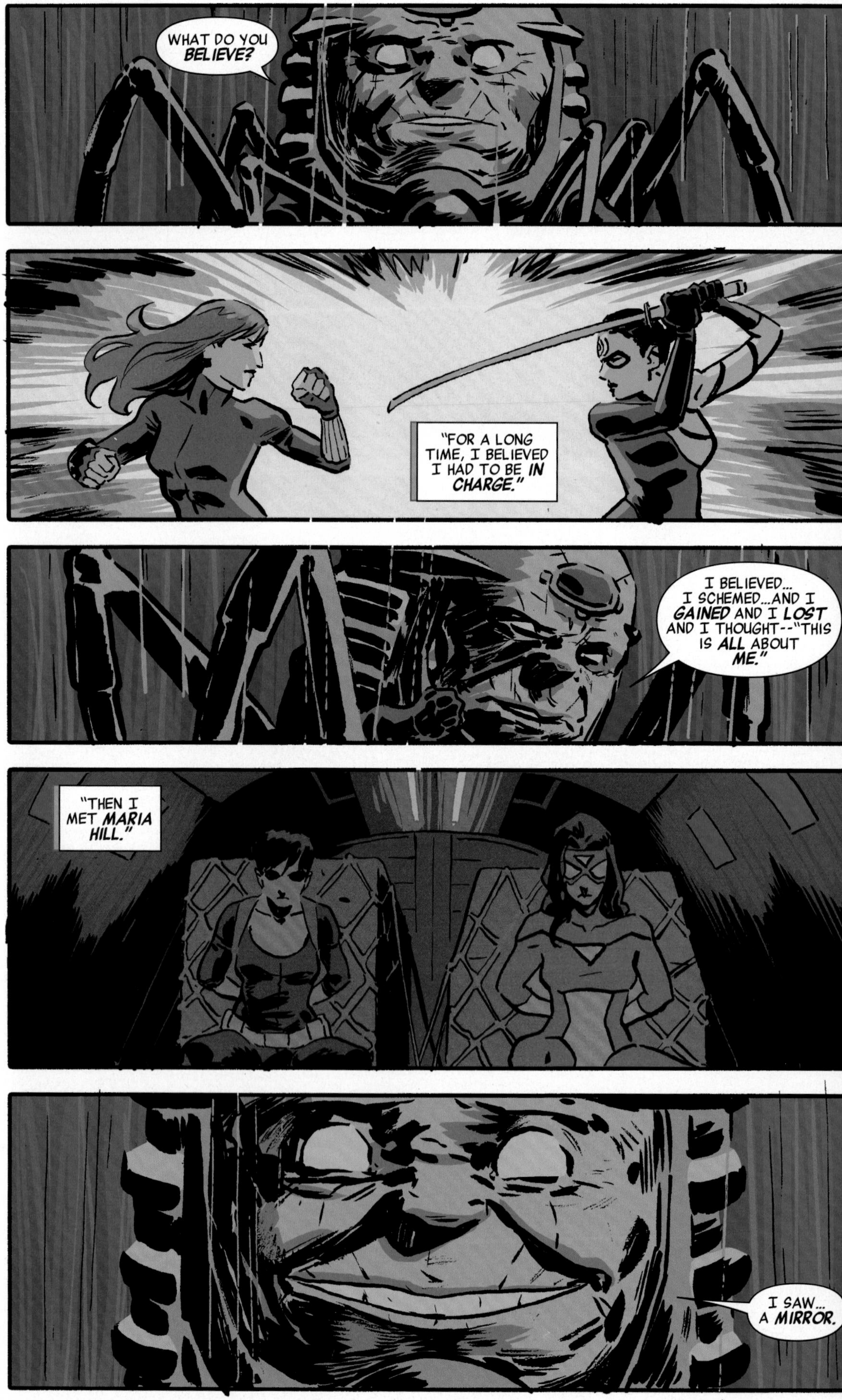

WHAT DO YOU BELIEVE?
"FOR A LONG TIME, I BELIEVED I HAD TO BE IN CHARGE."
I BELIEVED... I SCHEMED...AND I GAINED AND I LOST AND I THOUGHT--"THIS IS ALL ABOUT ME."
"THEN I MET MARIA HILL."
I SAW... A MIRROR.

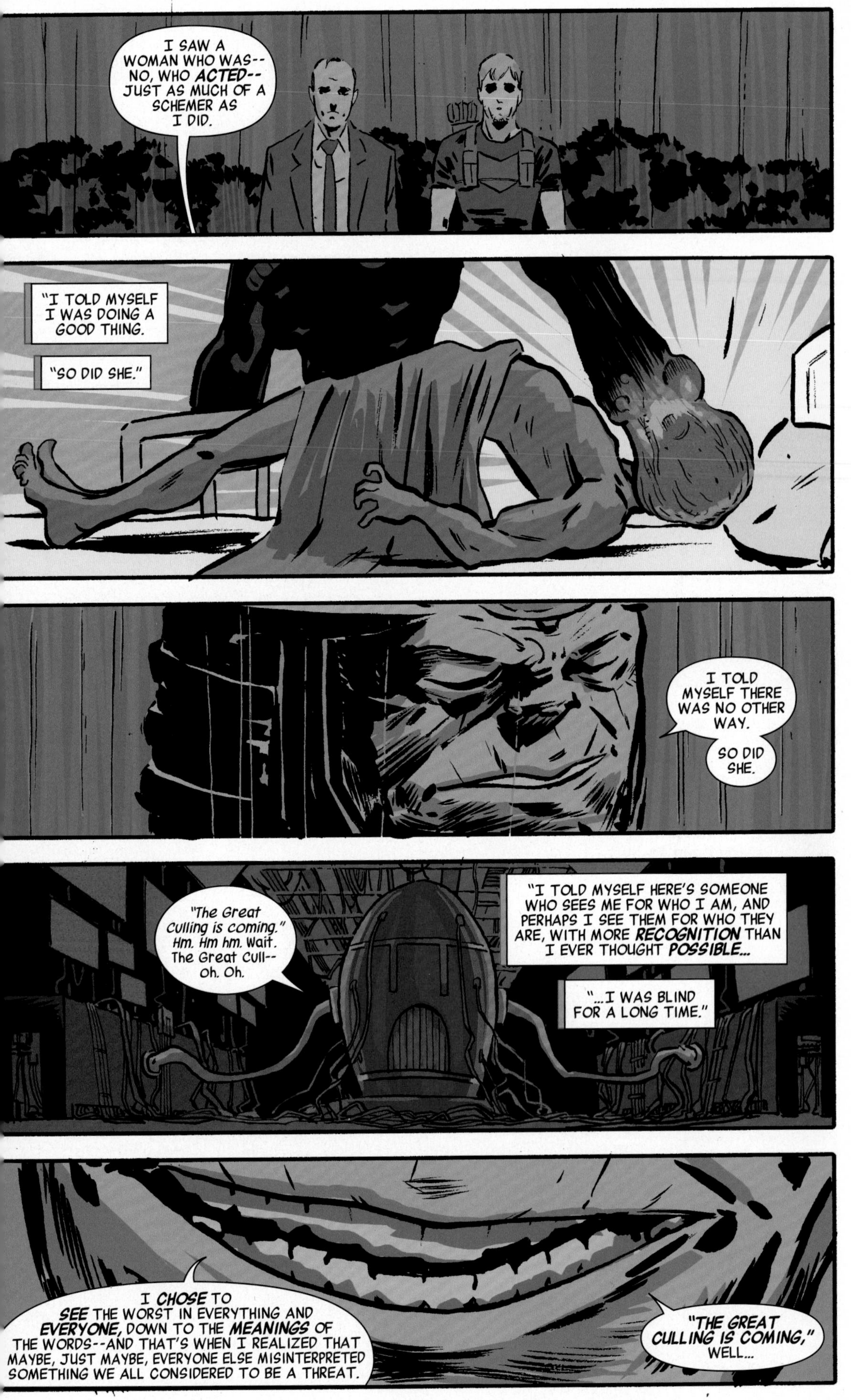
I SAW A WOMAN WHO WAS-- NO, WHO ACTED-- JUST AS MUCH OF A SCHEMER AS I DID.
"I TOLD MYSELF I WAS DOING A GOOD THING.
"SO DID SHE."
I TOLD MYSELF THERE WAS NO OTHER WAY.
SO DID SHE.
"The Great Culling is coming." Hm. Hm hm. Wait. The Great Cull-- Oh. Oh.
"I TOLD MYSELF HERE'S SOMEONE WHO SEES ME FOR WHO I AM, AND PERHAPS I SEE THEM FOR WHO THEY ARE, WITH MORE RECOGNITION THAN I EVER THOUGHT POSSIBLE...
"...I WAS BLIND FOR A LONG TIME."
I CHOSE TO SEE THE WORST IN EVERYTHING AND EVERYONE, DOWN TO THE MEANINGS OF THE WORDS--AND THAT'S WHEN I REALIZED THAT MAYBE, JUST MAYBE, EVERYONE ELSE MISINTERPRETED SOMETHING WE ALL CONSIDERED TO BE A THREAT.
"THE GREAT CULLING IS COMING," WELL...

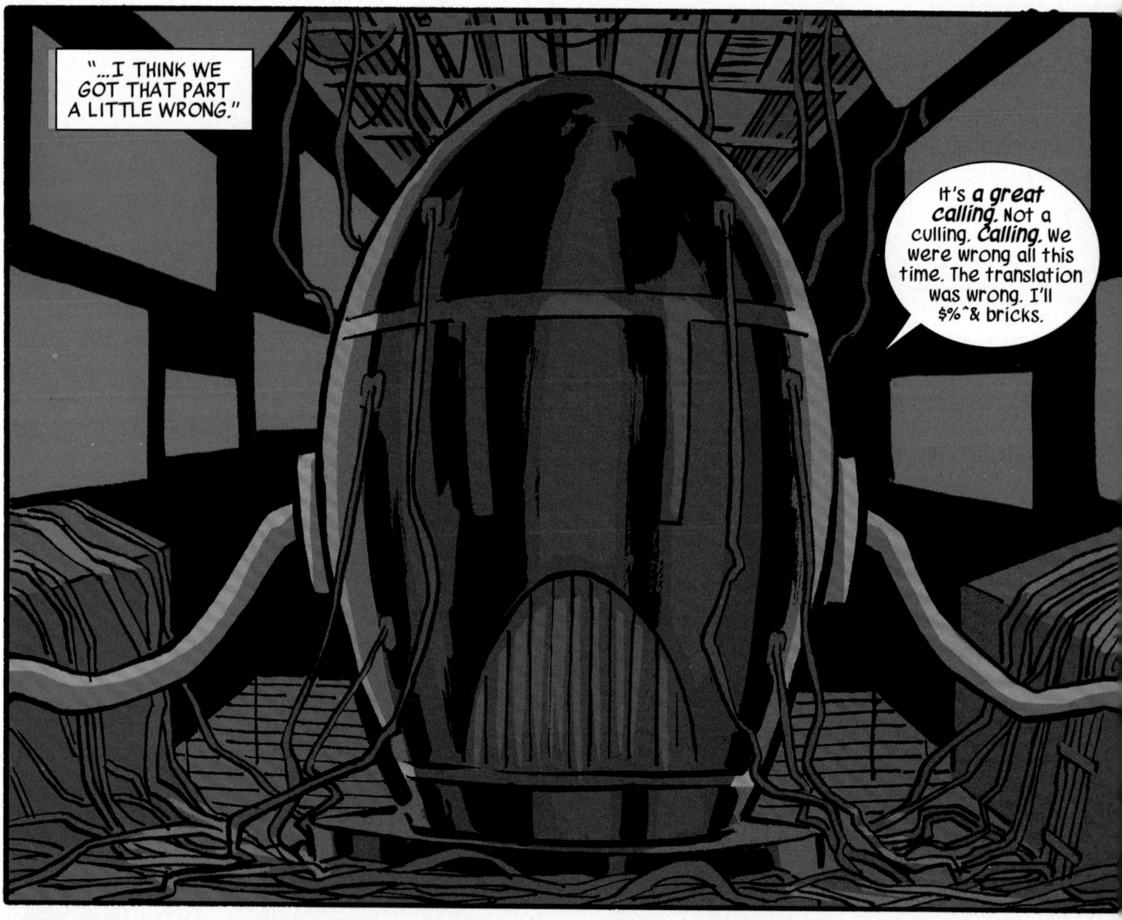
"...I THINK WE GOT THAT PART A LITTLE WRONG."
It's a great calling. Not a culling. Calling. We were wrong all this time. The translation was wrong. I'll $%^& bricks.

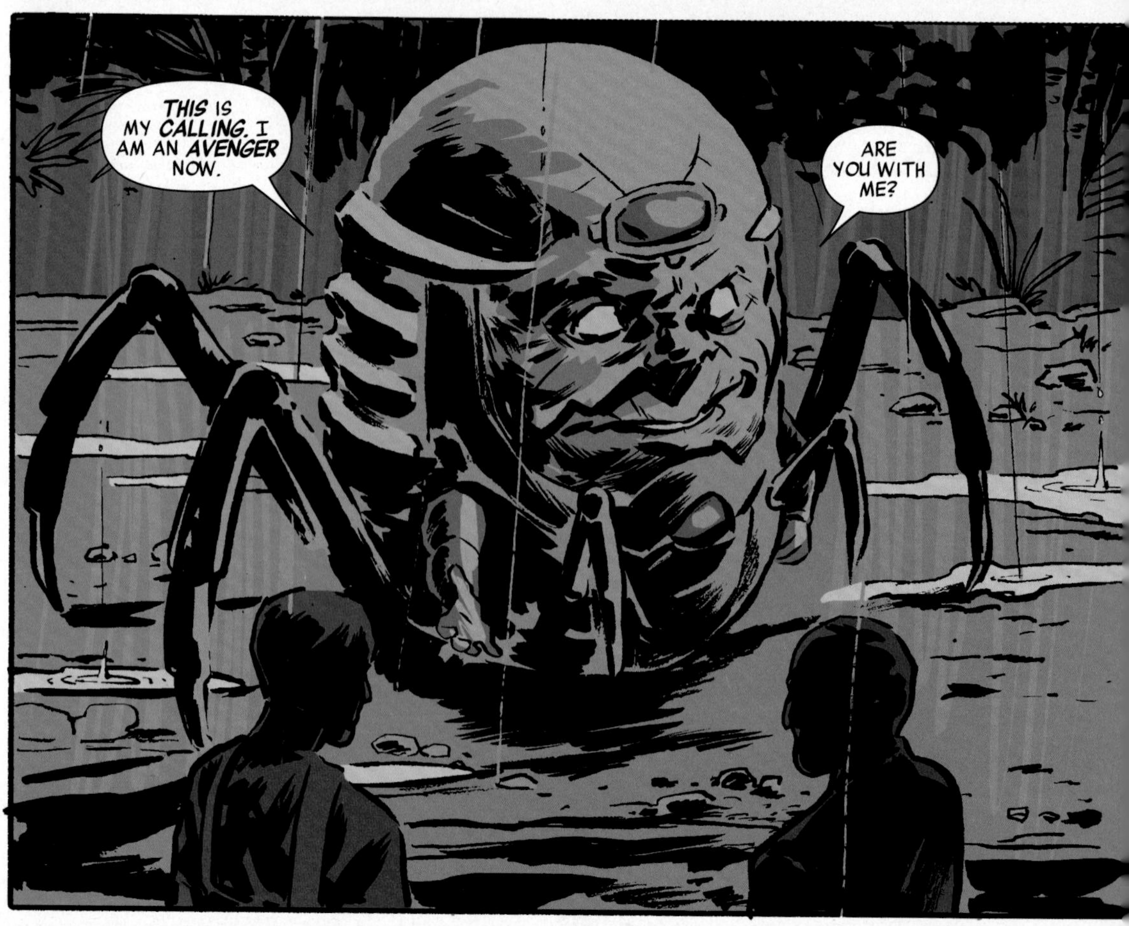
THIS IS MY CALLING. I AM AN AVENGER NOW.
ARE YOU WITH ME?

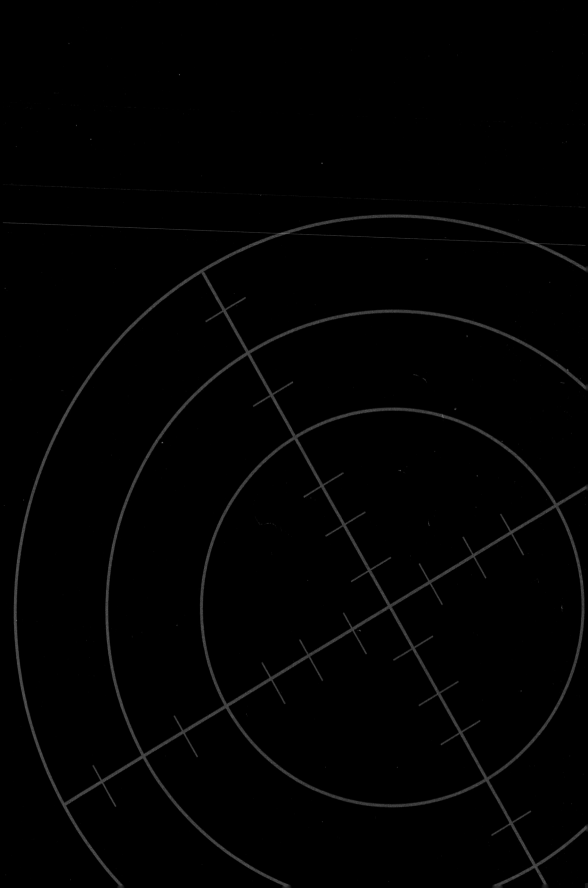

12

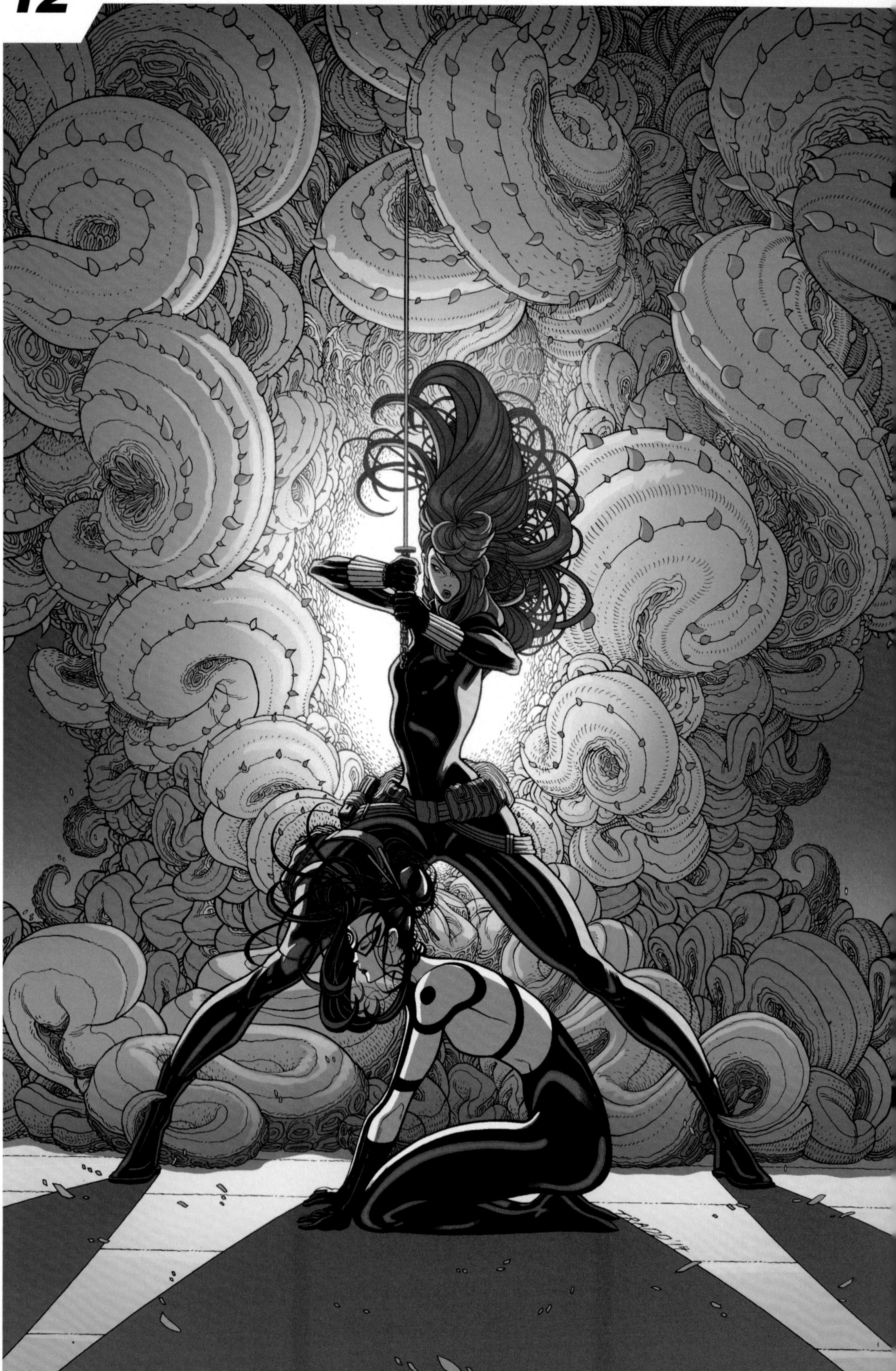

...AND WHAT DO YOU BELIEVE? PART TWO

VENEZUELAN RAINFOREST.

YOU WANTED TO *KILL* US.

HAWKEYE.
Clint Barton.
Secret Avenger.

YES.

M.O.D.O.K.
Master Of Delectable Operational Kaos. Not a Secret Avenger.

AND WE'RE SUPPOSED TO *TRUST* YOU NOW?

PHIL COULSON.
Secret Avenger.
Again.

IDEALLY, YES.

BECAUSE YOU LAID ALL THE BITS AND PIECES THAT LED US TO YOU IN THE END.

THAT IS A LITTLE BIT TOO GENEROUS A STATEMENT... BUT ALSO BASICALLY *CORRECT*.

BECAUSE OF YOUR *IDENTITY SPLIT* FOLLOWING... I CAN'T BELIEVE I'M SAYING THIS...

...FOLLOWING THE REALIZATION THAT I AM *IN LOVE* WITH MARIA HILL.

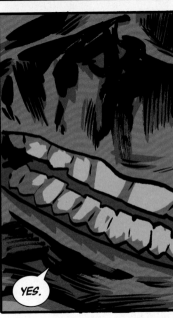

YES.

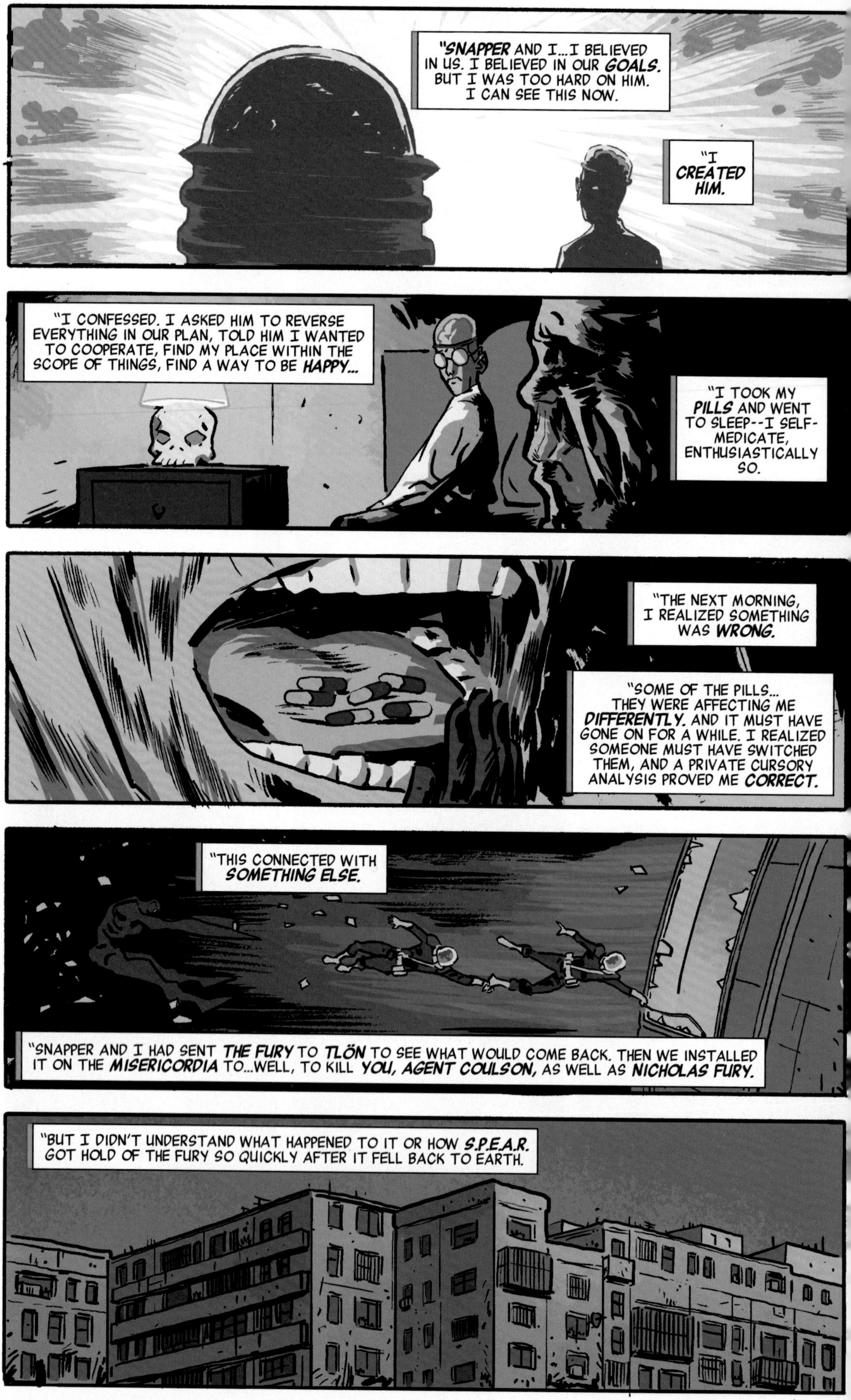
"SNAPPER AND I...I BELIEVED IN US. I BELIEVED IN OUR GOALS. BUT I WAS TOO HARD ON HIM. I CAN SEE THIS NOW.
"I CREATED HIM.
"I CONFESSED. I ASKED HIM TO REVERSE EVERYTHING IN OUR PLAN, TOLD HIM I WANTED TO COOPERATE, FIND MY PLACE WITHIN THE SCOPE OF THINGS, FIND A WAY TO BE HAPPY...
"I TOOK MY PILLS AND WENT TO SLEEP--I SELF-MEDICATE, ENTHUSIASTICALLY SO.
"THE NEXT MORNING, I REALIZED SOMETHING WAS WRONG.
"SOME OF THE PILLS... THEY WERE AFFECTING ME DIFFERENTLY. AND IT MUST HAVE GONE ON FOR A WHILE. I REALIZED SOMEONE MUST HAVE SWITCHED THEM, AND A PRIVATE CURSORY ANALYSIS PROVED ME CORRECT.
"THIS CONNECTED WITH SOMETHING ELSE.
"SNAPPER AND I HAD SENT THE FURY TO TLÖN TO SEE WHAT WOULD COME BACK. THEN WE INSTALLED IT ON THE MISERICORDIA TO...WELL, TO KILL YOU, AGENT COULSON, AS WELL AS NICHOLAS FURY.
"BUT I DIDN'T UNDERSTAND WHAT HAPPENED TO IT OR HOW S.P.E.A.R. GOT HOLD OF THE FURY SO QUICKLY AFTER IT FELL BACK TO EARTH.

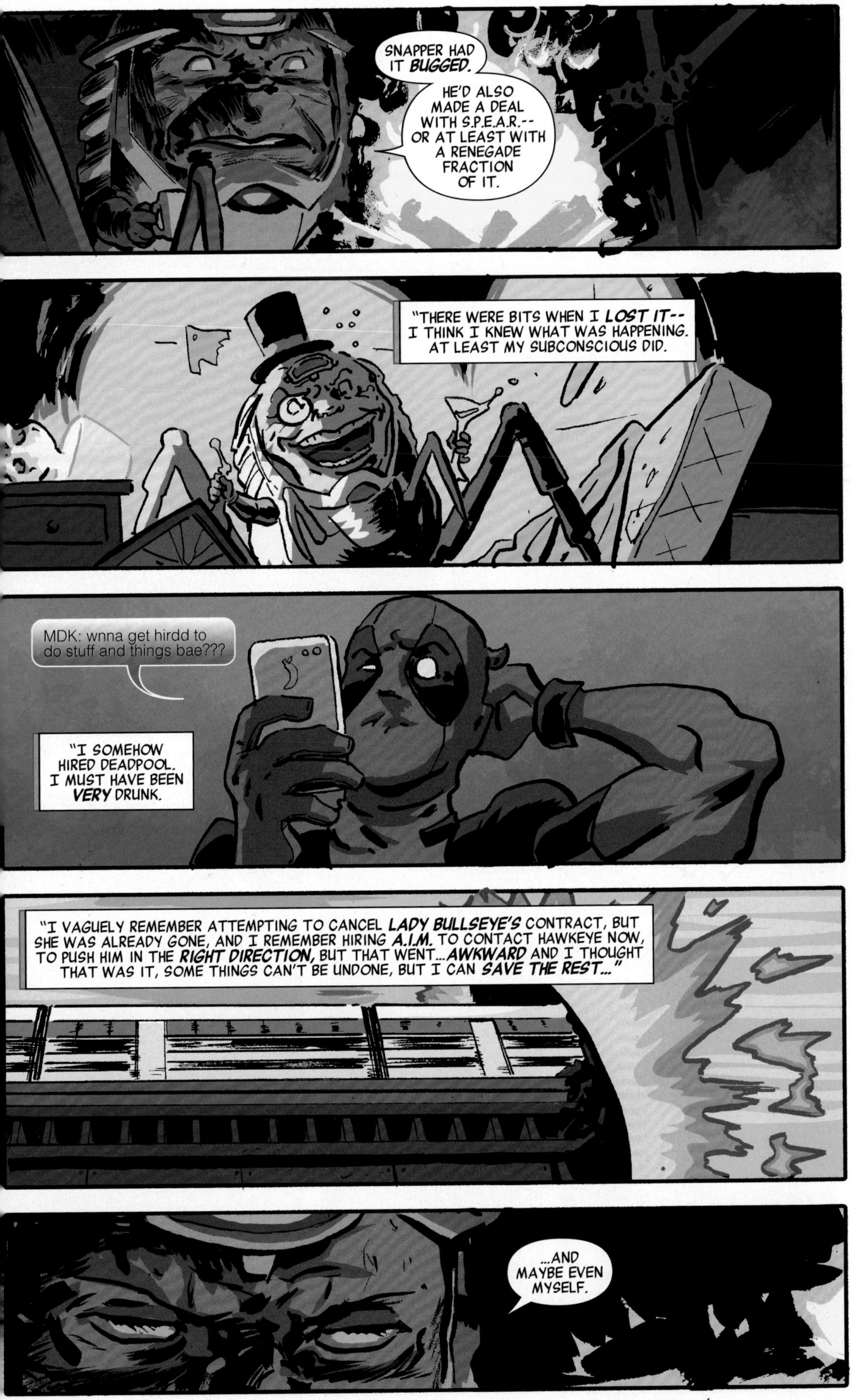
SNAPPER HAD IT BUGGED.
HE'D ALSO MADE A DEAL WITH S.P.E.A.R.-- OR AT LEAST WITH A RENEGADE FRACTION OF IT.
"THERE WERE BITS WHEN I LOST IT-- I THINK I KNEW WHAT WAS HAPPENING. AT LEAST MY SUBCONSCIOUS DID.
MDK: wnna get hirdd to do stuff and things bae???
"I SOMEHOW HIRED DEADPOOL. I MUST HAVE BEEN VERY DRUNK.
"I VAGUELY REMEMBER ATTEMPTING TO CANCEL LADY BULLSEYE'S CONTRACT, BUT SHE WAS ALREADY GONE, AND I REMEMBER HIRING A.I.M. TO CONTACT HAWKEYE NOW, TO PUSH HIM IN THE RIGHT DIRECTION, BUT THAT WENT...AWKWARD AND I THOUGHT THAT WAS IT, SOME THINGS CAN'T BE UNDONE, BUT I CAN SAVE THE REST..."
...AND MAYBE EVEN MYSELF.

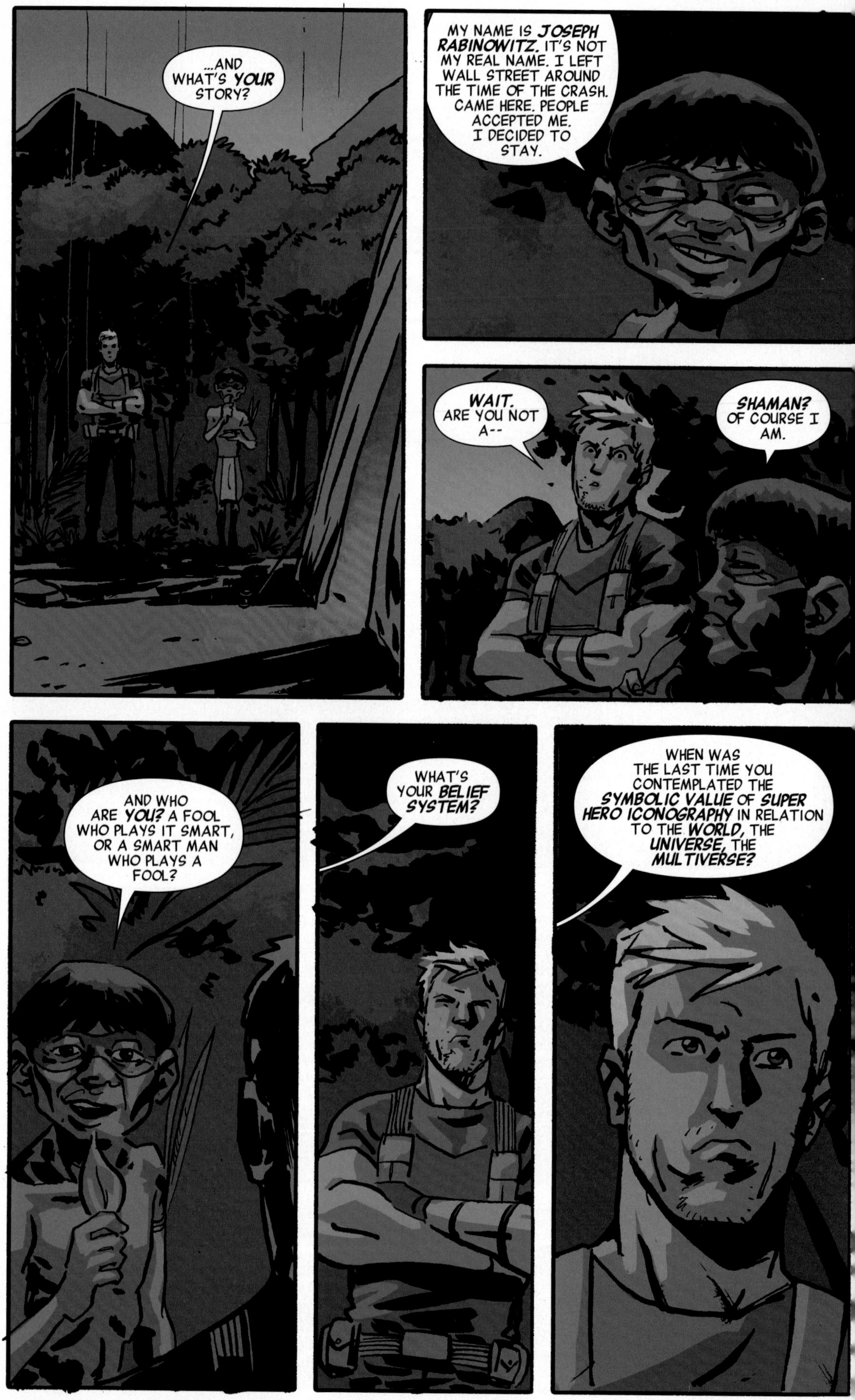
...AND WHAT'S YOUR STORY?
MY NAME IS JOSEPH RABINOWITZ. IT'S NOT MY REAL NAME. I LEFT WALL STREET AROUND THE TIME OF THE CRASH. CAME HERE. PEOPLE ACCEPTED ME. I DECIDED TO STAY.
WAIT. ARE YOU NOT A--
SHAMAN? OF COURSE I AM.
AND WHO ARE YOU? A FOOL WHO PLAYS IT SMART, OR A SMART MAN WHO PLAYS A FOOL?
WHAT'S YOUR BELIEF SYSTEM?
WHEN WAS THE LAST TIME YOU CONTEMPLATED THE SYMBOLIC VALUE OF SUPER HERO ICONOGRAPHY IN RELATION TO THE WORLD, THE UNIVERSE, THE MULTIVERSE?

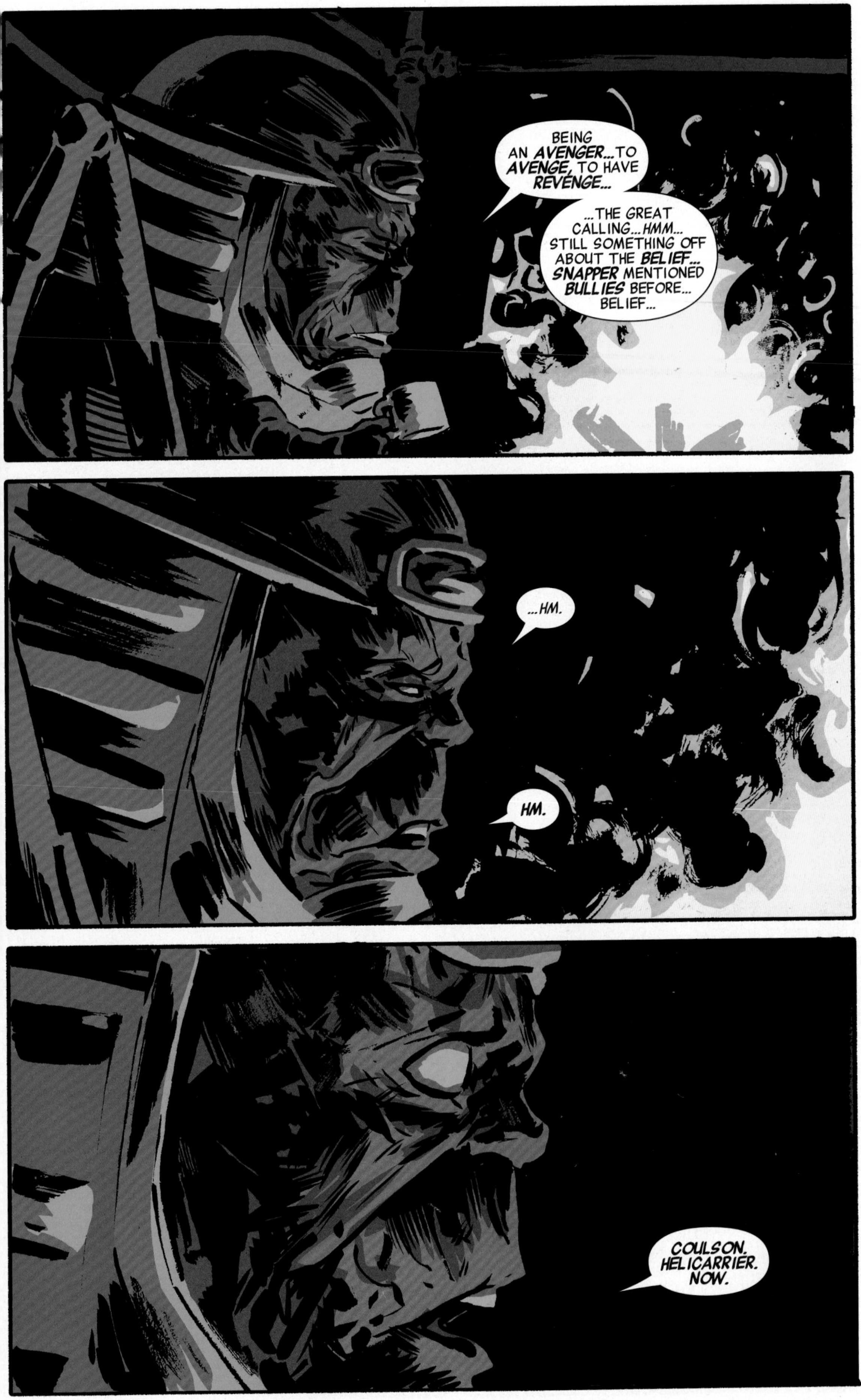
BEING AN AVENGER...TO AVENGE, TO HAVE REVENGE...
...THE GREAT CALLING...HMM... STILL SOMETHING OFF ABOUT THE BELIEF... SNAPPER MENTIONED BULLIES BEFORE... BELIEF...
...HM.
HM.
COULSON. HELICARRIER. NOW.

TLÖN.

BELIEVE ME.

I WILL KILL YOU.

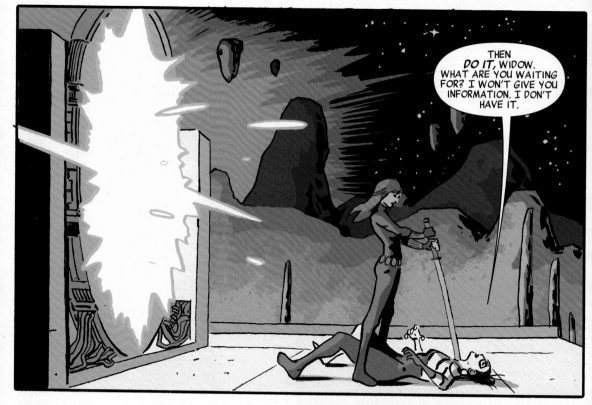

THEN *DO IT*, WIDOW. WHAT ARE YOU WAITING FOR? I WON'T GIVE YOU INFORMATION. I DON'T HAVE IT.

LOOK, LADY B--

DO NOT. CALL ME. THAT.

OH.

YOU DON'T LIKE BEING CALLED "LADY B.S."?

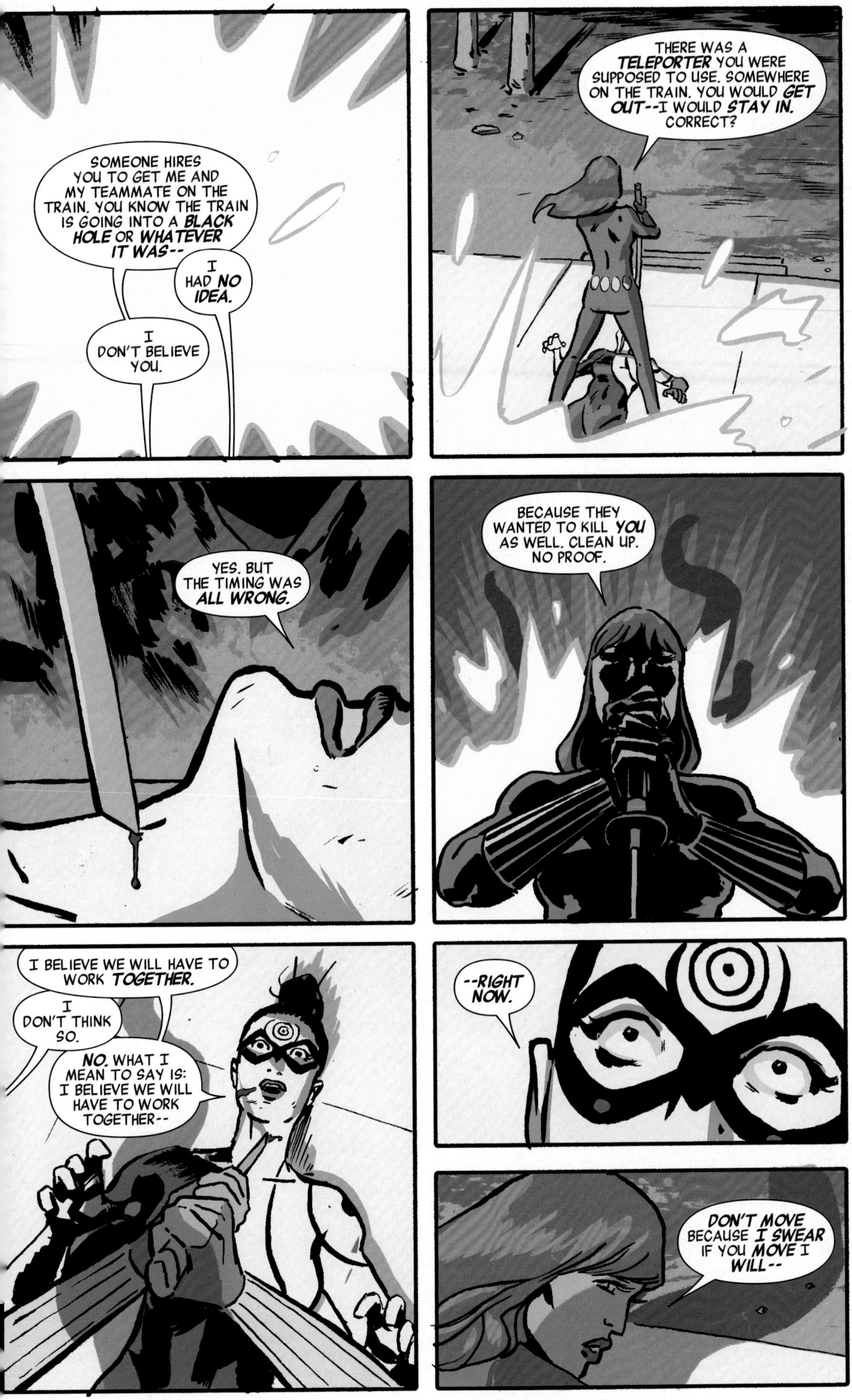
SOMEONE HIRES YOU TO GET ME AND MY TEAMMATE ON THE TRAIN. YOU KNOW THE TRAIN IS GOING INTO A BLACK HOLE OR WHATEVER IT WAS--
I HAD NO IDEA.
I DON'T BELIEVE YOU.
THERE WAS A TELEPORTER YOU WERE SUPPOSED TO USE. SOMEWHERE ON THE TRAIN. YOU WOULD GET OUT--I WOULD STAY IN. CORRECT?
YES. BUT THE TIMING WAS ALL WRONG.
BECAUSE THEY WANTED TO KILL YOU AS WELL. CLEAN UP. NO PROOF.
I BELIEVE WE WILL HAVE TO WORK TOGETHER.
I DON'T THINK SO.
NO. WHAT I MEAN TO SAY IS: I BELIEVE WE WILL HAVE TO WORK TOGETHER--
--RIGHT NOW.
DON'T MOVE BECAUSE I SWEAR IF YOU MOVE I WILL--

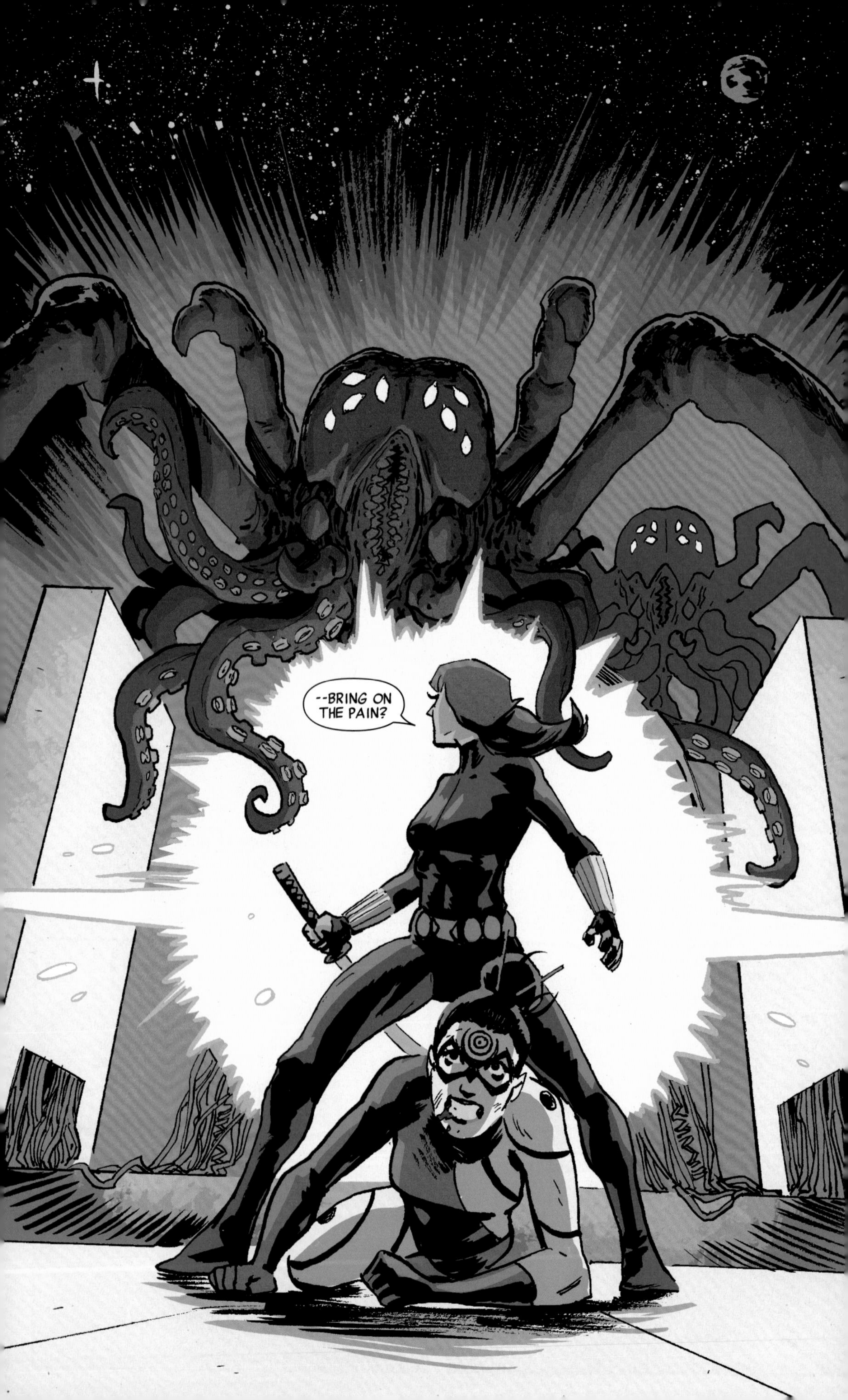
--BRING ON THE PAIN?

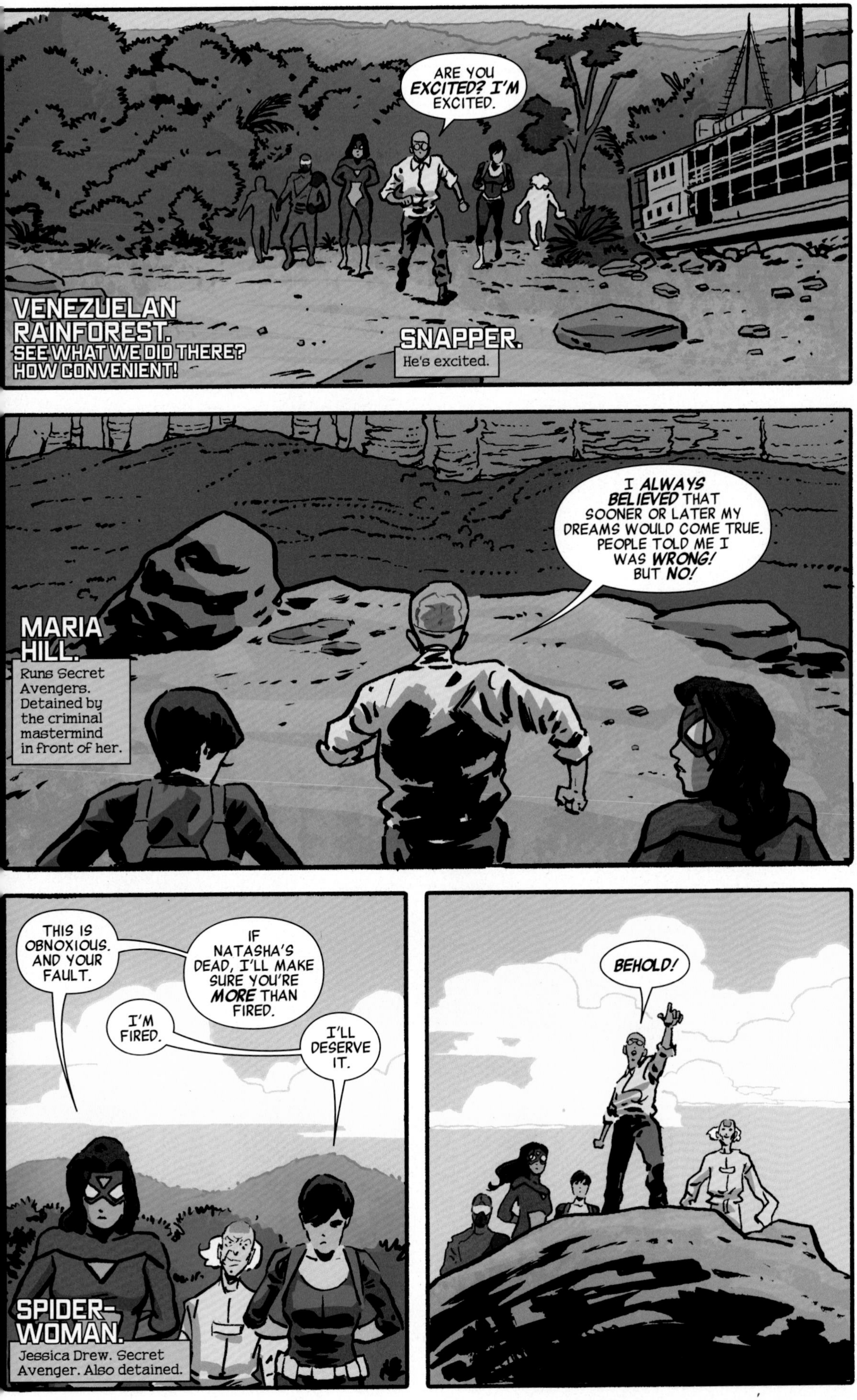
ARE YOU EXCITED? I'M EXCITED.
VENEZUELAN RAINFOREST.
SEE WHAT WE DID THERE? HOW CONVENIENT!
SNAPPER.
He's excited.
I ALWAYS BELIEVED THAT SOONER OR LATER MY DREAMS WOULD COME TRUE. PEOPLE TOLD ME I WAS WRONG! BUT NO!
MARIA HILL.
Runs Secret Avengers. Detained by the criminal mastermind in front of her.
THIS IS OBNOXIOUS. AND YOUR FAULT.
IF NATASHA'S DEAD, I'LL MAKE SURE YOU'RE MORE THAN FIRED.
I'M FIRED.
I'LL DESERVE IT.
SPIDER-WOMAN.
Jessica Drew. Secret Avenger. Also detained.
BEHOLD!

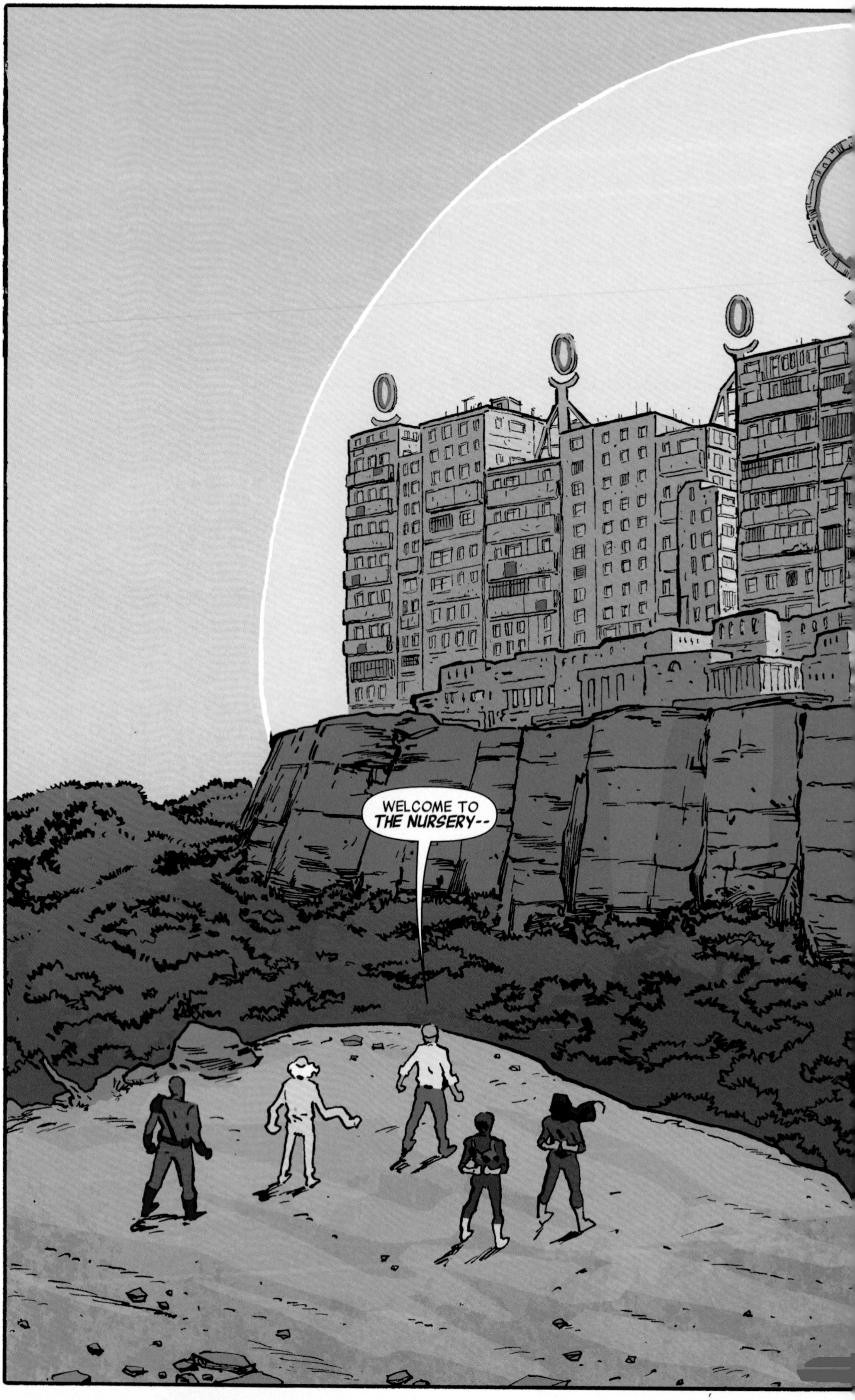
WELCOME TO THE NURSERY--

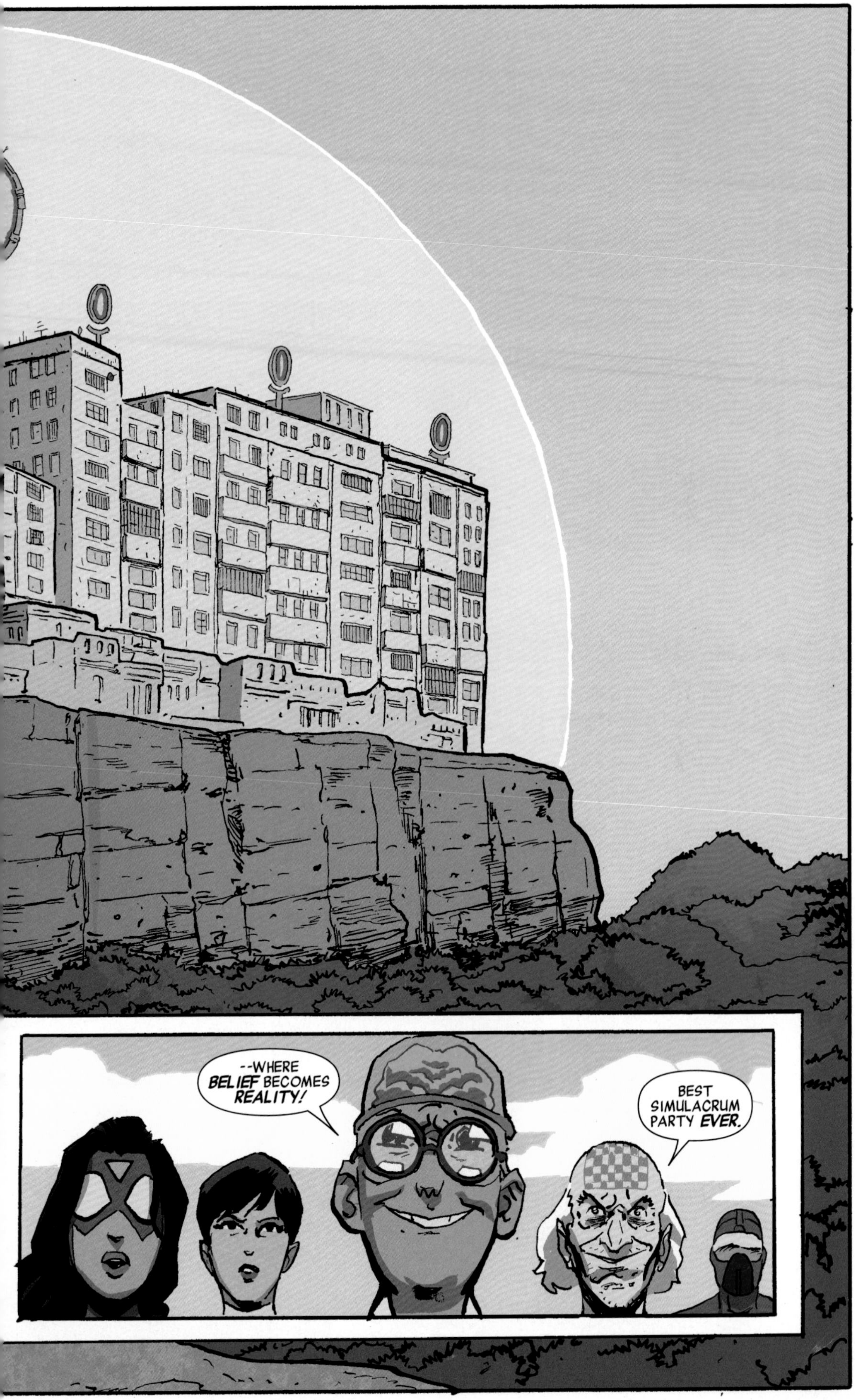
--WHERE BELIEF BECOMES REALITY!
BEST SIMULACRUM PARTY EVER.

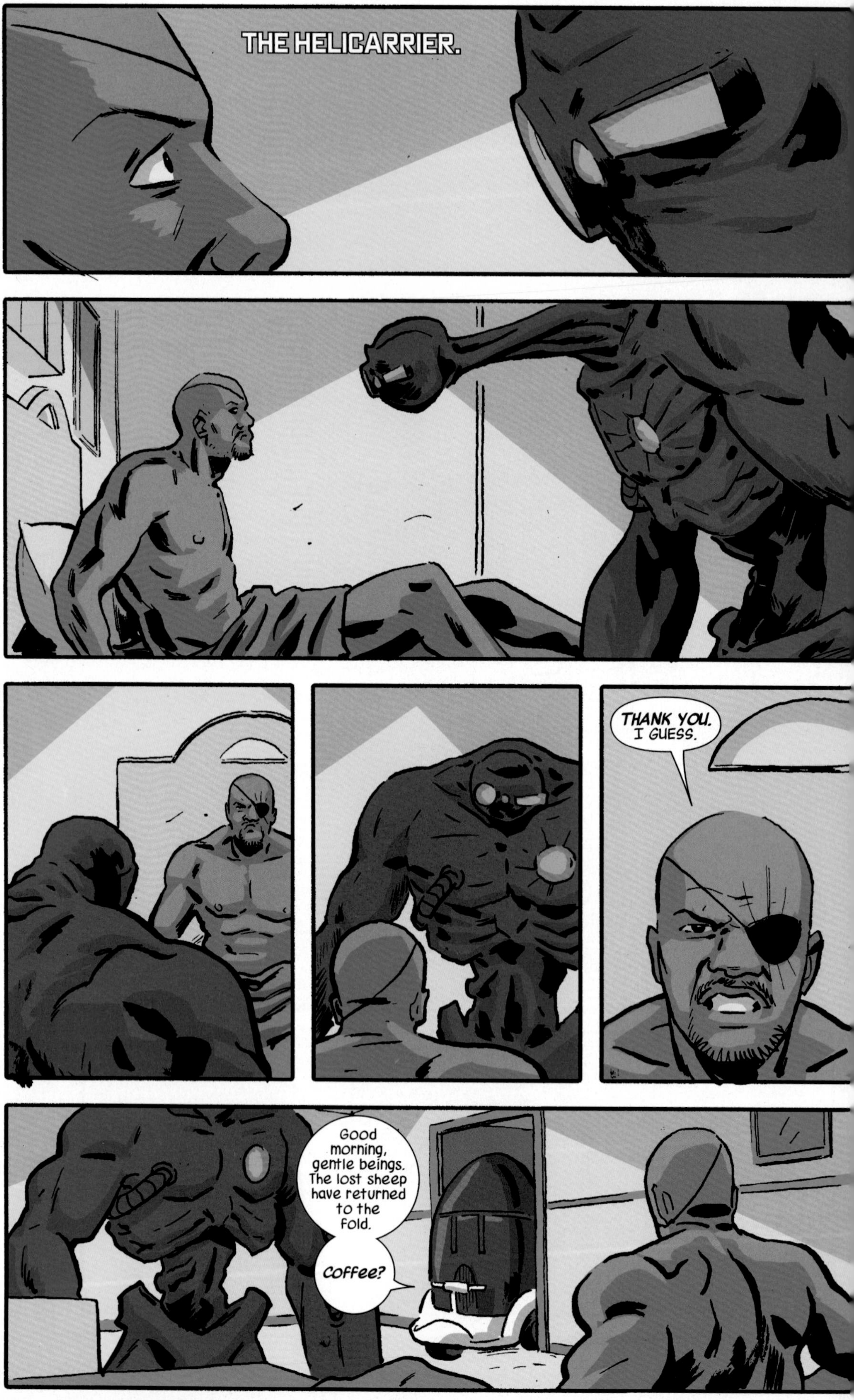
THE HELICARRIER.
THANK YOU. I GUESS.
Good morning, gentle beings. The lost sheep have returned to the fold.
Coffee?

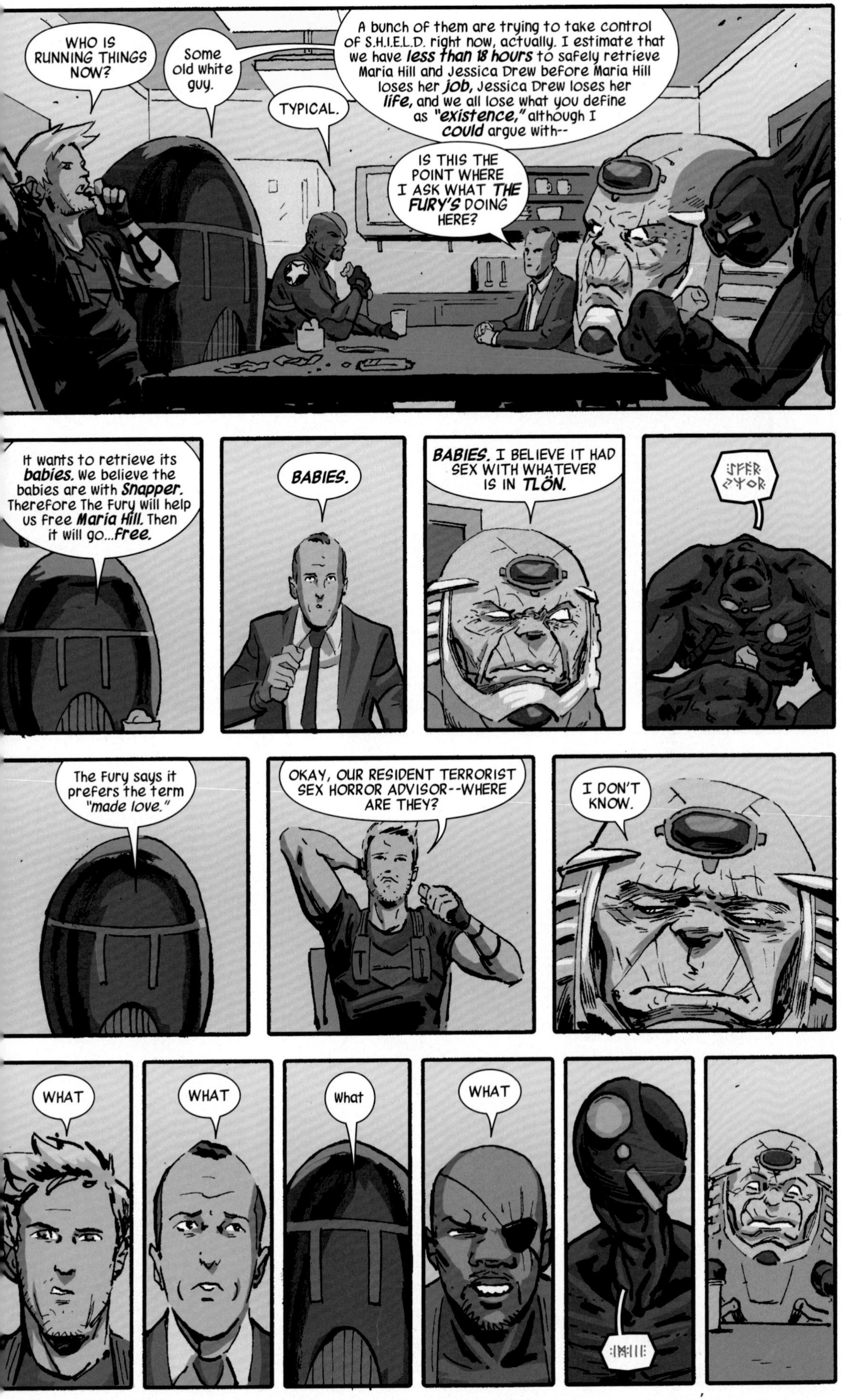
WHO IS RUNNING THINGS NOW?
Some old white guy.
TYPICAL.
A bunch of them are trying to take control of S.H.I.E.L.D. right now, actually. I estimate that we have less than 18 hours to safely retrieve Maria Hill and Jessica Drew before Maria Hill loses her job, Jessica Drew loses her life, and we all lose what you define as "existence," although I could argue with--
IS THIS THE POINT WHERE I ASK WHAT THE FURY'S DOING HERE?
It wants to retrieve its babies. We believe the babies are with Snapper. Therefore The Fury will help us free Maria Hill. Then it will go...free.
BABIES.
BABIES. I BELIEVE IT HAD SEX WITH WHATEVER IS IN TLÖN.
The Fury says it prefers the term "made love."
OKAY, OUR RESIDENT TERRORIST SEX HORROR ADVISOR--WHERE ARE THEY?
I DON'T KNOW.
WHAT
WHAT
What
WHAT

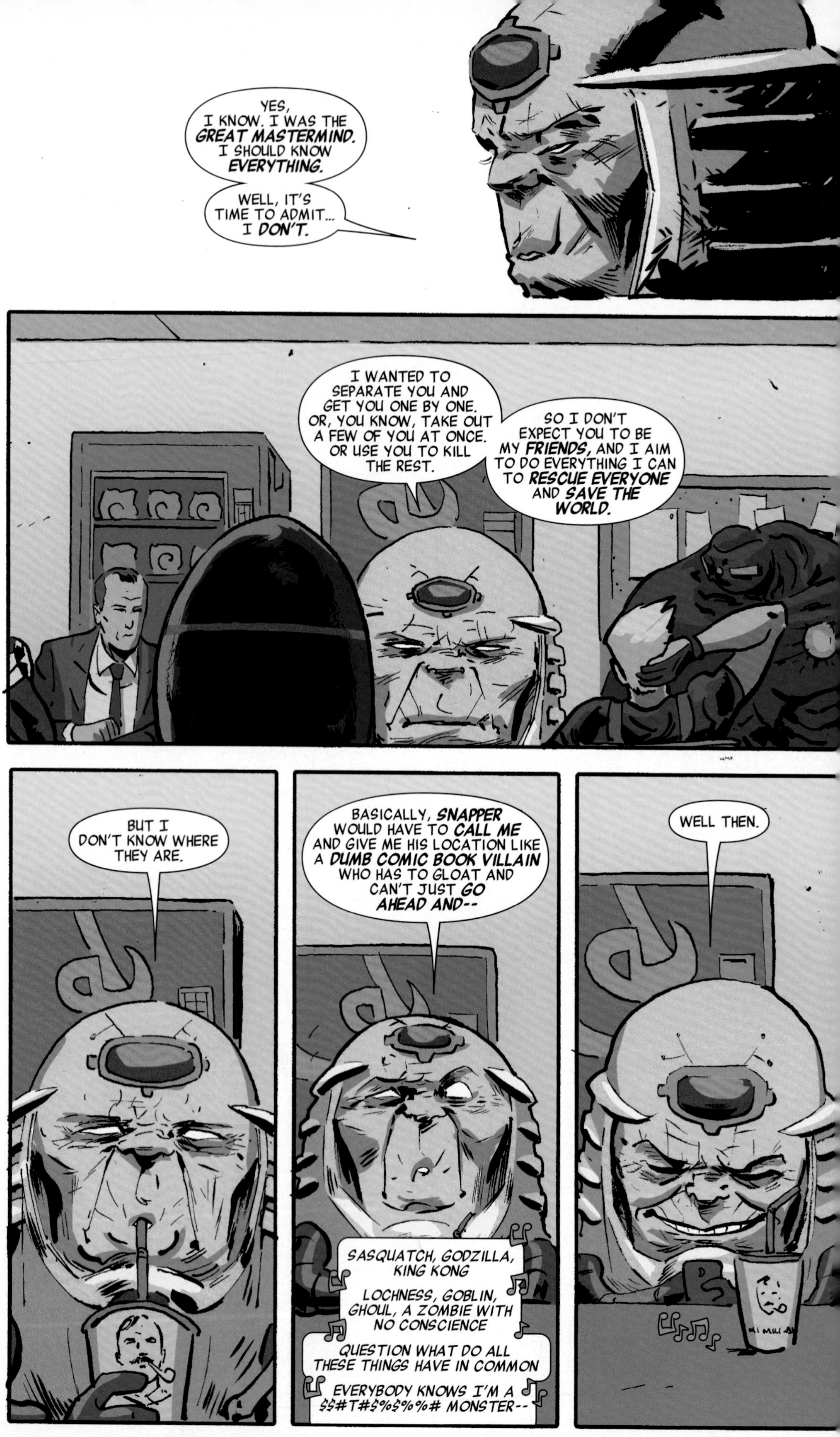
YES, I KNOW. I WAS THE GREAT MASTERMIND. I SHOULD KNOW EVERYTHING.
WELL, IT'S TIME TO ADMIT... I DON'T.
I WANTED TO SEPARATE YOU AND GET YOU ONE BY ONE. OR, YOU KNOW, TAKE OUT A FEW OF YOU AT ONCE. OR USE YOU TO KILL THE REST.
SO I DON'T EXPECT YOU TO BE MY FRIENDS, AND I AIM TO DO EVERYTHING I CAN TO RESCUE EVERYONE AND SAVE THE WORLD.
BUT I DON'T KNOW WHERE THEY ARE.
BASICALLY, SNAPPER WOULD HAVE TO CALL ME AND GIVE ME HIS LOCATION LIKE A DUMB COMIC BOOK VILLAIN WHO HAS TO GLOAT AND CAN'T JUST GO AHEAD AND--
SASQUATCH, GODZILLA, KING KONG
LOCHNESS, GOBLIN, GHOUL, A ZOMBIE WITH NO CONSCIENCE
QUESTION WHAT DO ALL THESE THINGS HAVE IN COMMON
EVERYBODY KNOWS I'M A $$#T#$%$%%# MONSTER--
WELL THEN.

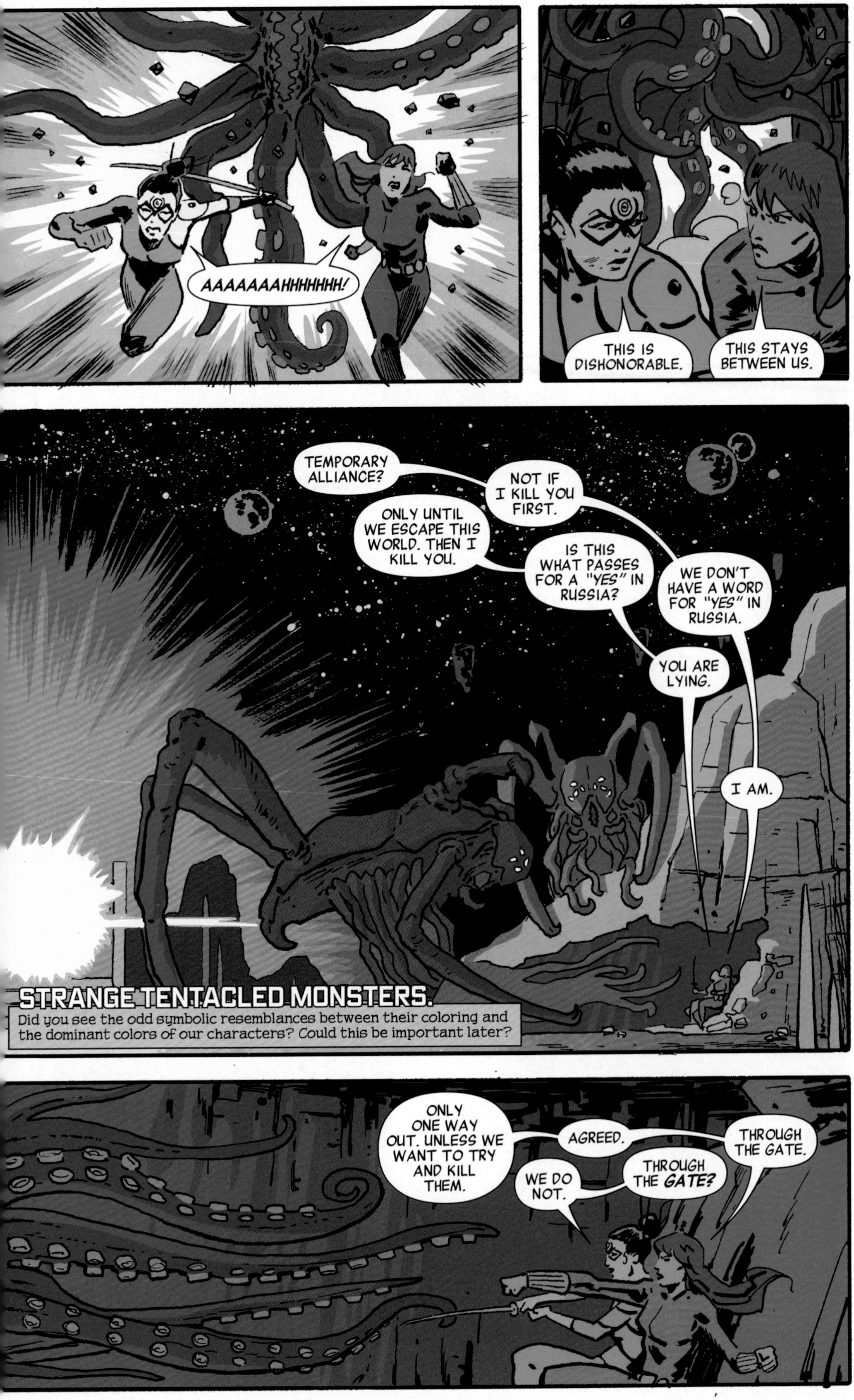
AAAAAAAHHHHHHH!
THIS IS DISHONORABLE.
THIS STAYS BETWEEN US.
TEMPORARY ALLIANCE?
NOT IF I KILL YOU FIRST.
ONLY UNTIL WE ESCAPE THIS WORLD. THEN I KILL YOU.
IS THIS WHAT PASSES FOR A "YES" IN RUSSIA?
WE DON'T HAVE A WORD FOR "YES" IN RUSSIA.
YOU ARE LYING.
I AM.
STRANGE TENTACLED MONSTERS.
Did you see the odd symbolic resemblances between their coloring and the dominant colors of our characters? Could this be important later?
ONLY ONE WAY OUT. UNLESS WE WANT TO TRY AND KILL THEM.
WE DO NOT.
AGREED.
THROUGH THE GATE.
THROUGH THE GATE?

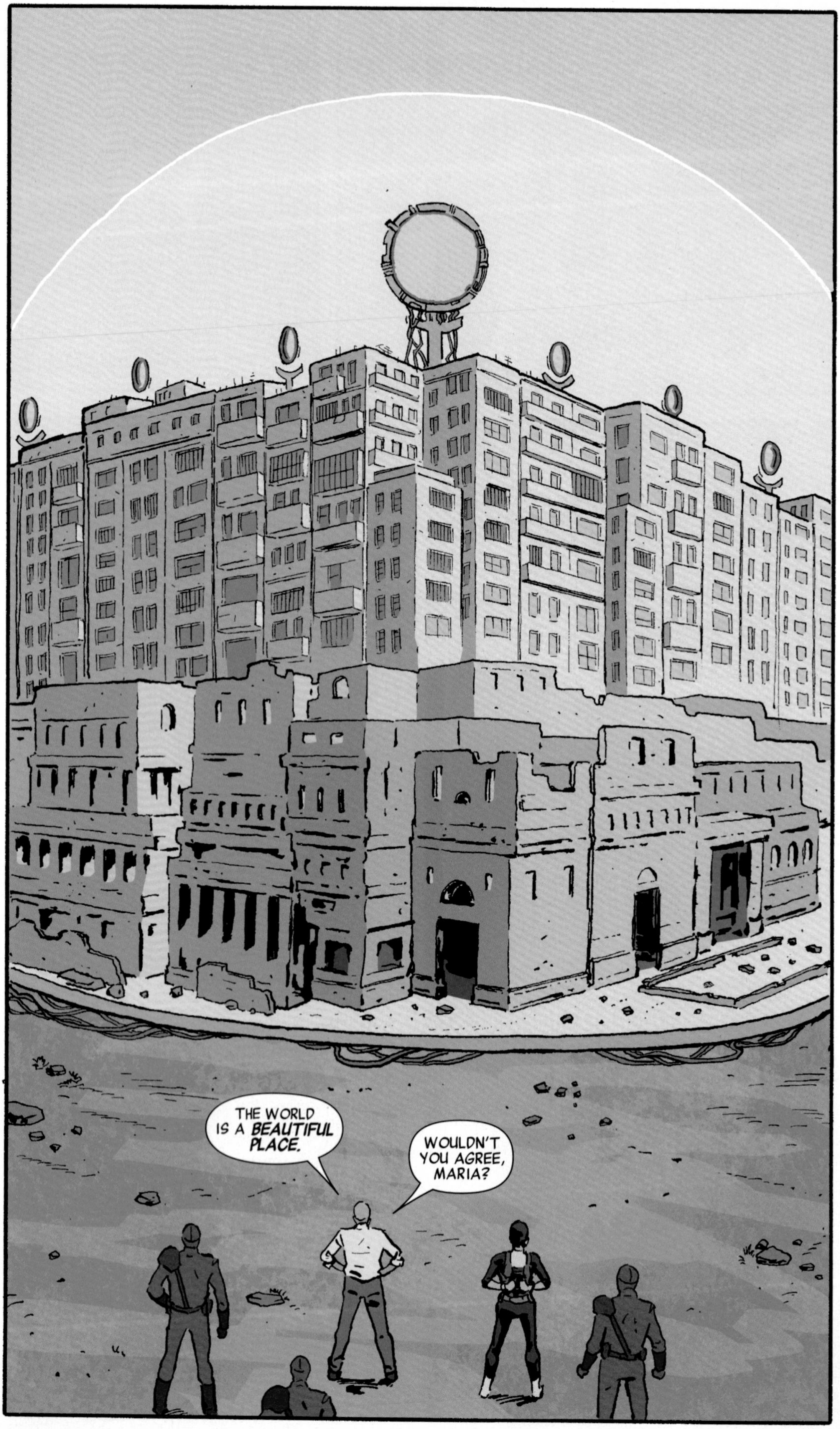
THE WORLD IS A BEAUTIFUL PLACE.
WOULDN'T YOU AGREE, MARIA?

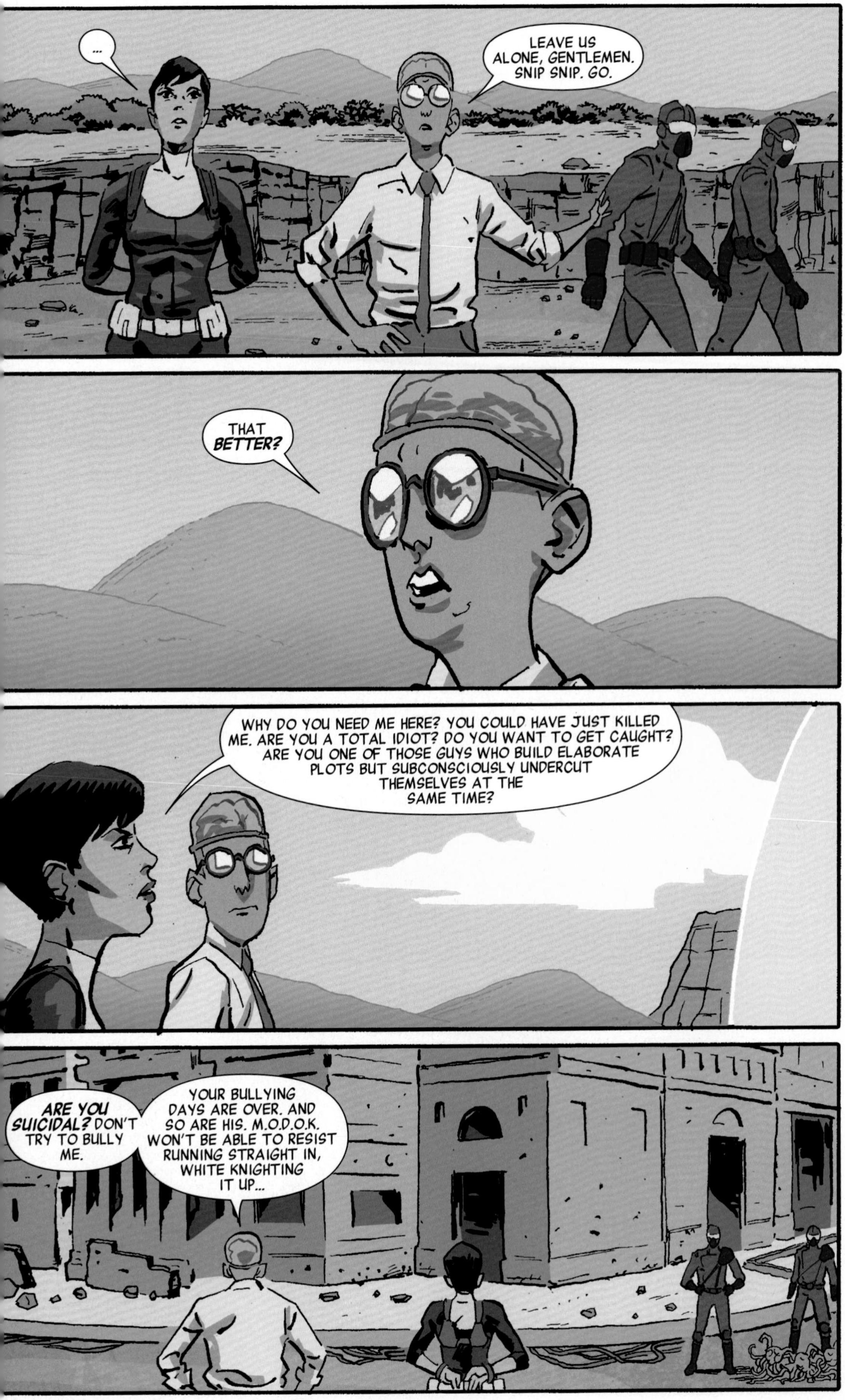

...
LEAVE US ALONE, GENTLEMEN. SNIP SNIP. GO.
THAT BETTER?
WHY DO YOU NEED ME HERE? YOU COULD HAVE JUST KILLED ME. ARE YOU A TOTAL IDIOT? DO YOU WANT TO GET CAUGHT? ARE YOU ONE OF THOSE GUYS WHO BUILD ELABORATE PLOTS BUT SUBCONSCIOUSLY UNDERCUT THEMSELVES AT THE SAME TIME?
ARE YOU SUICIDAL? DON'T TRY TO BULLY ME.
YOUR BULLYING DAYS ARE OVER. AND SO ARE HIS. M.O.D.O.K. WON'T BE ABLE TO RESIST RUNNING STRAIGHT IN, WHITE KNIGHTING IT UP...

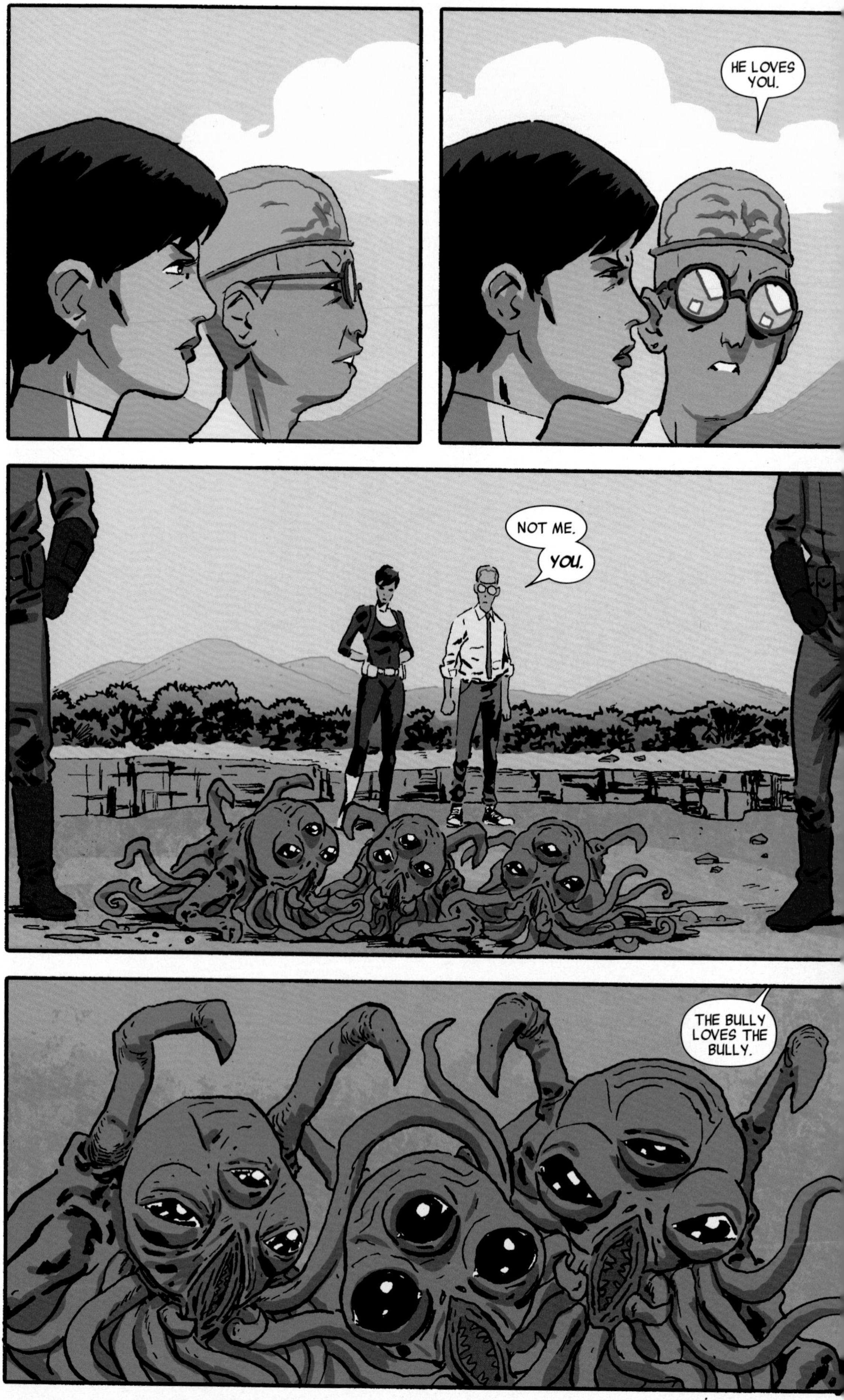
HE LOVES YOU.
NOT ME.
YOU.
THE BULLY LOVES THE BULLY.

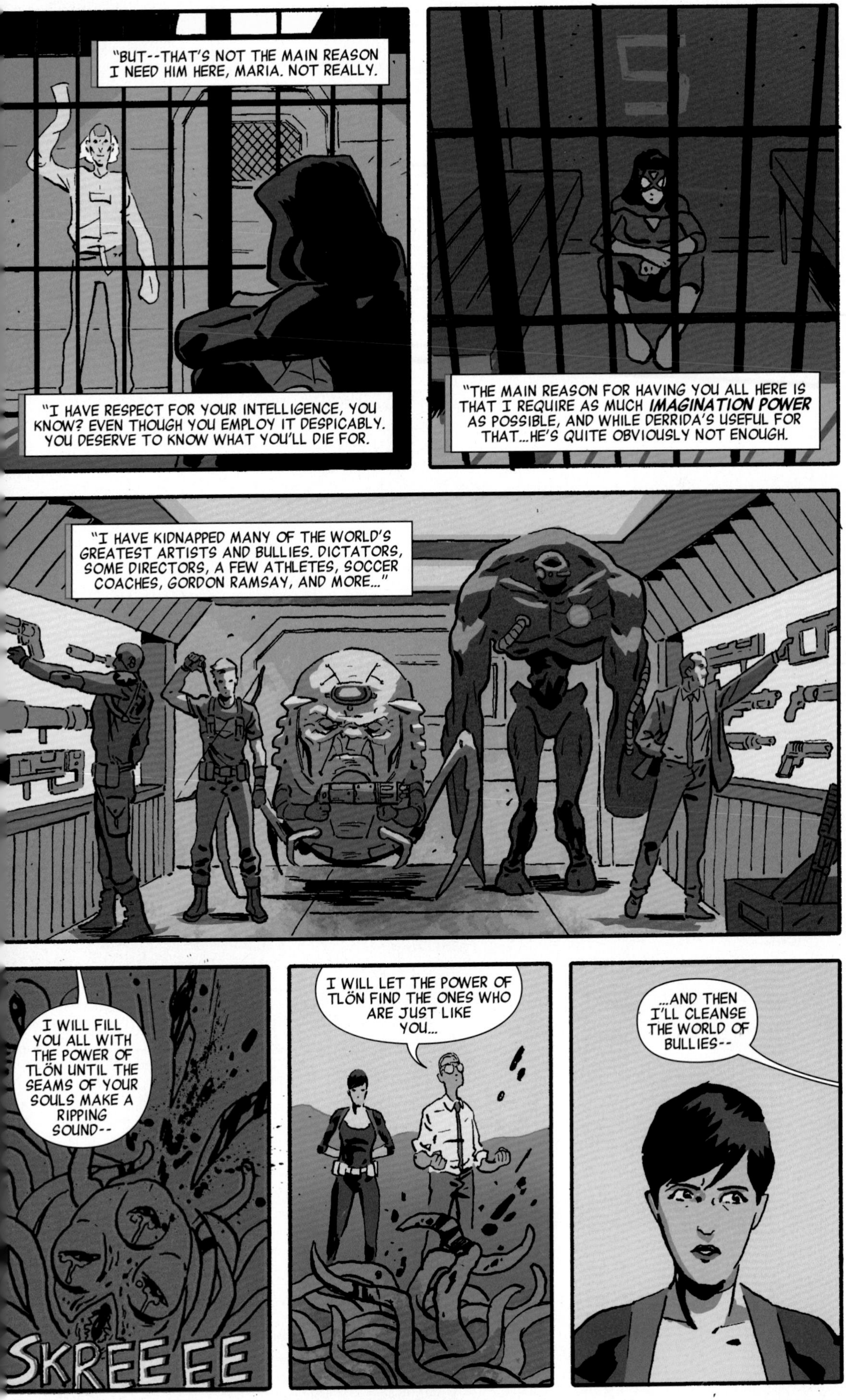
"BUT--THAT'S NOT THE MAIN REASON I NEED HIM HERE, MARIA. NOT REALLY.
"I HAVE RESPECT FOR YOUR INTELLIGENCE, YOU KNOW? EVEN THOUGH YOU EMPLOY IT DESPICABLY. YOU DESERVE TO KNOW WHAT YOU'LL DIE FOR.
"THE MAIN REASON FOR HAVING YOU ALL HERE IS THAT I REQUIRE AS MUCH *IMAGINATION POWER* AS POSSIBLE, AND WHILE DERRIDA'S USEFUL FOR THAT...HE'S QUITE OBVIOUSLY NOT ENOUGH.
"I HAVE KIDNAPPED MANY OF THE WORLD'S GREATEST ARTISTS AND BULLIES. DICTATORS, SOME DIRECTORS, A FEW ATHLETES, SOCCER COACHES, GORDON RAMSAY, AND MORE..."
I WILL FILL YOU ALL WITH THE POWER OF TLÖN UNTIL THE SEAMS OF YOUR SOULS MAKE A RIPPING SOUND--
SKREEEEE
I WILL LET THE POWER OF TLÖN FIND THE ONES WHO ARE JUST LIKE YOU...
...AND THEN I'LL CLEANSE THE WORLD OF BULLIES--

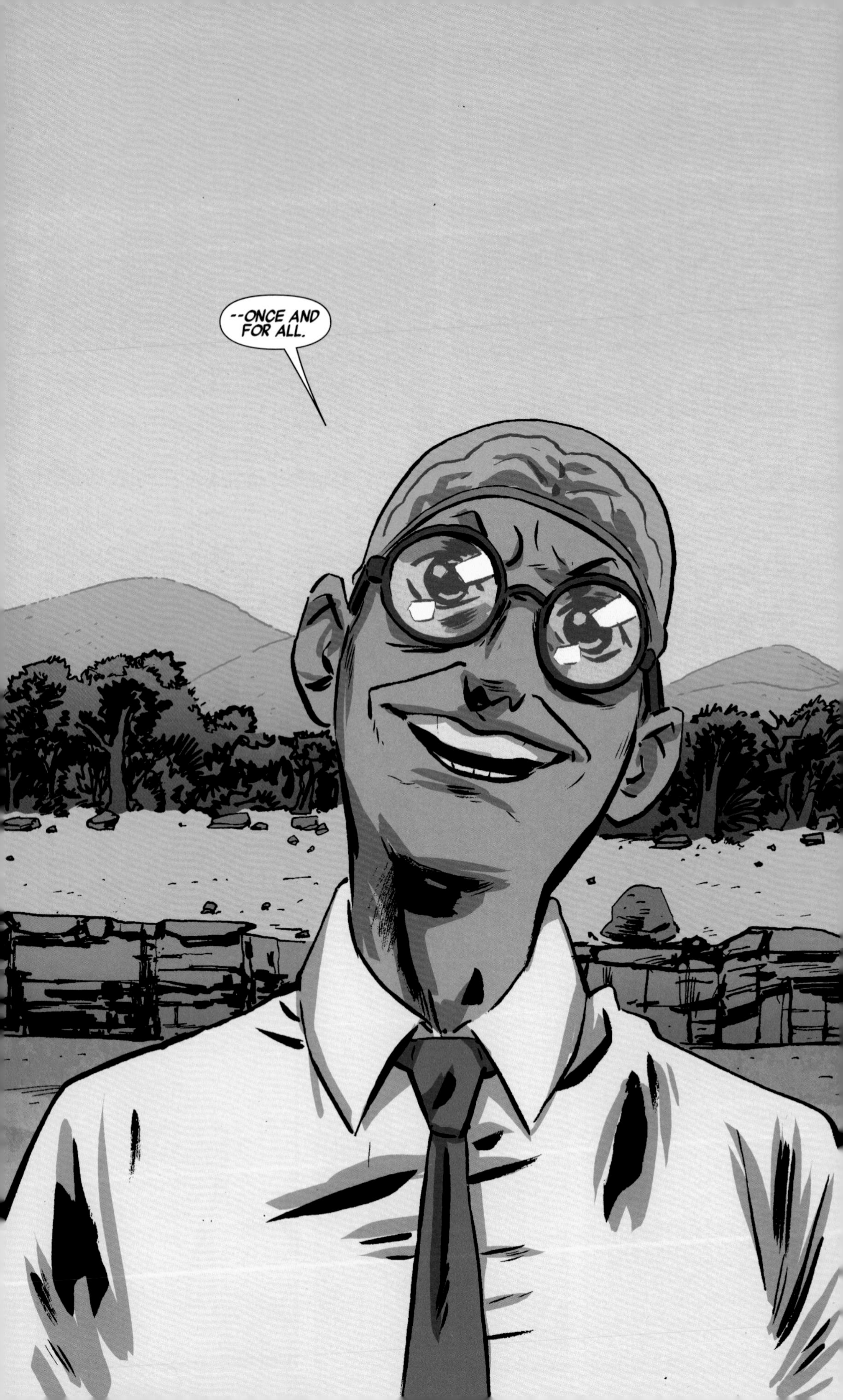
--ONCE AND FOR ALL.

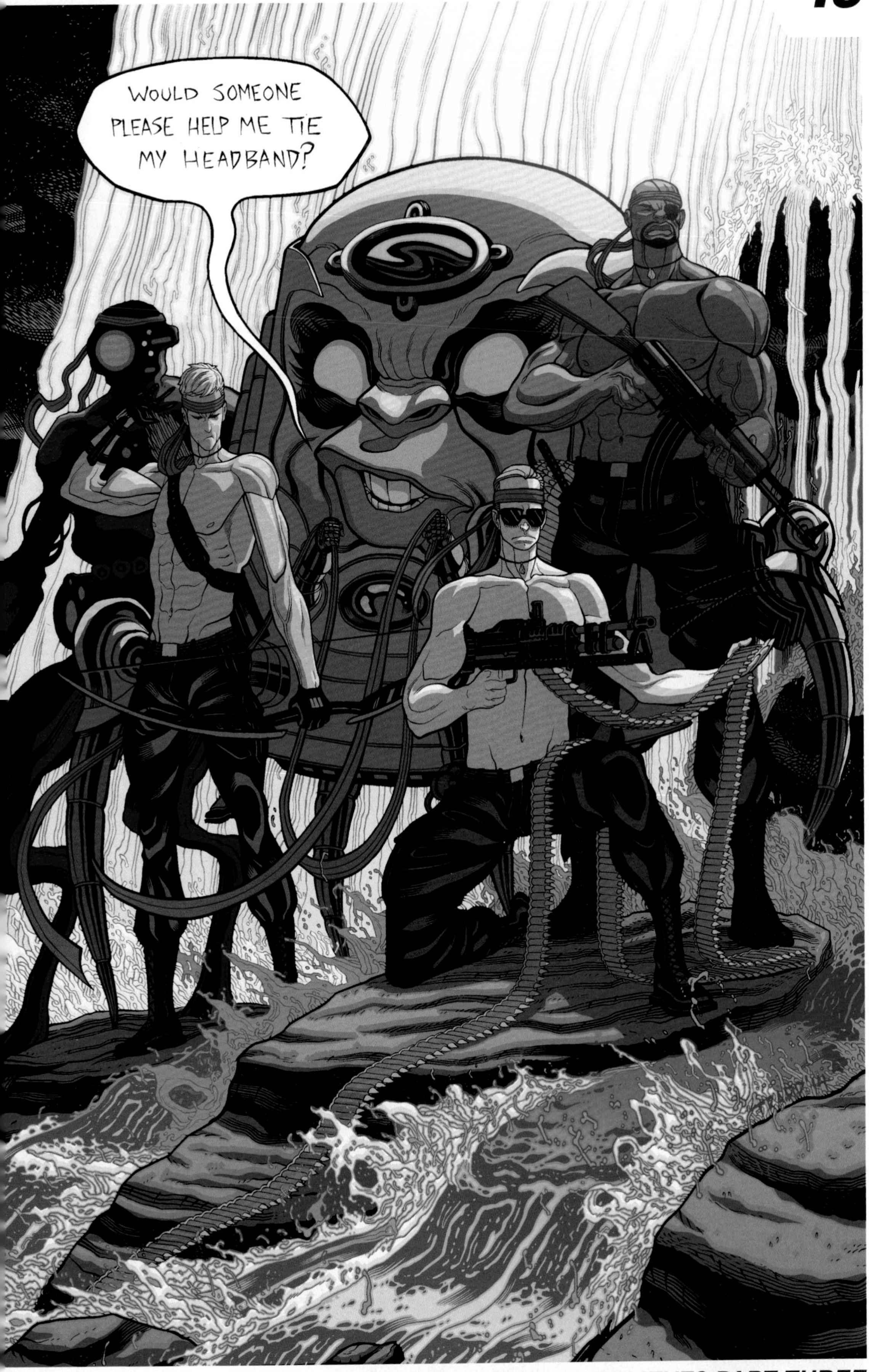
WOULD SOMEONE PLEASE HELP ME TIE MY HEADBAND?

...AND WHAT DO YOU BELIEVE? PART THREE

VENEZUELAN RAINFOREST.
THE NURSERY.

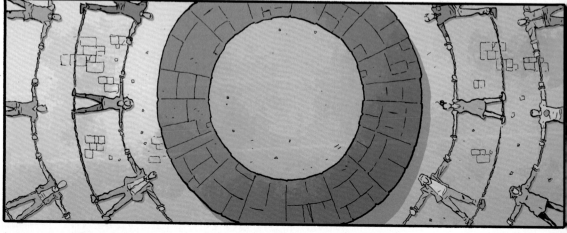

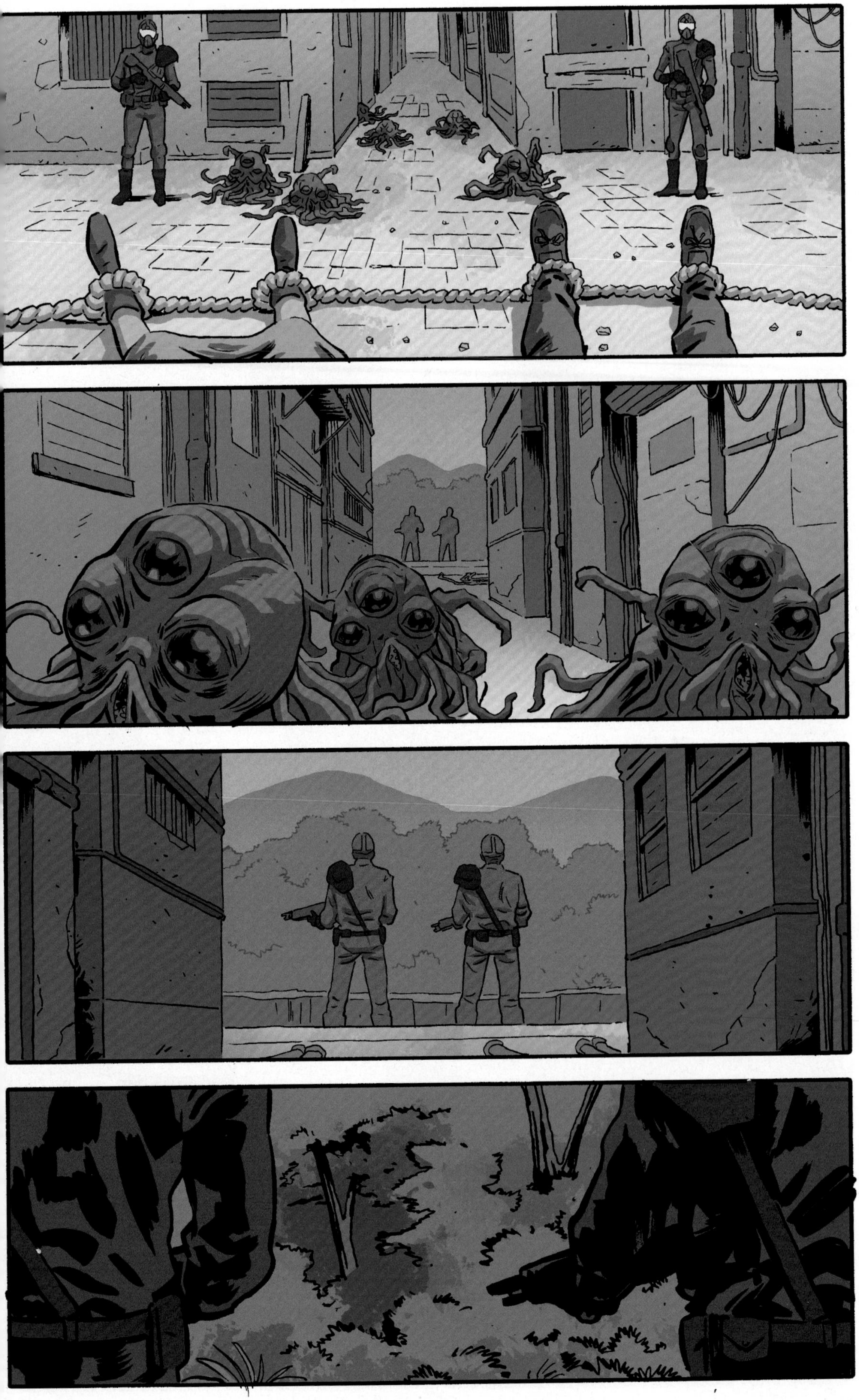

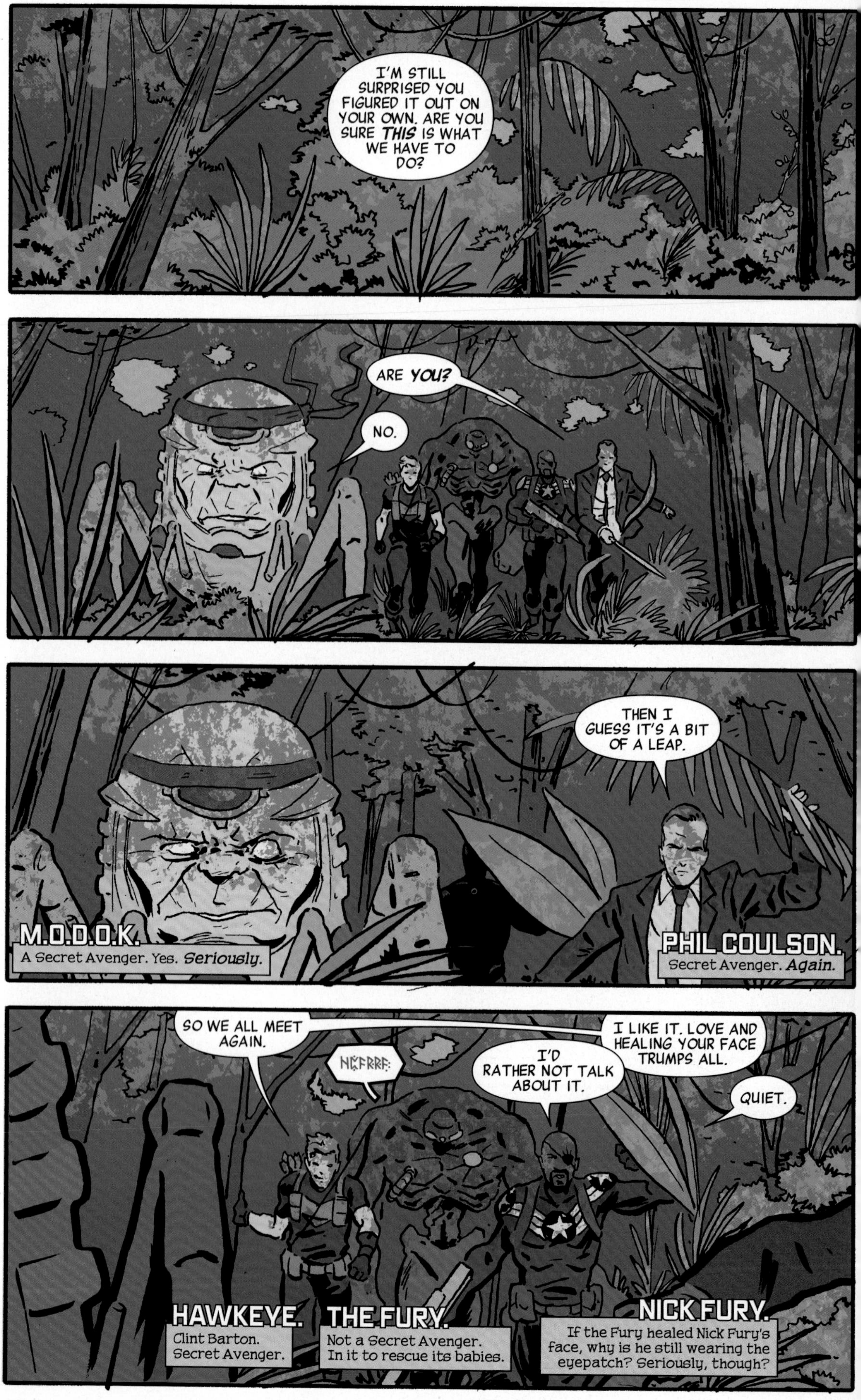
I'M STILL SURPRISED YOU FIGURED IT OUT ON YOUR OWN. ARE YOU SURE *THIS* IS WHAT WE HAVE TO DO?
ARE *YOU?*
NO.
THEN I GUESS IT'S A BIT OF A LEAP.
M.O.D.O.K.
A Secret Avenger. Yes. *Seriously.*
PHIL COULSON.
Secret Avenger. *Again.*
SO WE ALL MEET AGAIN.
I LIKE IT. LOVE AND HEALING YOUR FACE TRUMPS ALL.
I'D RATHER NOT TALK ABOUT IT.
QUIET.
HAWKEYE.
Clint Barton. Secret Avenger.
THE FURY.
Not a Secret Avenger. In it to rescue its babies.
NICK FURY.
If the Fury healed Nick Fury's face, why is he still wearing the eyepatch? Seriously, though?

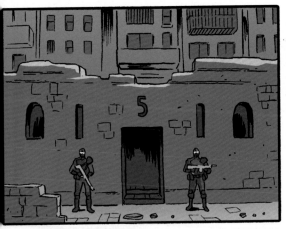

IS THIS A GOOD TIME TO TELL YOU THAT I FIND YOU **VERY** ATTRACTIVE?

ARTAUD DERRIDA.
A deranged poet. Not a feminist.

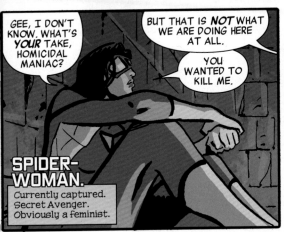

GEE, I DON'T KNOW. WHAT'S **YOUR** TAKE, HOMICIDAL MANIAC?

BUT THAT IS **NOT** WHAT WE ARE DOING HERE AT ALL.

YOU WANTED TO KILL ME.

SPIDER-WOMAN.
Currently captured. Secret Avenger. Obviously a feminist.

THAT WAS BEFORE I FULLY REALIZED HOW YOUR **CONTOURS** INTERACT WITH THE LIGHT. I BEGGED **THE MASTER** TO **SAVE YOU.**

HAVE YOU CONSIDERED LOSING A LITTLE WEIGHT? BECAUSE YOU ARE **ALMOST** PERFECT. ALMOST A **GODDESS.**

YOU SEE ME AS A VILLAIN, BUT I AM HERE TO EMBOLDEN FRAIL, YOUNG POETS AND GAMERS WITH SWOLLEN CYSTS IN THEIR FACES! I AM HERE TO SAY, "JUST BECAUSE YOU'RE TOO AFRAID TO TALK TO THE GIRLS DOESN'T MEAN YOU DON'T DESERVE THEM ALREADY!"

I AM HERE TO SAY, "YOU ALL DESERVE THE SEXY, SEXY GIRL!"

THEY HURT YOU WHEN YOU WERE YOUNG, DIDN'T THEY?

...I'D RATHER NOT TALK ABOUT IT.

I WAS BULLIED WHEN I WAS IN SCHOOL, ACTUALLY.

THERE WAS THIS GIRL--JOAN GELLHORN? SHE MADE FUN OF MY HAIR. SHE TOLD ME I LOOKED LIKE A MOP, AND OTHER KIDS WENT WITH IT.

IT SUCKED. NO ONE WANTED TO KISS ME.

AND I WANTED TO BE KISSED.

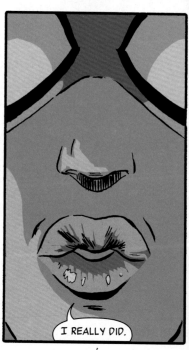

I REALLY DID.

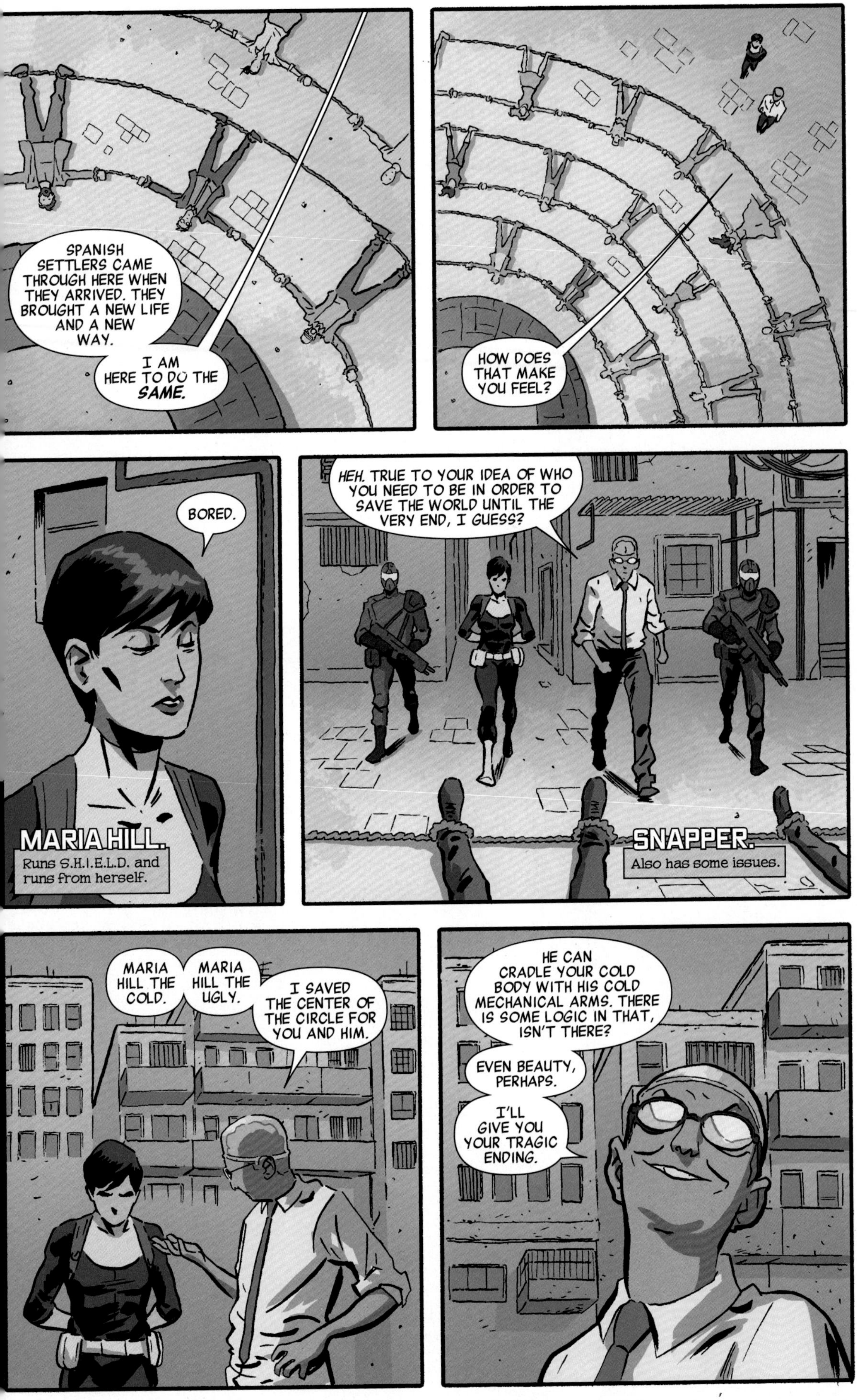
SPANISH SETTLERS CAME THROUGH HERE WHEN THEY ARRIVED. THEY BROUGHT A NEW LIFE AND A NEW WAY.
I AM HERE TO DO THE *SAME.*
HOW DOES THAT MAKE YOU FEEL?
BORED.
MARIA HILL.
Runs S.H.I.E.L.D. and runs from herself.
HEH. TRUE TO YOUR IDEA OF WHO YOU NEED TO BE IN ORDER TO SAVE THE WORLD UNTIL THE VERY END, I GUESS?
SNAPPER.
Also has some issues.
MARIA HILL THE COLD.
MARIA HILL THE UGLY.
I SAVED THE CENTER OF THE CIRCLE FOR YOU AND HIM.
HE CAN CRADLE YOUR COLD BODY WITH HIS COLD MECHANICAL ARMS. THERE IS SOME LOGIC IN THAT, ISN'T THERE?
EVEN BEAUTY, PERHAPS.
I'LL GIVE YOU YOUR TRAGIC ENDING.

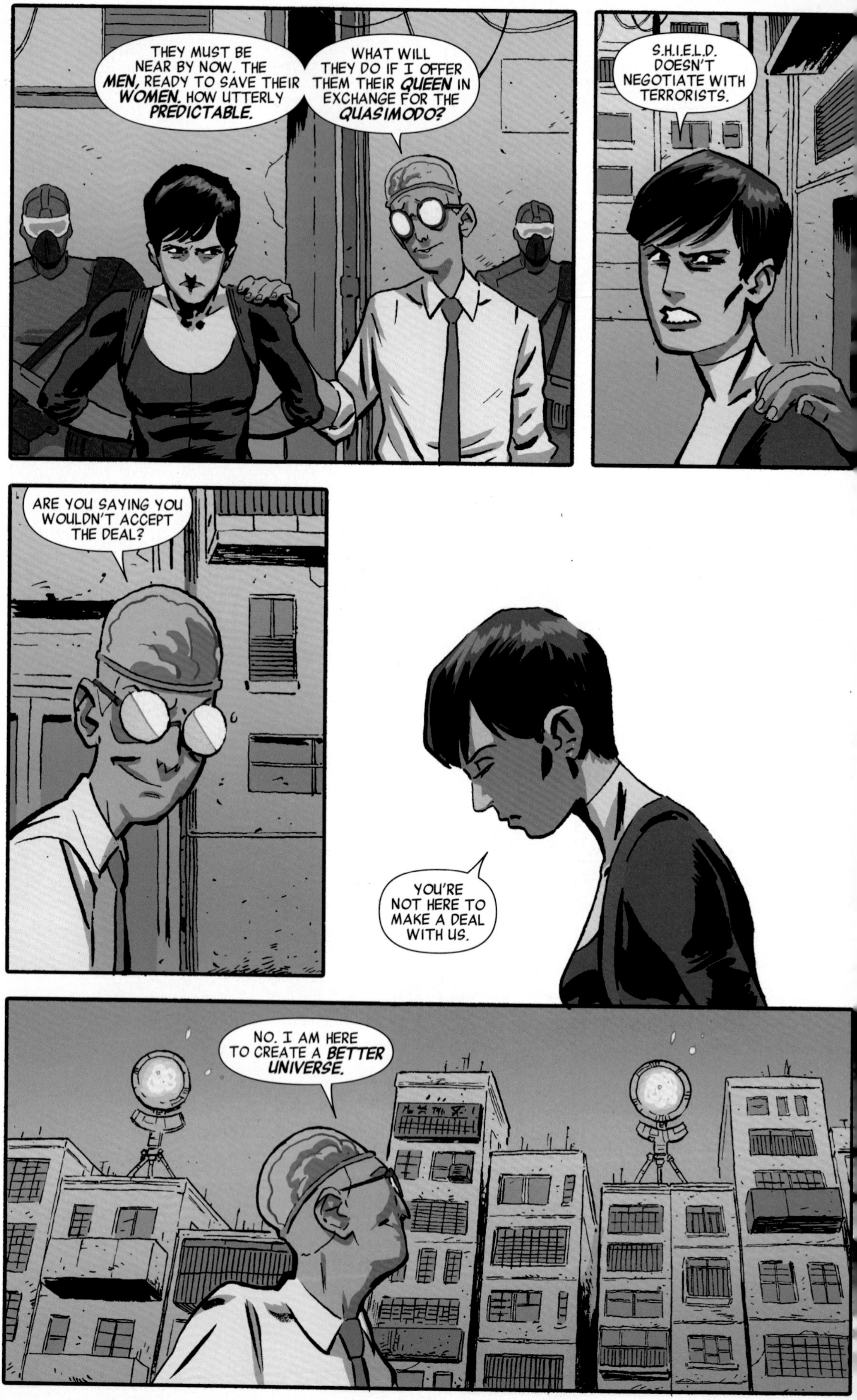
THEY MUST BE NEAR BY NOW. THE MEN, READY TO SAVE THEIR WOMEN. HOW UTTERLY PREDICTABLE.
WHAT WILL THEY DO IF I OFFER THEM THEIR QUEEN IN EXCHANGE FOR THE QUASIMODO?
S.H.I.E.L.D. DOESN'T NEGOTIATE WITH TERRORISTS.
ARE YOU SAYING YOU WOULDN'T ACCEPT THE DEAL?
YOU'RE NOT HERE TO MAKE A DEAL WITH US.
NO. I AM HERE TO CREATE A BETTER UNIVERSE.

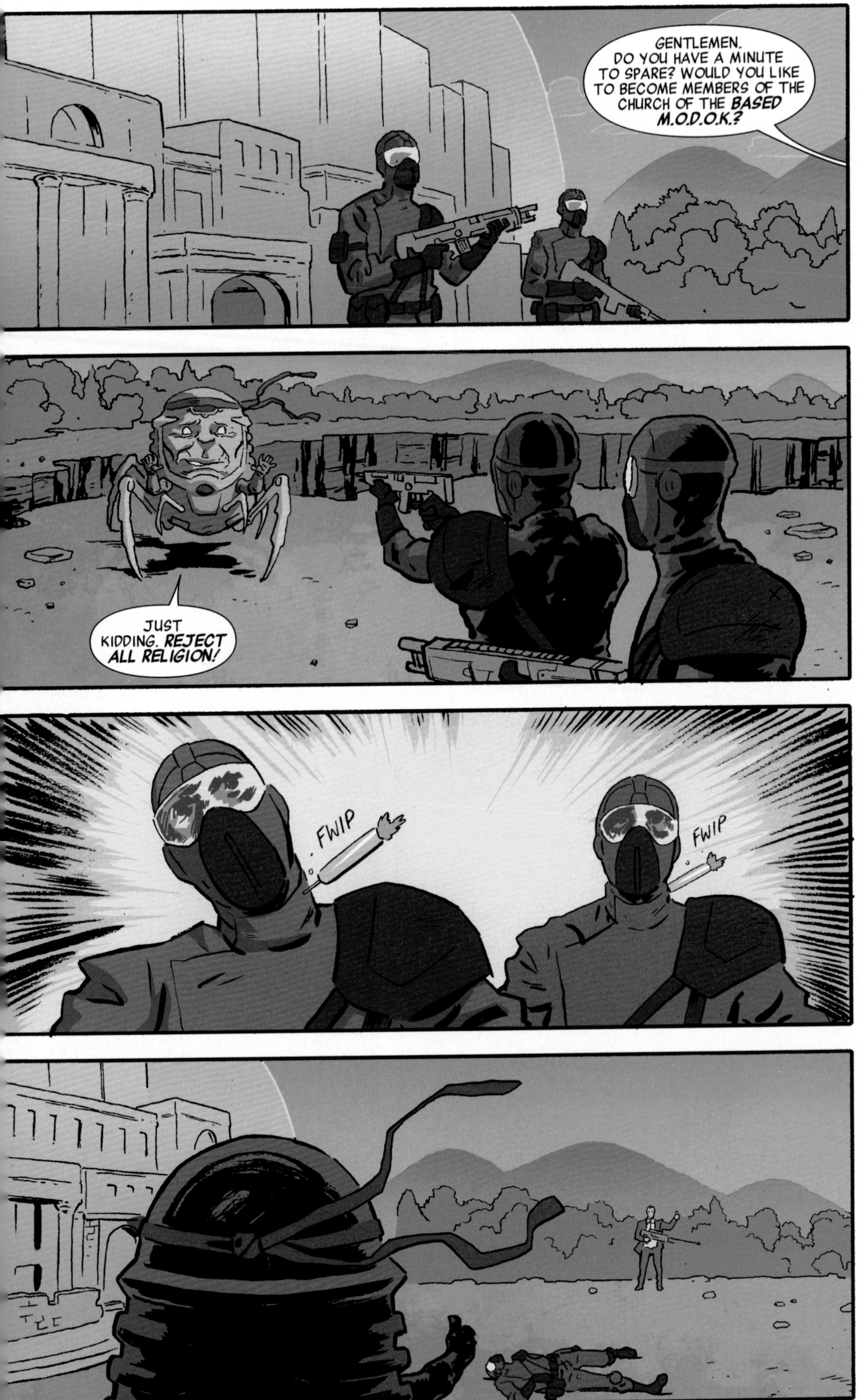
GENTLEMEN. DO YOU HAVE A MINUTE TO SPARE? WOULD YOU LIKE TO BECOME MEMBERS OF THE CHURCH OF THE BASED M.O.D.O.K.?
JUST KIDDING. REJECT ALL RELIGION!
FWIP
FWIP

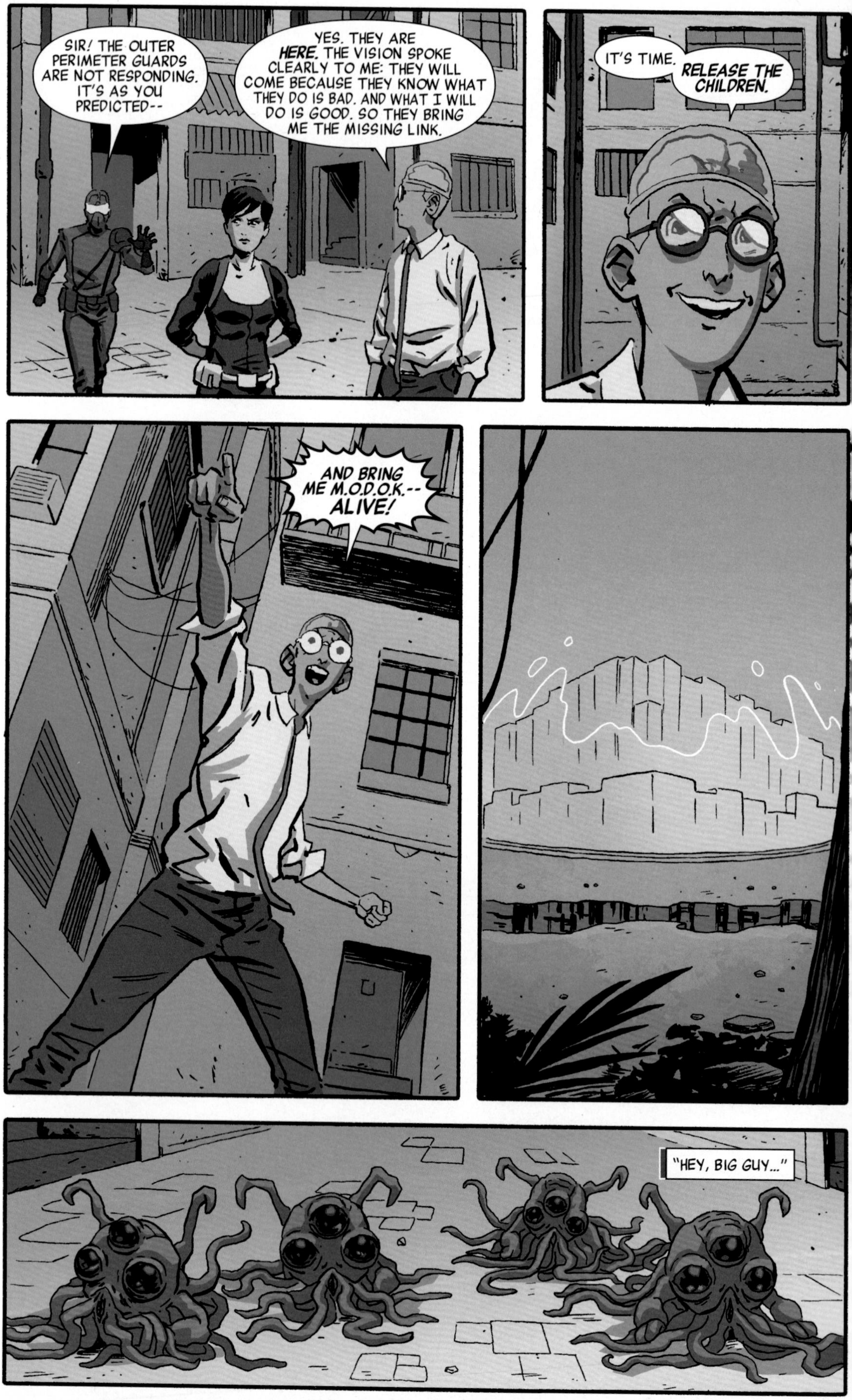
SIR! THE OUTER PERIMETER GUARDS ARE NOT RESPONDING. IT'S AS YOU PREDICTED--
YES. THEY ARE HERE. THE VISION SPOKE CLEARLY TO ME: THEY WILL COME BECAUSE THEY KNOW WHAT THEY DO IS BAD. AND WHAT I WILL DO IS GOOD. SO THEY BRING ME THE MISSING LINK.
IT'S TIME.
RELEASE THE CHILDREN.
AND BRING ME M.O.D.O.K.-- ALIVE!
"HEY, BIG GUY..."

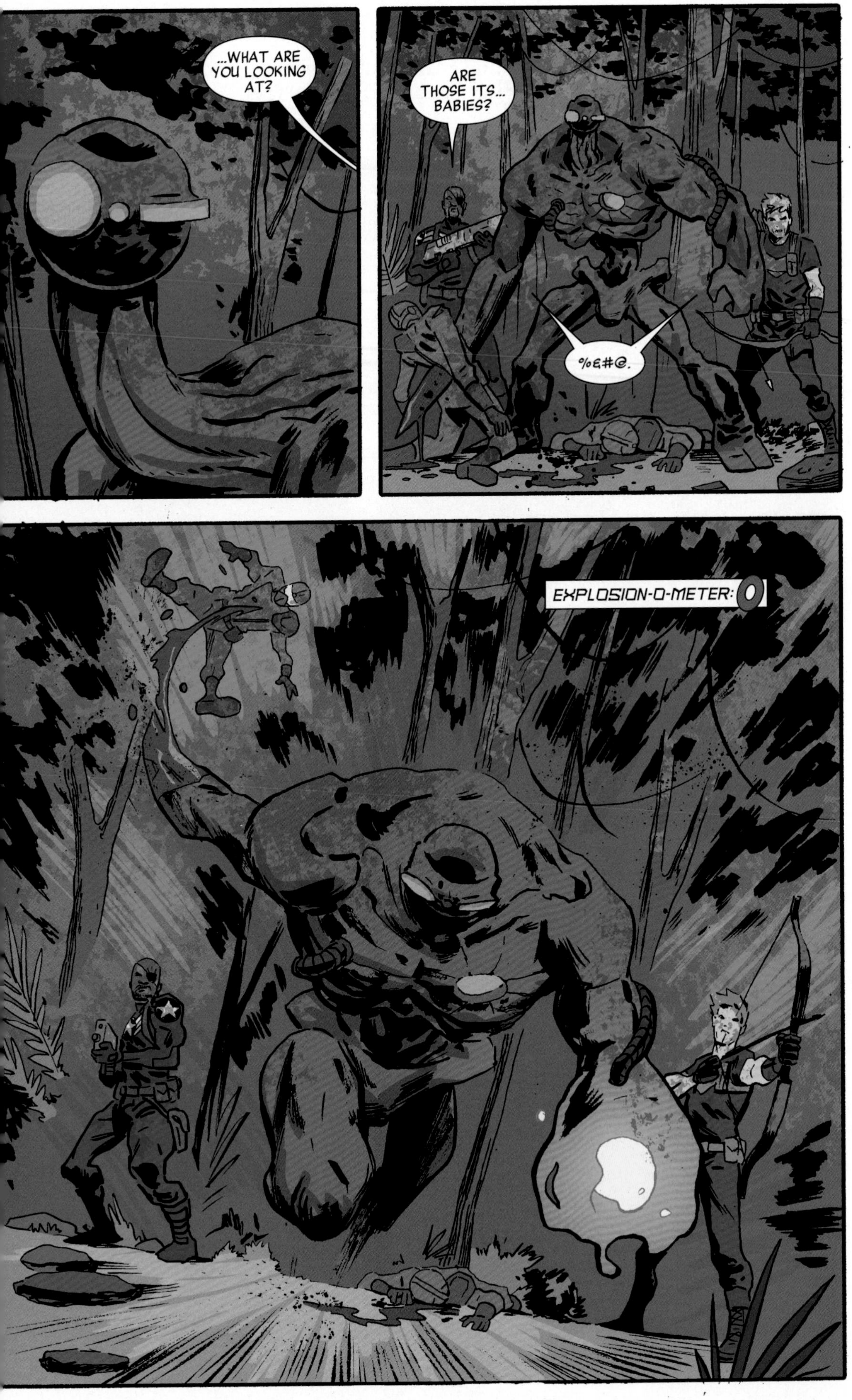
...WHAT ARE YOU LOOKING AT?
ARE THOSE ITS... BABIES?
%&#@.
EXPLOSION-O-METER: 0

AND NOW FOR SOMETHING COMPLETELY DIFFERENT!

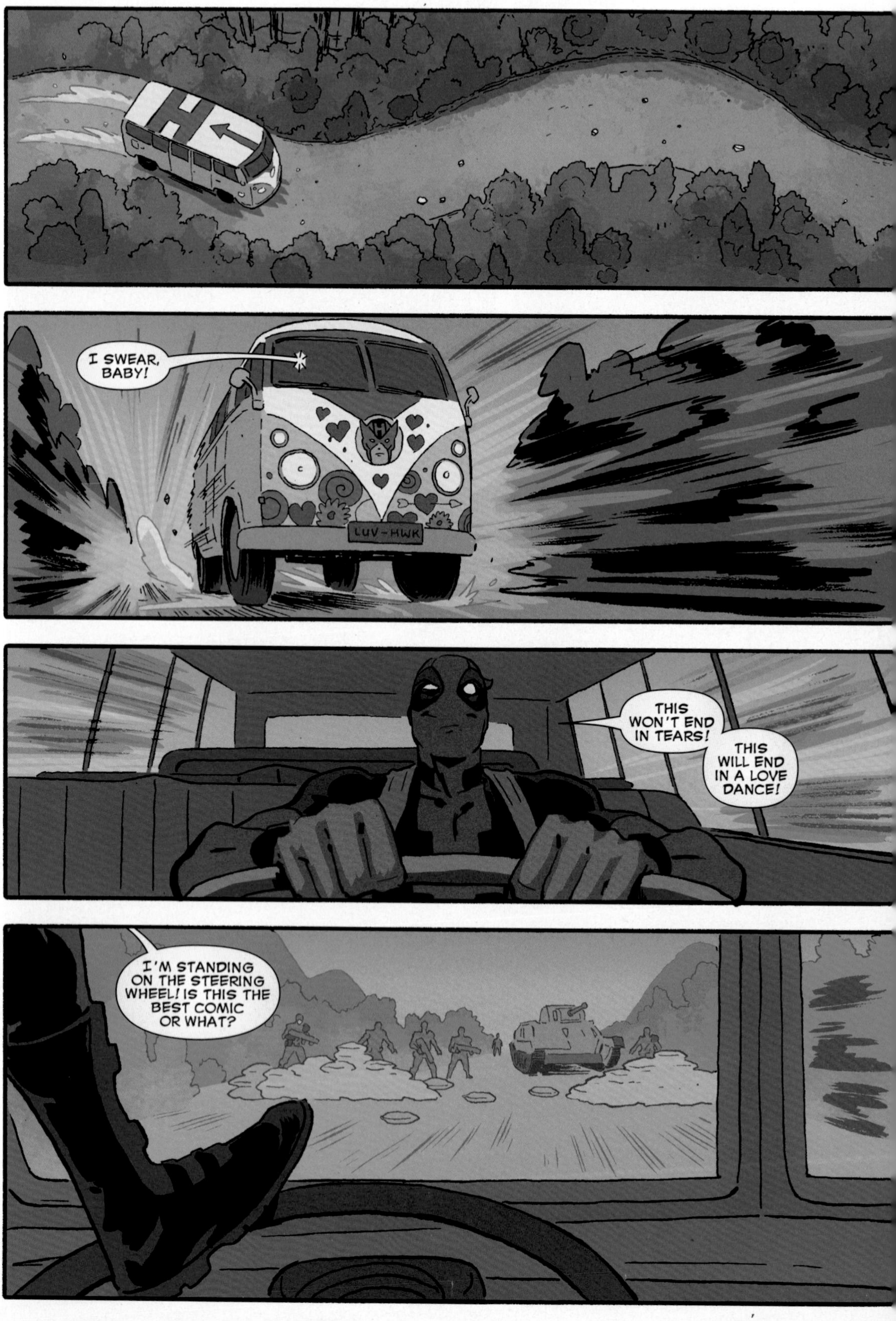
I SWEAR, BABY!
LUV-HWK
THIS WON'T END IN TEARS!
THIS WILL END IN A LOVE DANCE!
I'M STANDING ON THE STEERING WHEEL! IS THIS THE BEST COMIC OR WHAT?

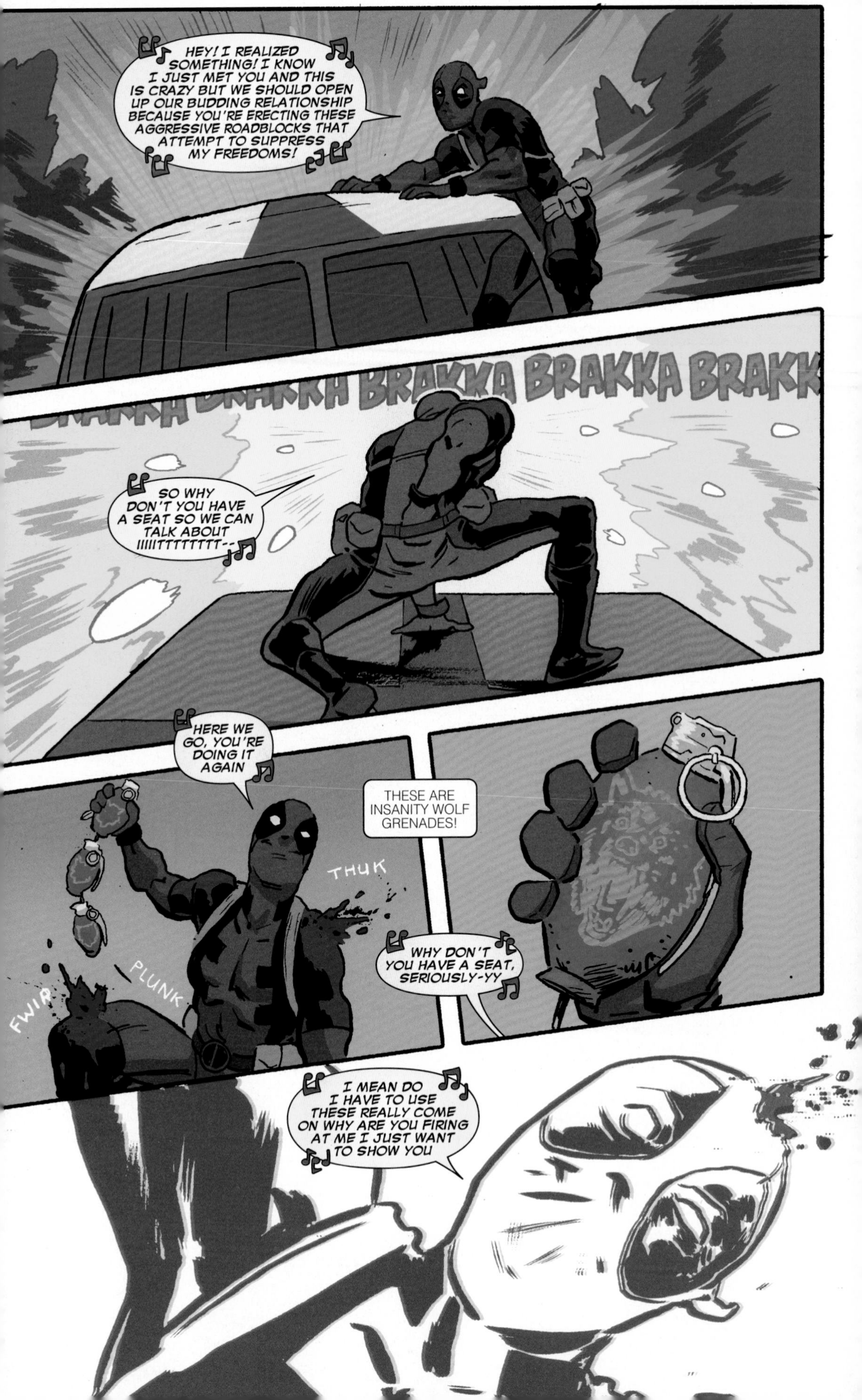

HEY! I REALIZED SOMETHING! I KNOW I JUST MET YOU AND THIS IS CRAZY BUT WE SHOULD OPEN UP OUR BUDDING RELATIONSHIP BECAUSE YOU'RE ERECTING THESE AGGRESSIVE ROADBLOCKS THAT ATTEMPT TO SUPPRESS MY FREEDOMS!
BRAKKA BRAKKA BRAKKA BRAKK
SO WHY DON'T YOU HAVE A SEAT SO WE CAN TALK ABOUT IIIIITTTTTTTT--
HERE WE GO, YOU'RE DOING IT AGAIN
THUK
PLUNK
FWIP
THESE ARE INSANITY WOLF GRENADES!
WHY DON'T YOU HAVE A SEAT, SERIOUSLY-YY
I MEAN DO I HAVE TO USE THESE REALLY COME ON WHY ARE YOU FIRING AT ME I JUST WANT TO SHOW YOU

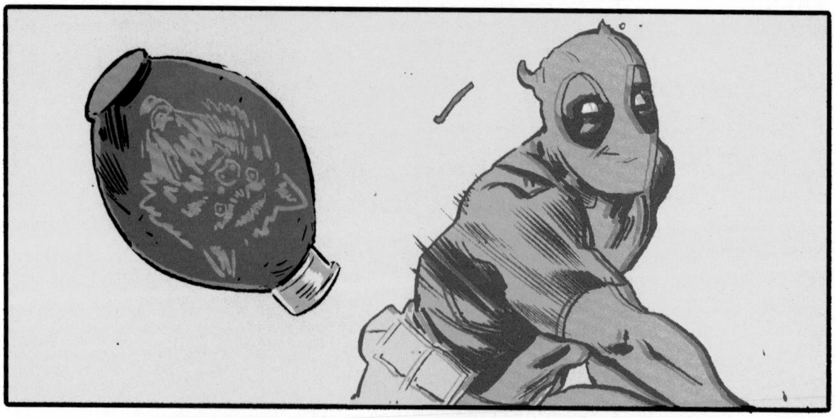

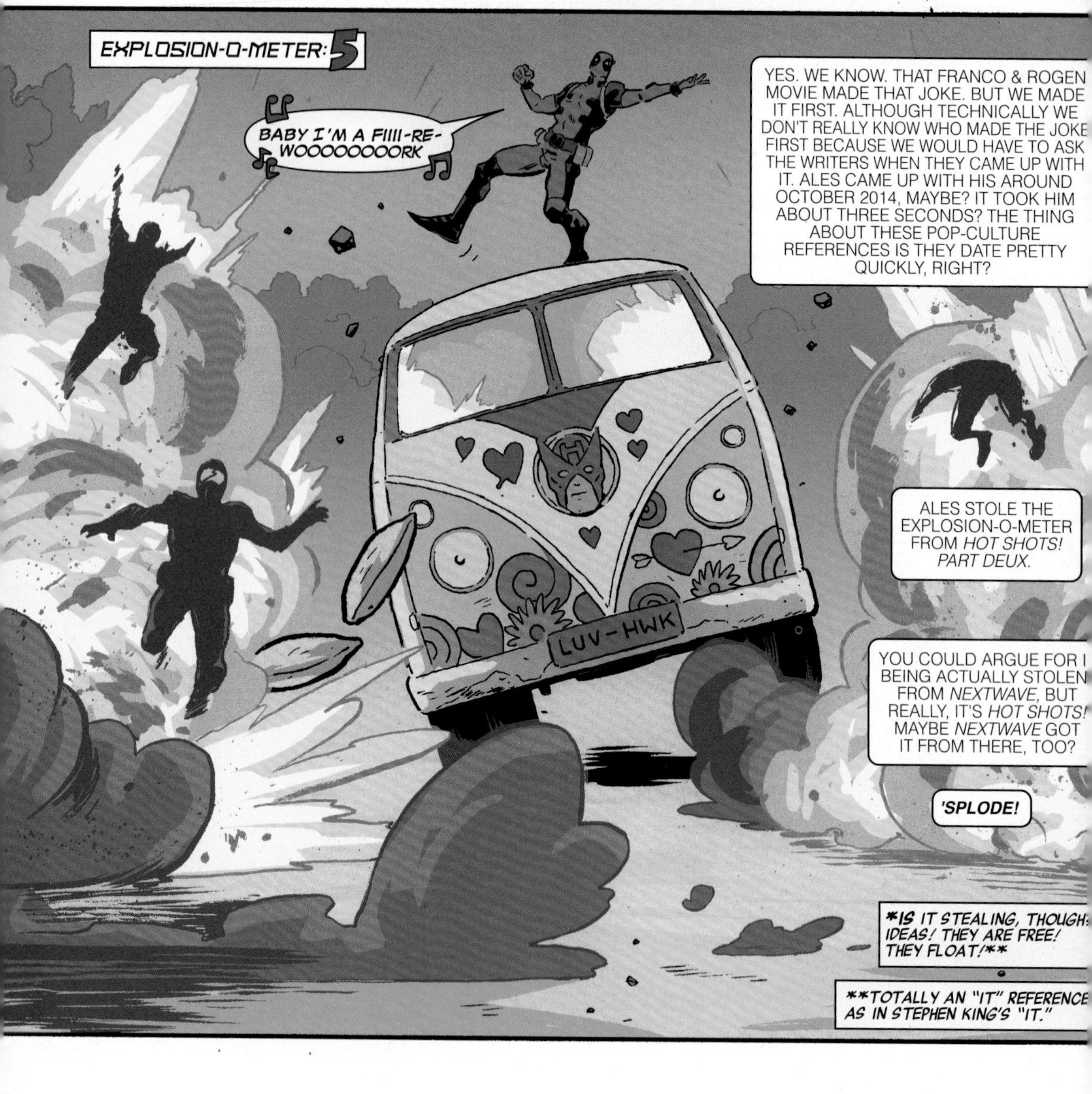
EXPLOSION-O-METER: 5
BABY I'M A FIIII-RE-WOOOOOOOORK
YES. WE KNOW. THAT FRANCO & ROGEN MOVIE MADE THAT JOKE. BUT WE MADE IT FIRST. ALTHOUGH TECHNICALLY WE DON'T REALLY KNOW WHO MADE THE JOKE FIRST BECAUSE WE WOULD HAVE TO ASK THE WRITERS WHEN THEY CAME UP WITH IT. ALES CAME UP WITH HIS AROUND OCTOBER 2014, MAYBE? IT TOOK HIM ABOUT THREE SECONDS? THE THING ABOUT THESE POP-CULTURE REFERENCES IS THEY DATE PRETTY QUICKLY, RIGHT?
LUV-HWK
ALES STOLE THE EXPLOSION-O-METER FROM *HOT SHOTS! PART DEUX.*
YOU COULD ARGUE FOR I BEING ACTUALLY STOLEN FROM *NEXTWAVE*, BUT REALLY, IT'S *HOT SHOTS!* MAYBE *NEXTWAVE* GOT IT FROM THERE, TOO?
'SPLODE!
*IS IT STEALING, THOUGH: IDEAS! THEY ARE FREE! THEY FLOAT!**
**TOTALLY AN "IT" REFERENCE AS IN STEPHEN KING'S "IT."

CONSIDER THIS A PRELUDE.

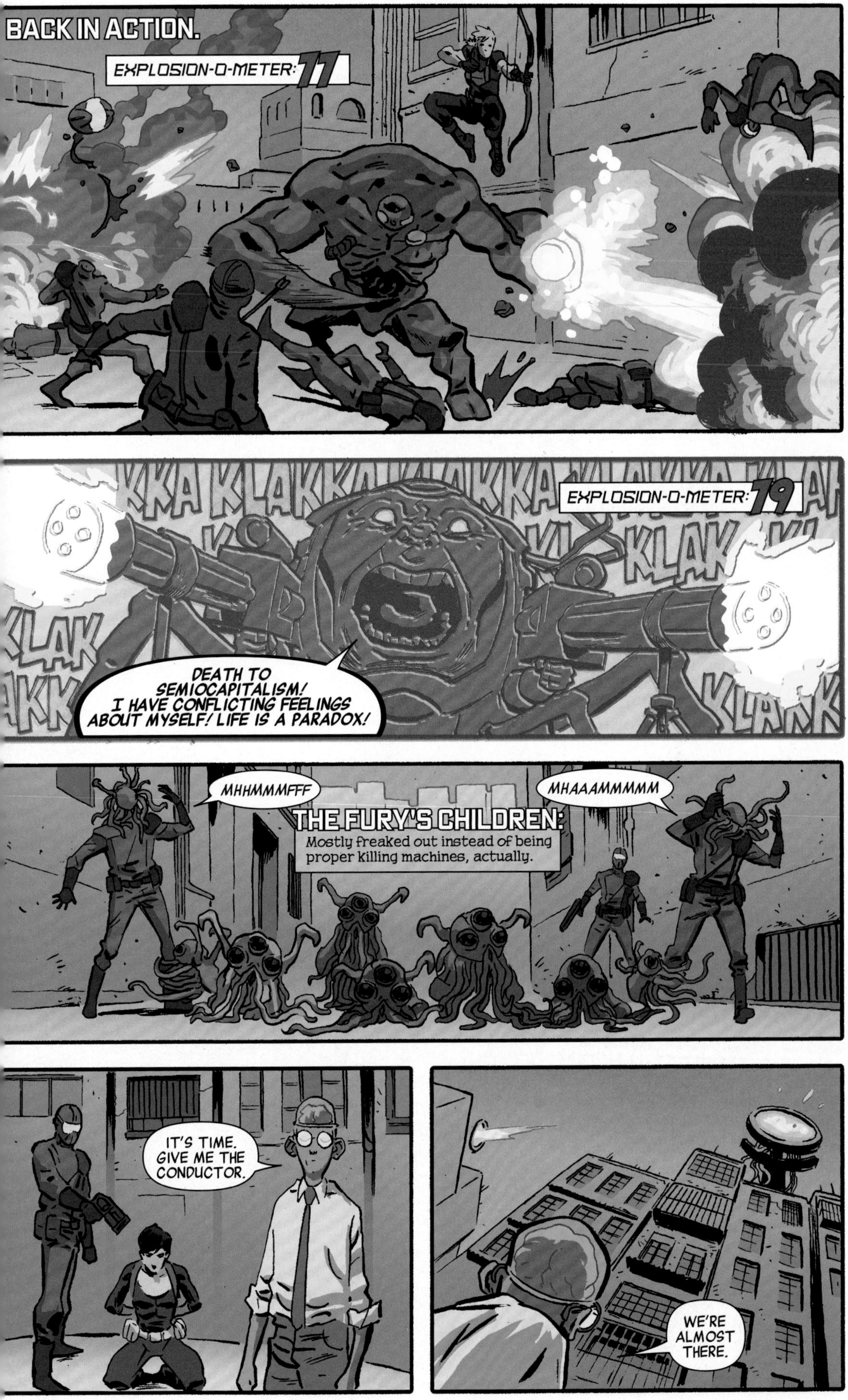
BACK IN ACTION.
EXPLOSION-O-METER: 17
KLAKKA KLAKKA KLAK KLAK
EXPLOSION-O-METER: 19
DEATH TO SEMIOCAPITALISM! I HAVE CONFLICTING FEELINGS ABOUT MYSELF! LIFE IS A PARADOX!
MHHMMMFFF
MHAAAMMMMM
THE FURY'S CHILDREN:
Mostly freaked out instead of being proper killing machines, actually.
IT'S TIME. GIVE ME THE CONDUCTOR.
WE'RE ALMOST THERE.

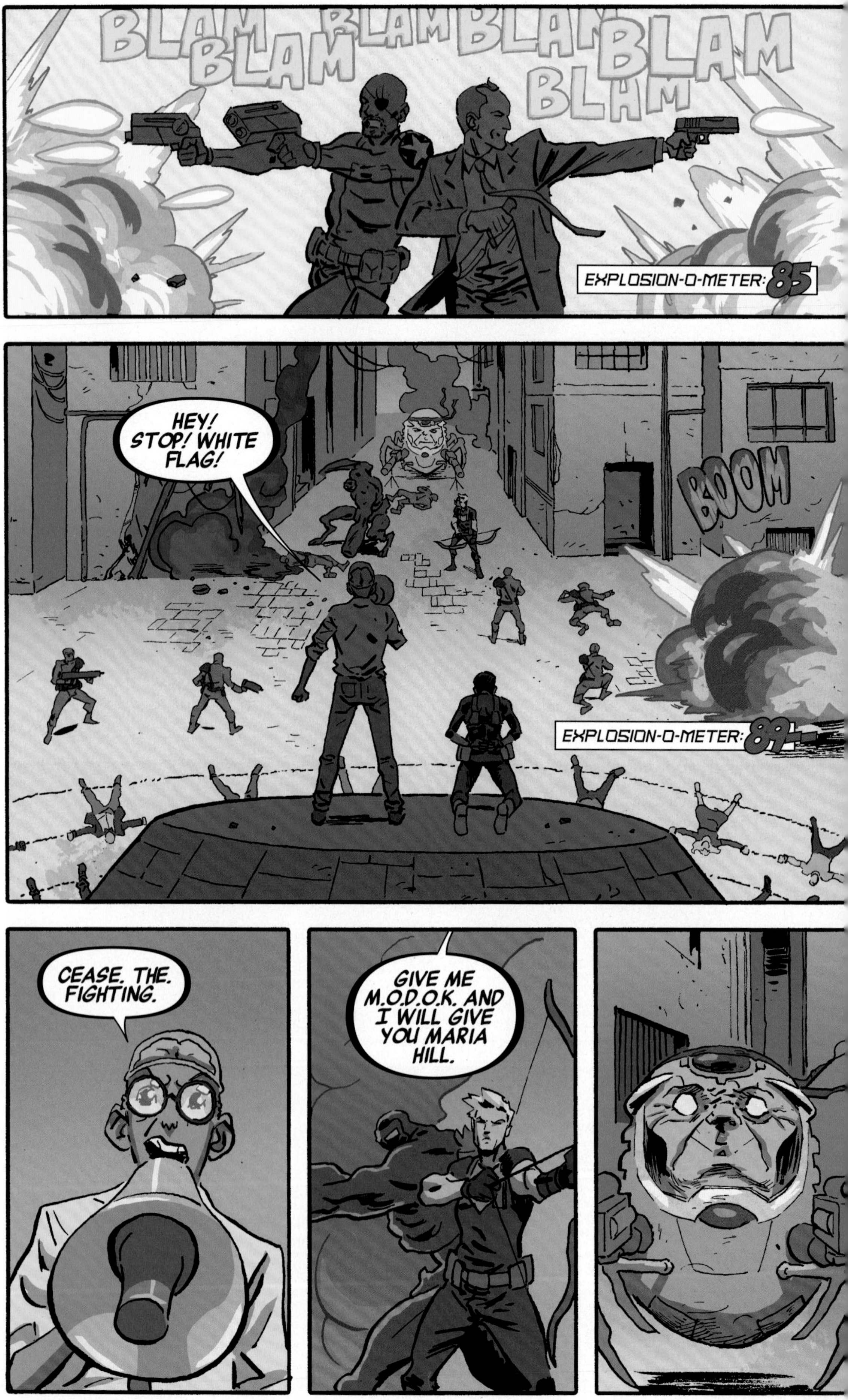
BLAM BLAM BLAM BLAM BLAM BLAM
EXPLOSION-O-METER: 85
HEY! STOP! WHITE FLAG!
BOOM
EXPLOSION-O-METER: 89
CEASE. THE. FIGHTING.
GIVE ME M.O.D.O.K. AND I WILL GIVE YOU MARIA HILL.

NEED AN INCENTIVE?
THUNK
UNGGHHH
NO. JUST STOP.

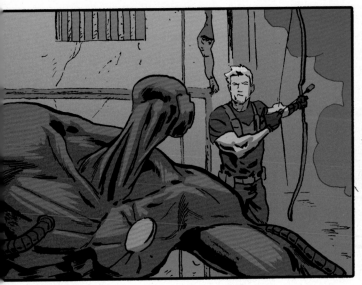

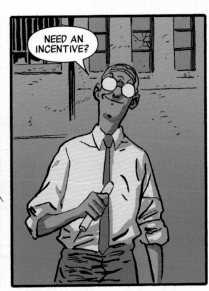

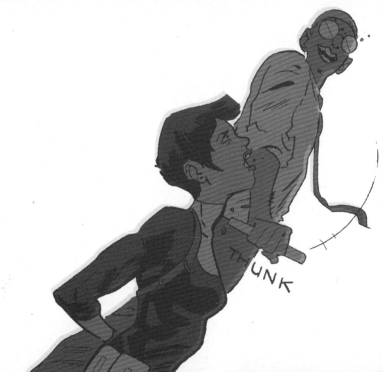

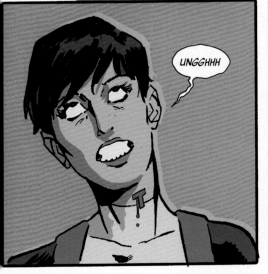

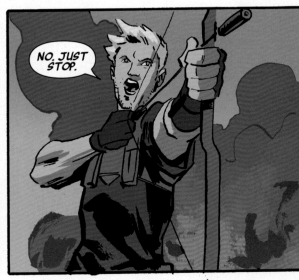

MR. BARTON, THANK YOU. I WILL STOP SOON ENOUGH.

THE PROPHECY IS CLEAR.

I JUST NEEDED HIM TO STAY STILL.

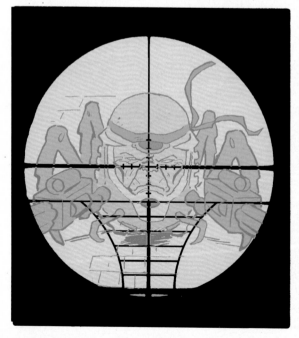

PHOOM

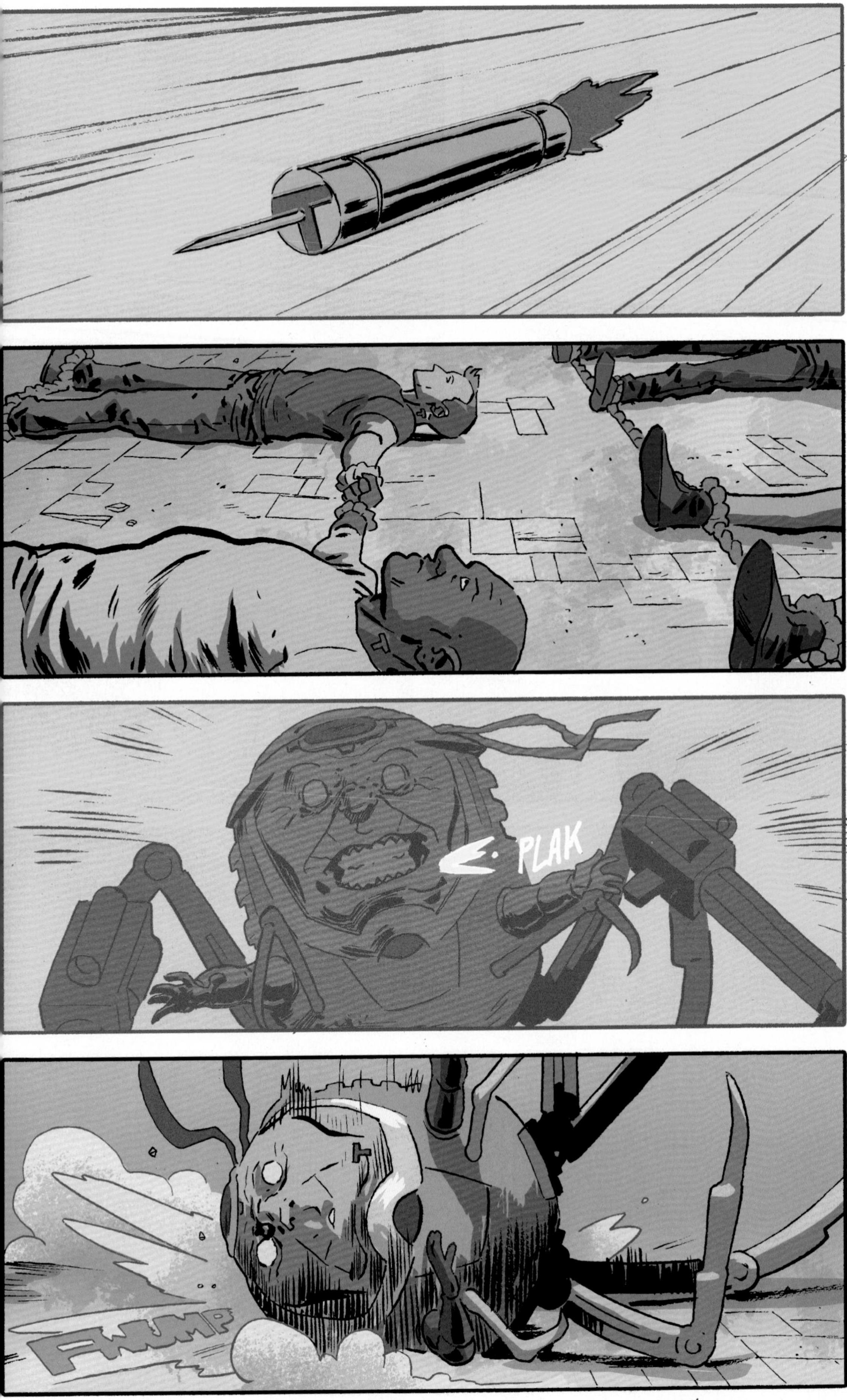
PLAK
FWUMP

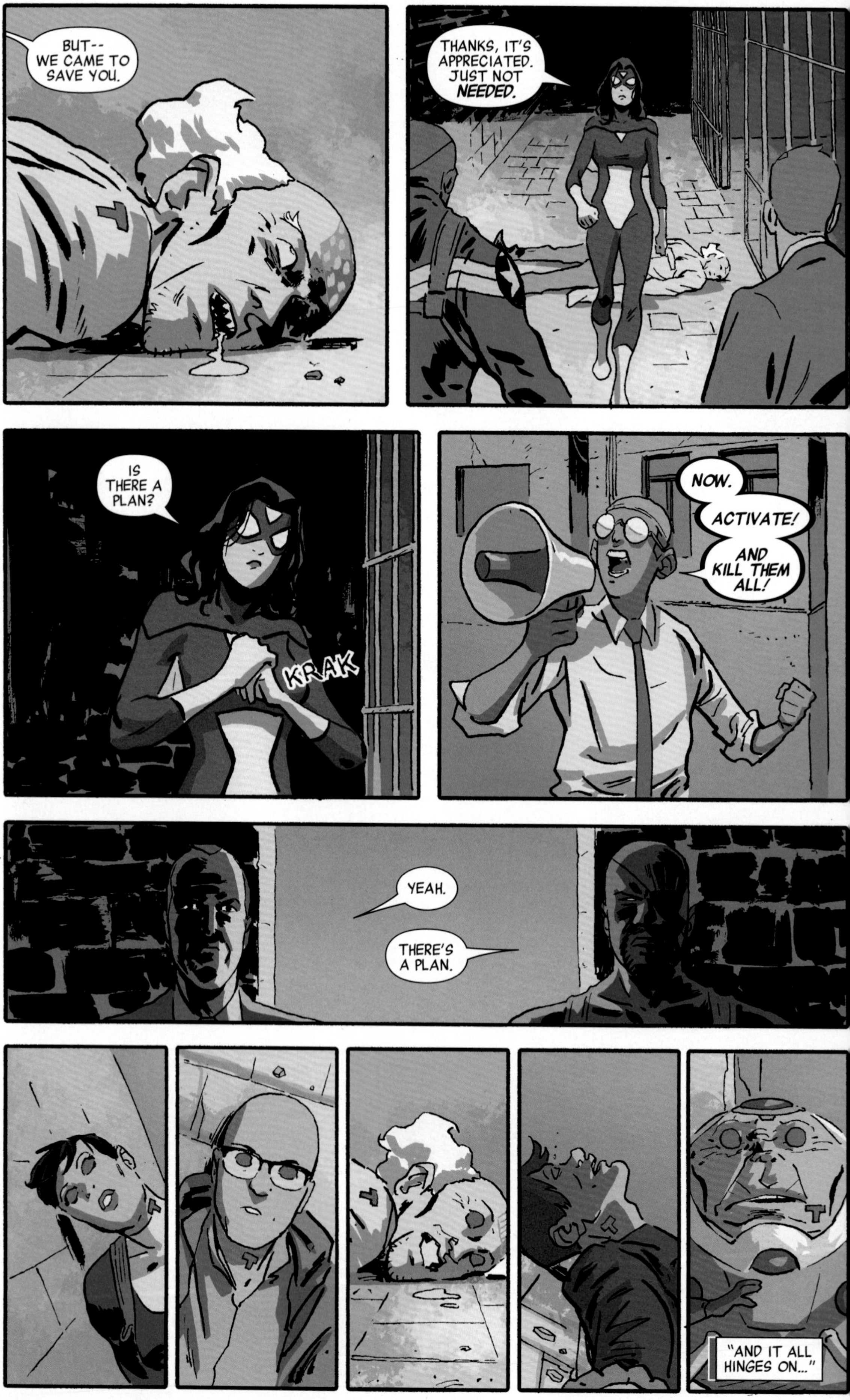
BUT-- WE CAME TO SAVE YOU.
THANKS, IT'S APPRECIATED. JUST NOT NEEDED.
IS THERE A PLAN?
KRAK
NOW.
ACTIVATE!
AND KILL THEM ALL!
YEAH.
THERE'S A PLAN.
"AND IT ALL HINGES ON..."

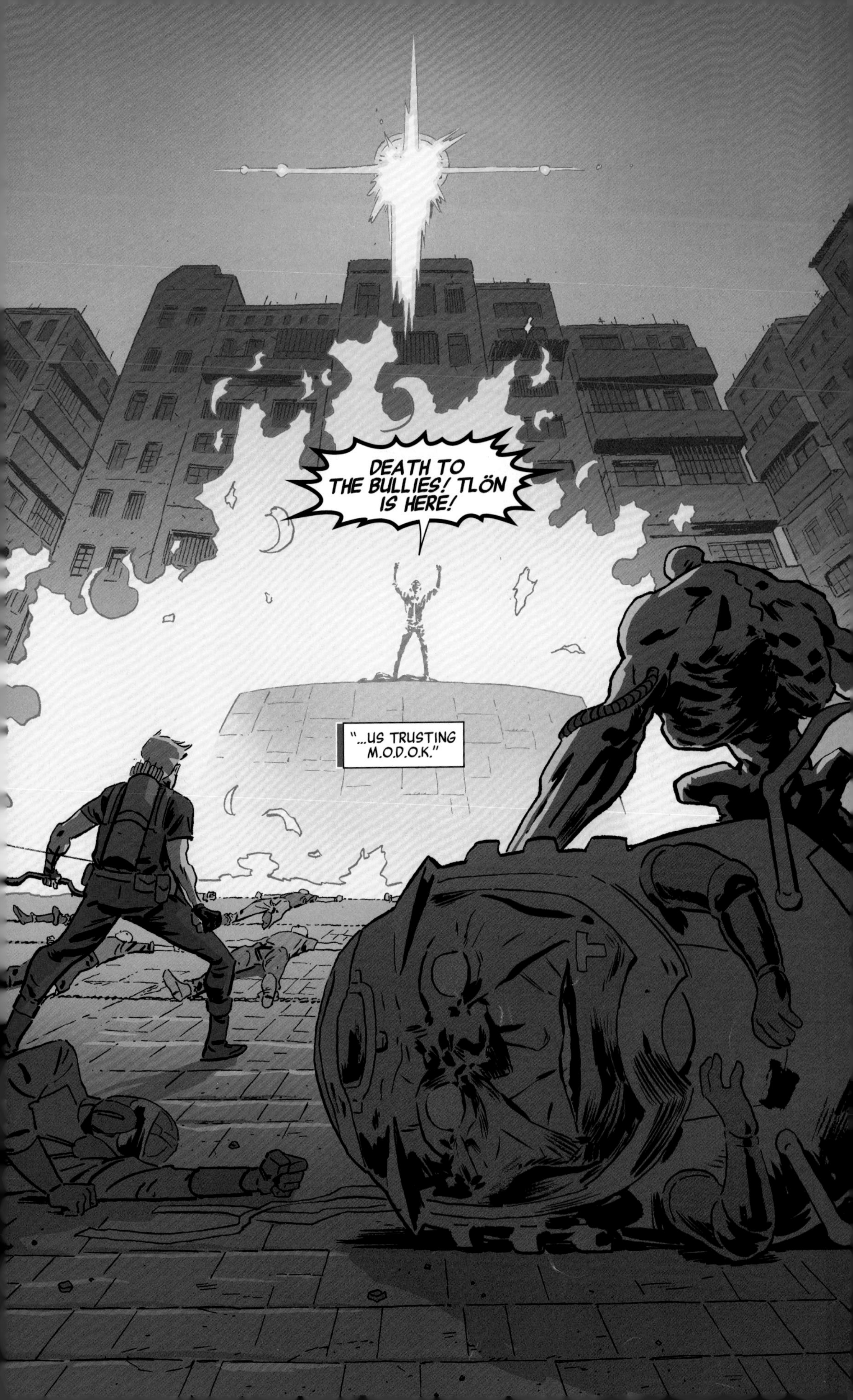
DEATH TO THE BULLIES! TLÖN IS HERE!
"...US TRUSTING M.O.D.O.K."

14

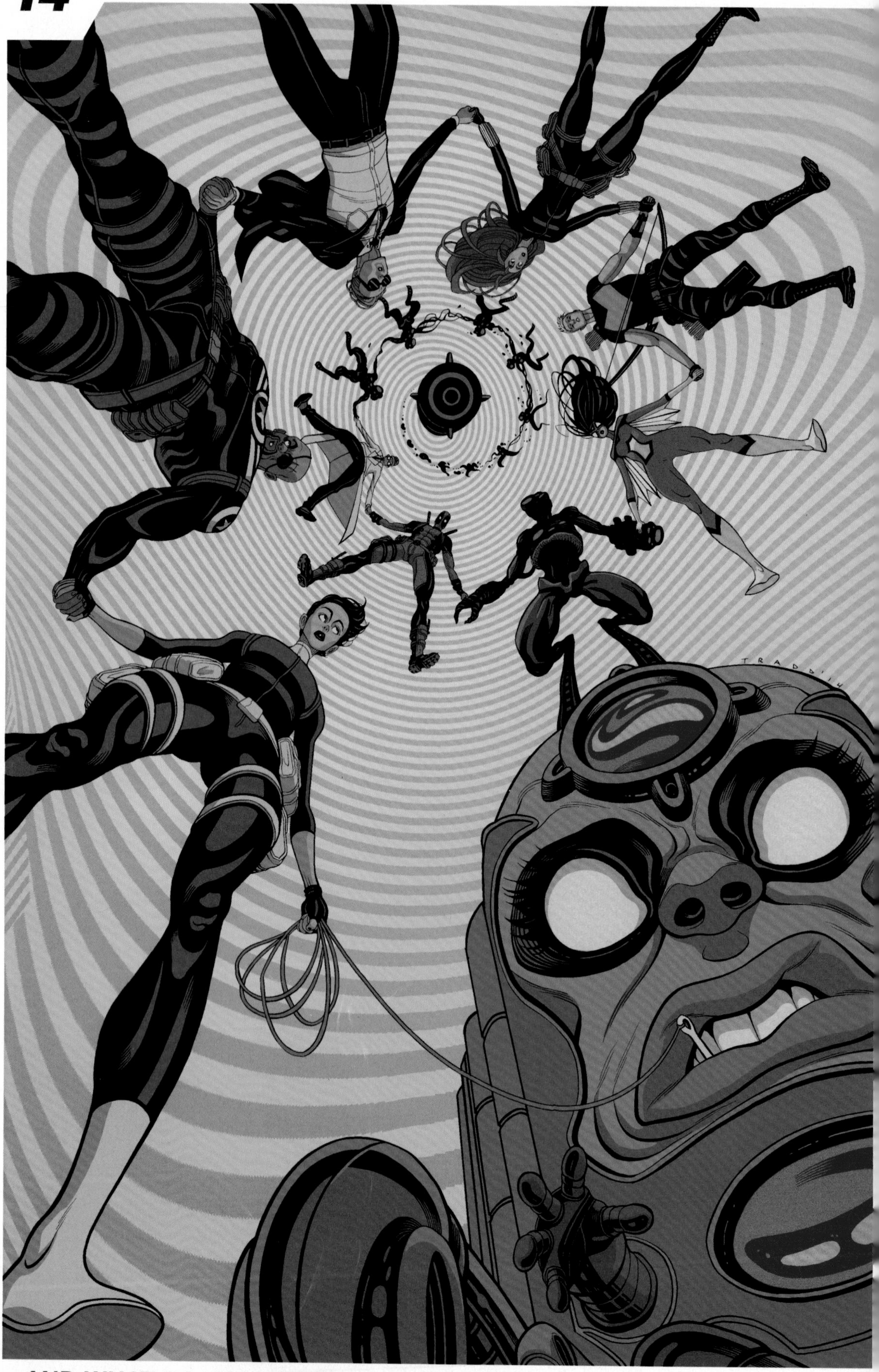

...AND WHAT DO YOU BELIEVE? PART FOUR

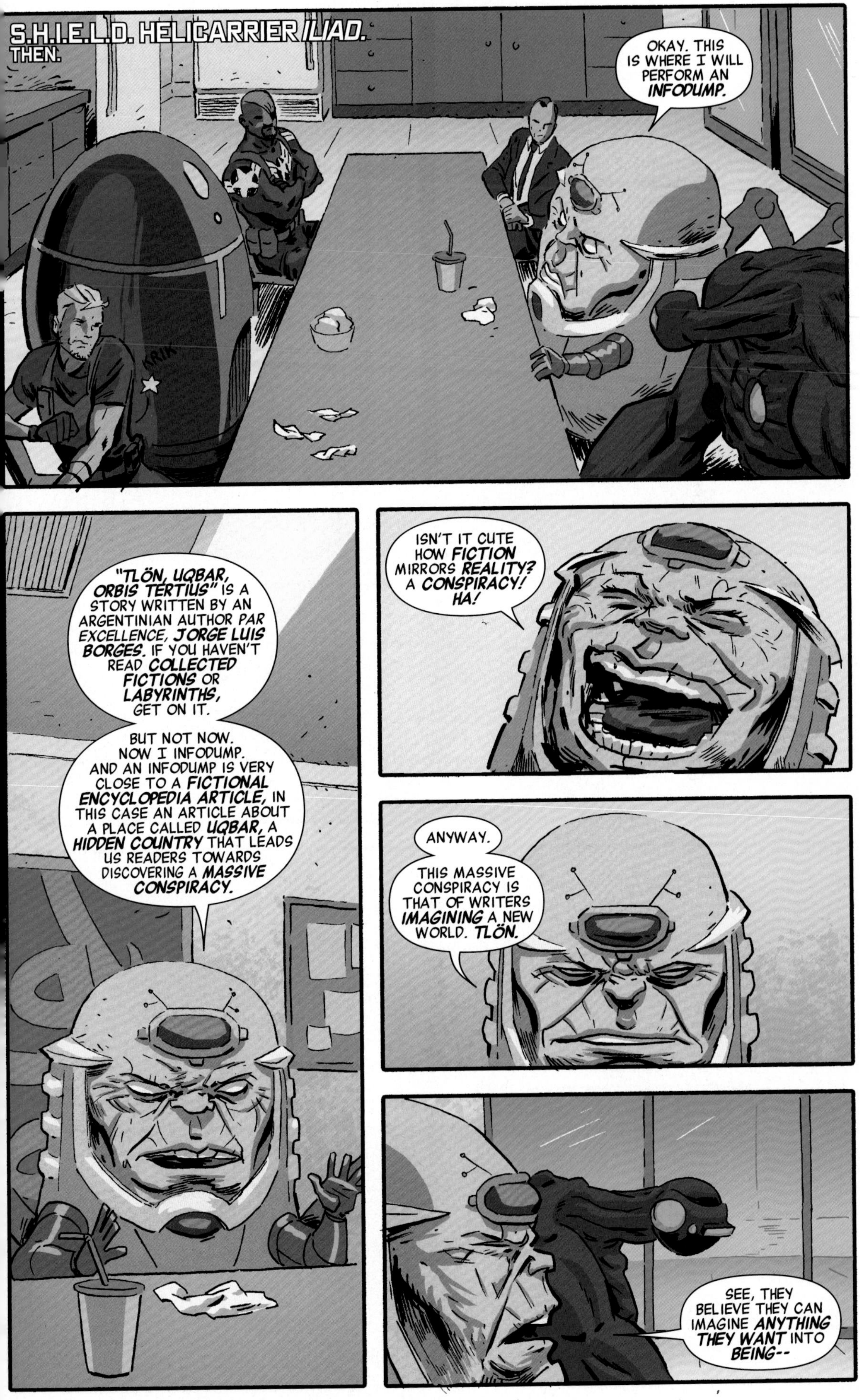
S.H.I.E.L.D. HELICARRIER ILIAD.
THEN.
OKAY. THIS IS WHERE I WILL PERFORM AN INFODUMP.
KRIK
"TLÖN, UQBAR, ORBIS TERTIUS" IS A STORY WRITTEN BY AN ARGENTINIAN AUTHOR PAR EXCELLENCE, JORGE LUIS BORGES. IF YOU HAVEN'T READ COLLECTED FICTIONS OR LABYRINTHS, GET ON IT.
BUT NOT NOW. NOW I INFODUMP. AND AN INFODUMP IS VERY CLOSE TO A FICTIONAL ENCYCLOPEDIA ARTICLE, IN THIS CASE AN ARTICLE ABOUT A PLACE CALLED UQBAR, A HIDDEN COUNTRY THAT LEADS US READERS TOWARDS DISCOVERING A MASSIVE CONSPIRACY.
ISN'T IT CUTE HOW FICTION MIRRORS REALITY? A CONSPIRACY! HA!
ANYWAY.
THIS MASSIVE CONSPIRACY IS THAT OF WRITERS IMAGINING A NEW WORLD. TLÖN.
SEE, THEY BELIEVE THEY CAN IMAGINE ANYTHING THEY WANT INTO BEING--

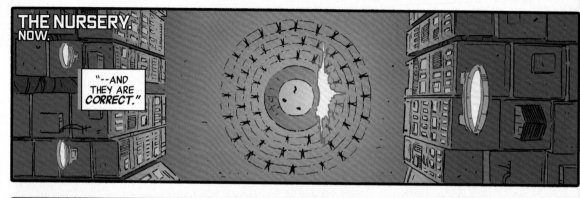

THE NURSERY.
NOW.

"--AND THEY ARE CORRECT."

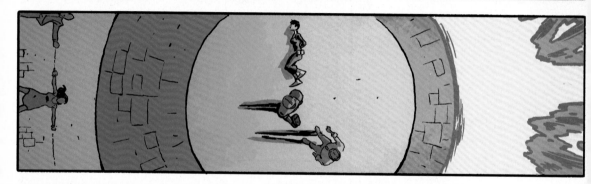

MARIA HILL.
Used to run S.H.I.E.L.D. but got kidnapped--

--now she's (unwillingly) helping *Tlön* rise.

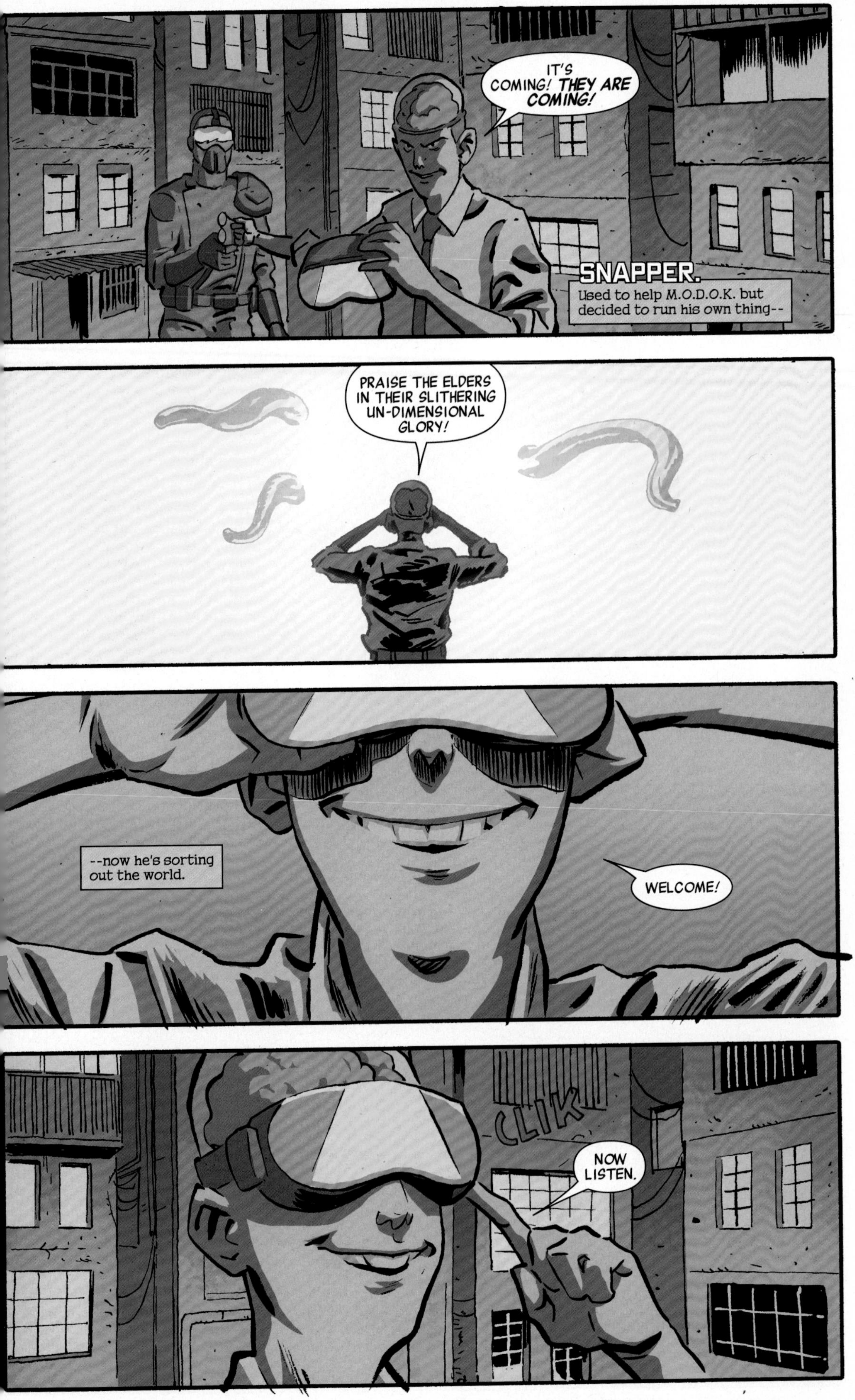
IT'S COMING! THEY ARE COMING!
SNAPPER.
Used to help M.O.D.O.K. but decided to run his own thing--
PRAISE THE ELDERS IN THEIR SLITHERING UN-DIMENSIONAL GLORY!
--now he's sorting out the world.
WELCOME!
CLIK
NOW LISTEN.

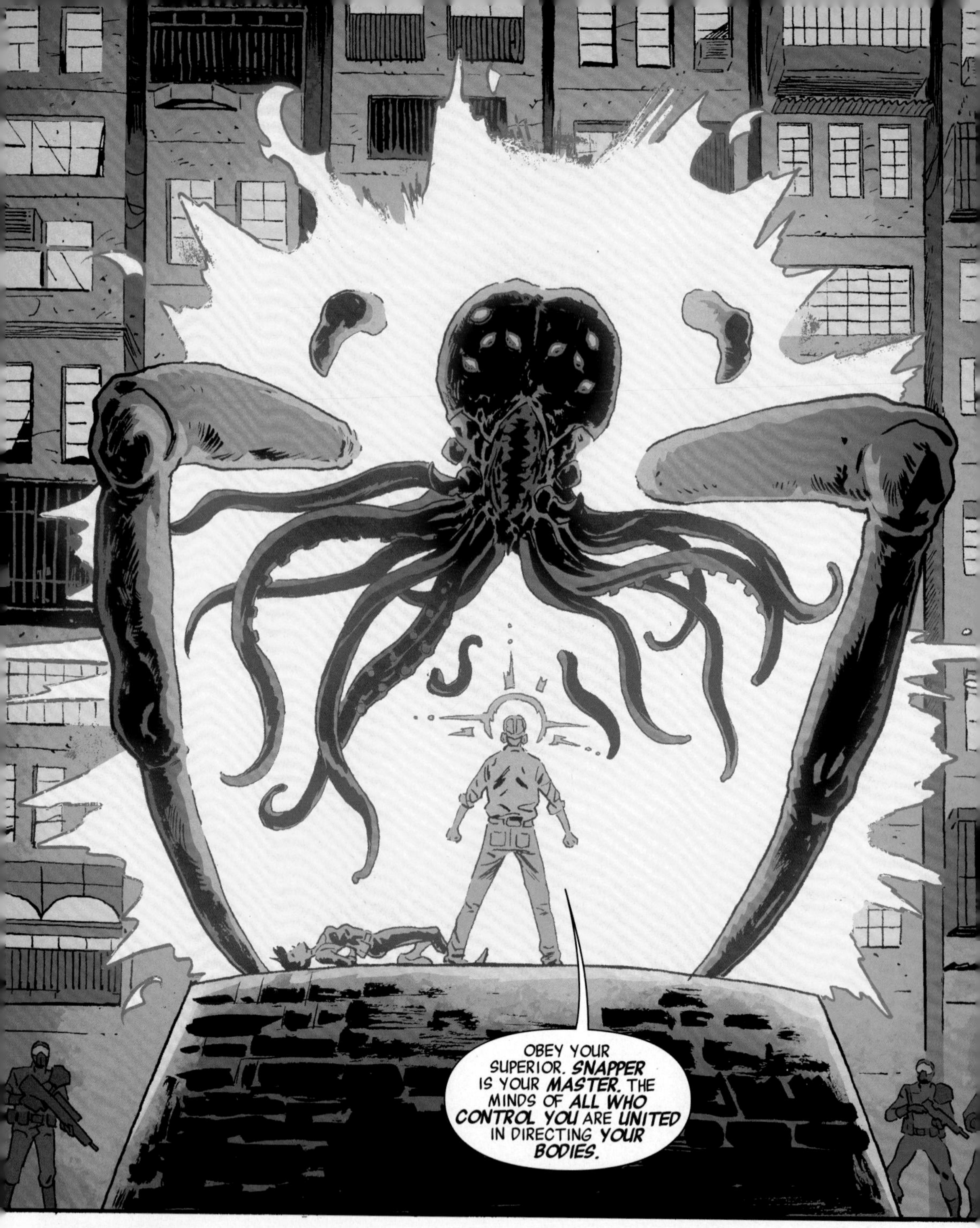
OBEY YOUR SUPERIOR. SNAPPER IS YOUR MASTER. THE MINDS OF ALL WHO CONTROL YOU ARE UNITED IN DIRECTING YOUR BODIES.

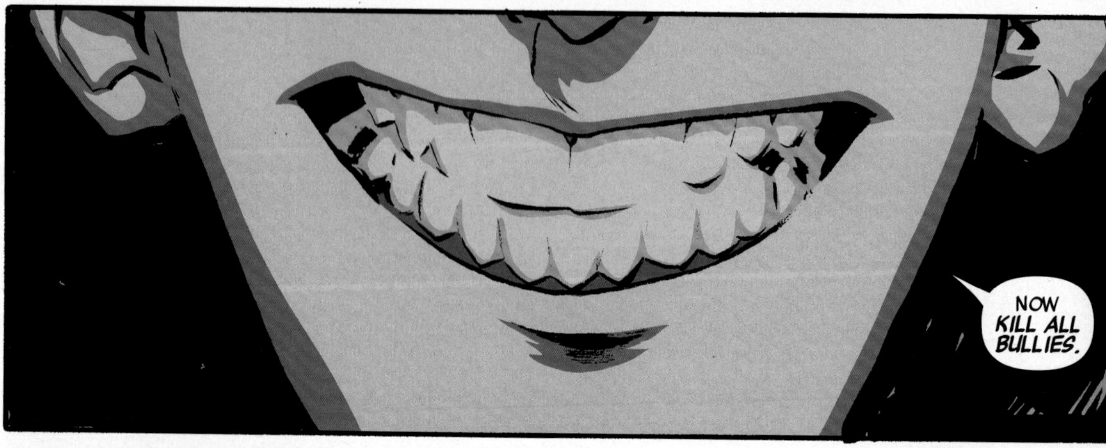
NOW KILL ALL BULLIES.

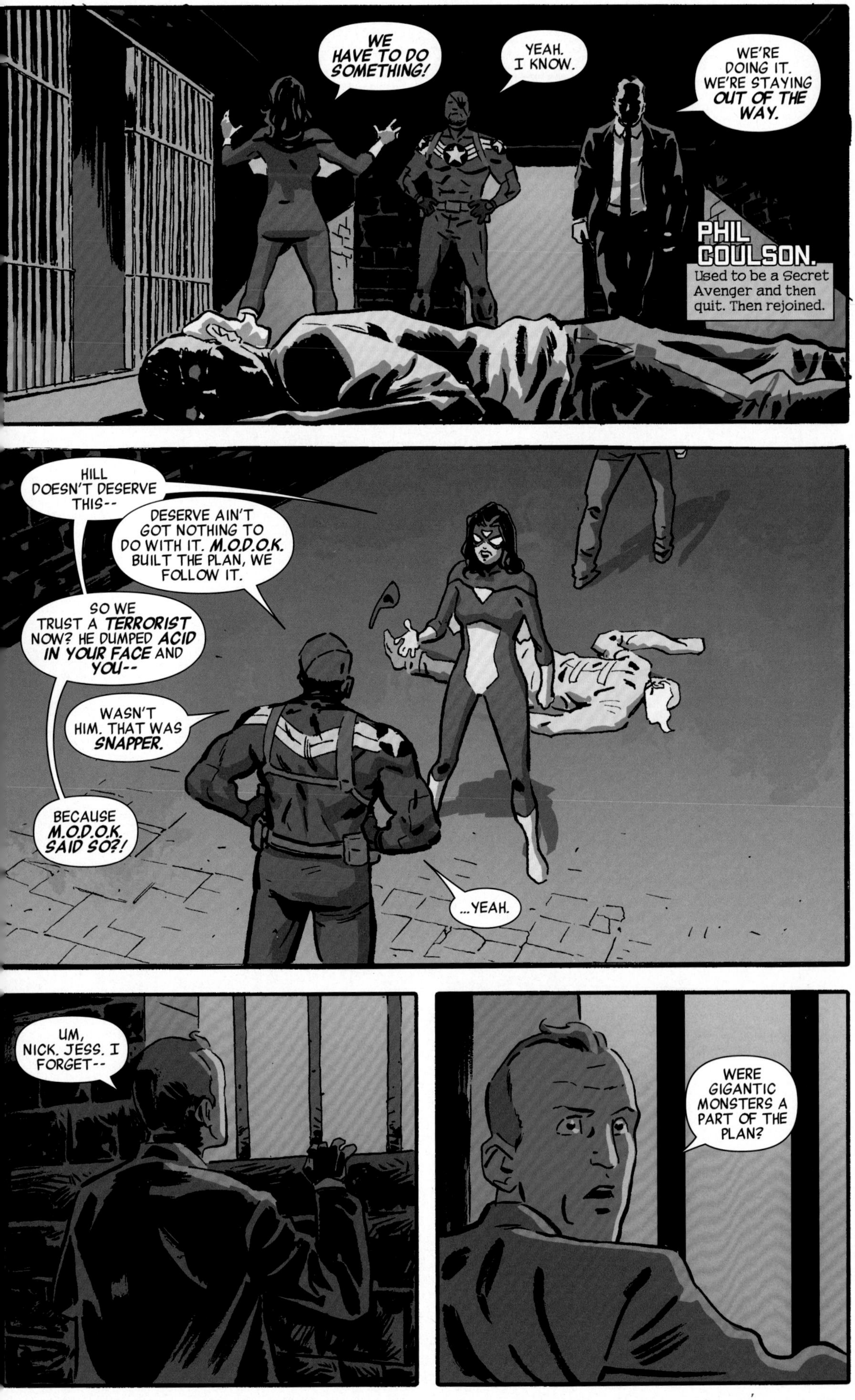
WE HAVE TO DO SOMETHING!
YEAH. I KNOW.
WE'RE DOING IT. WE'RE STAYING OUT OF THE WAY.
PHIL COULSON.
Used to be a Secret Avenger and then quit. Then rejoined.
HILL DOESN'T DESERVE THIS--
DESERVE AIN'T GOT NOTHING TO DO WITH IT. M.O.D.O.K. BUILT THE PLAN, WE FOLLOW IT.
SO WE TRUST A TERRORIST NOW? HE DUMPED ACID IN YOUR FACE AND YOU--
WASN'T HIM. THAT WAS SNAPPER.
BECAUSE M.O.D.O.K. SAID SO?!
...YEAH.
UM, NICK. JESS. I FORGET--
WERE GIGANTIC MONSTERS A PART OF THE PLAN?

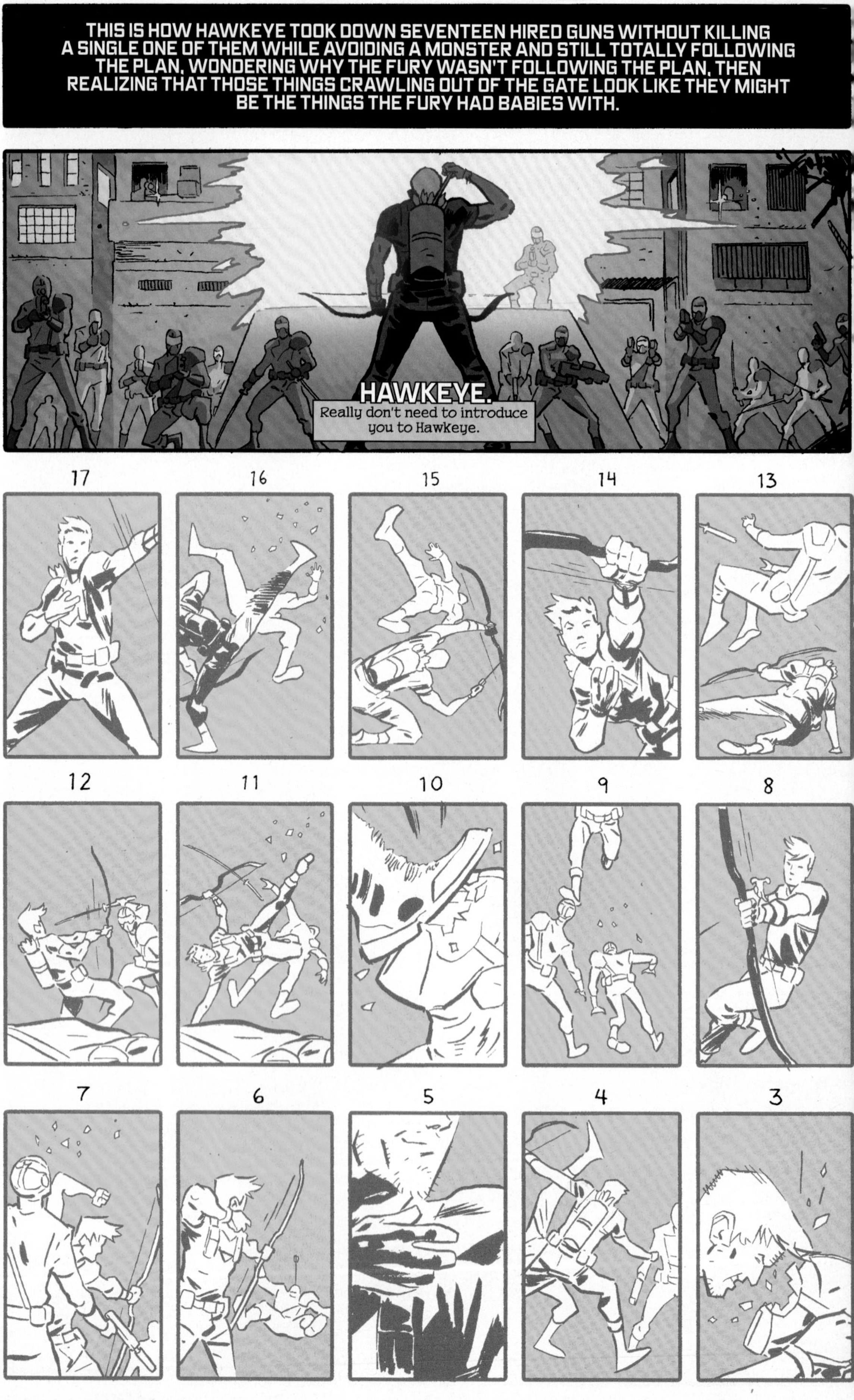
THIS IS HOW HAWKEYE TOOK DOWN SEVENTEEN HIRED GUNS WITHOUT KILLING A SINGLE ONE OF THEM WHILE AVOIDING A MONSTER AND STILL TOTALLY FOLLOWING THE PLAN, WONDERING WHY THE FURY WASN'T FOLLOWING THE PLAN, THEN REALIZING THAT THOSE THINGS CRAWLING OUT OF THE GATE LOOK LIKE THEY MIGHT BE THE THINGS THE FURY HAD BABIES WITH.
HAWKEYE.
Really don't need to introduce you to Hawkeye.
17
16
15
14
13
12
11
10
9
8
7
6
5
4
3

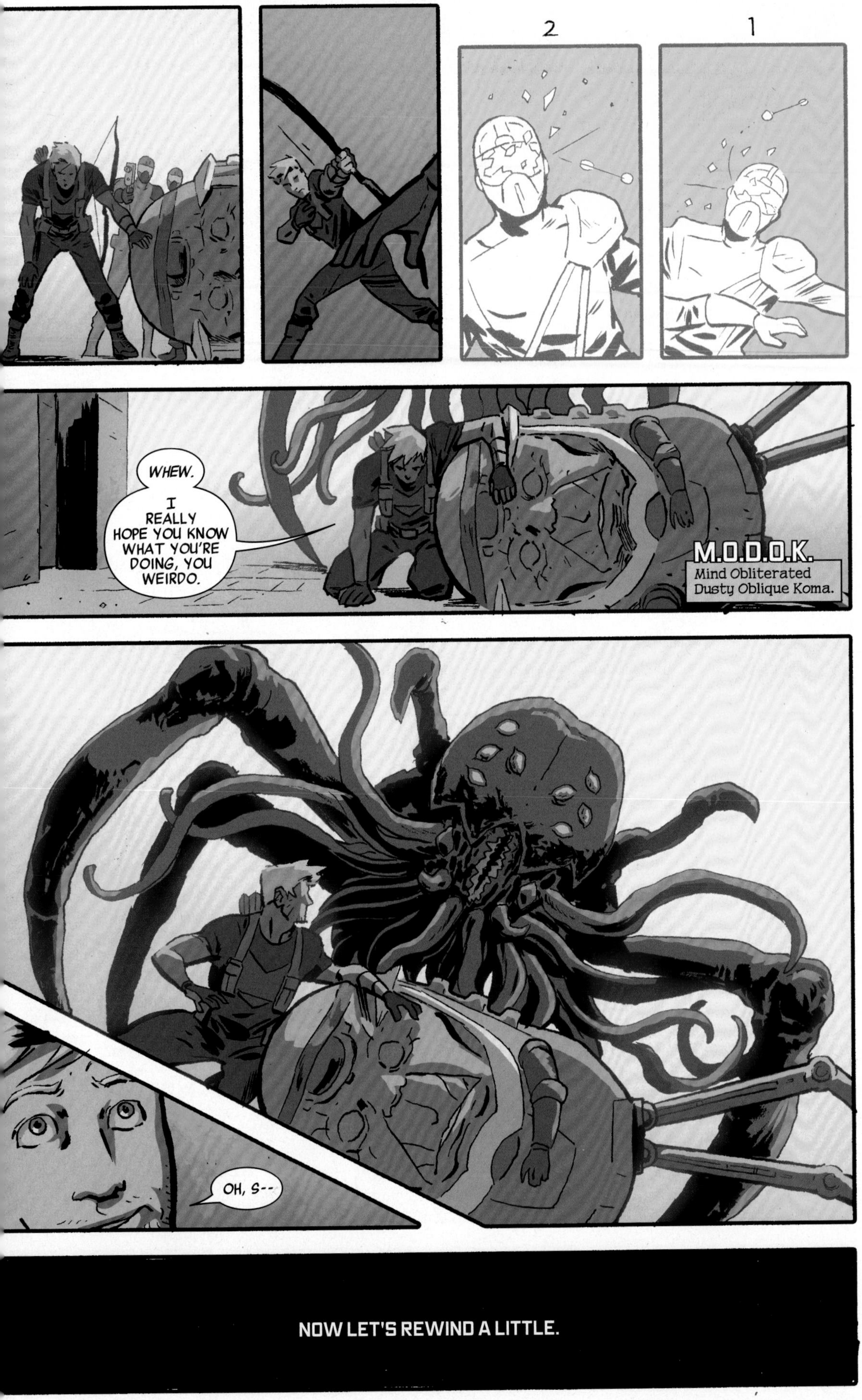
2
1
WHEW.
I REALLY HOPE YOU KNOW WHAT YOU'RE DOING, YOU WEIRDO.
M.O.D.O.K.
Mind Obliterated Dusty Oblique Koma.
OH, S--
NOW LET'S REWIND A LITTLE.

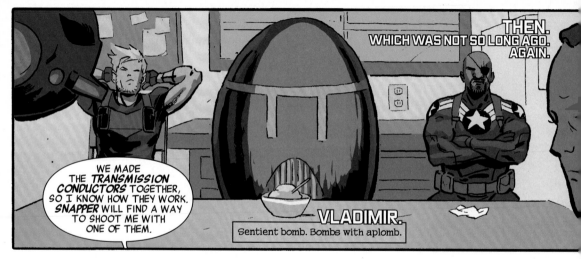

THEN.
WHICH WAS NOT SO LONG AGO. AGAIN.
WE MADE THE TRANSMISSION CONDUCTORS TOGETHER, SO I KNOW HOW THEY WORK. SNAPPER WILL FIND A WAY TO SHOOT ME WITH ONE OF THEM.
VLADIMIR.
Sentient bomb. Bombs with aplomb.
AND YOU HAVE TO LET HIM DO IT.
EXCUSE ME?
NICK FURY.
Couldn't come up with anything good here in time for the deadline.
YOU HAVE TO LET HIM DO IT BECAUSE I AM A GENIUS OF THE IDEASPACE AND HE NEEDS ME TO FINISH HIS MASTERPIECE.
ALSO BECAUSE HE STOLE EVERY SINGLE TRANSMITTER WE BUILT AND I DON'T HAVE THE TIME AND RESOURCES TO BUILD OUR OWN AND FLIP THE SCENARIO THAT WAY.
WE SIMPLY HAVE TO GO WITH THE FLOW AND IMAGINE A BETTER GAME. HAVE YOU NOT HEARD OF TAOISM?
NOW LET'S GO FORWARD AGAIN.
BUT NOT TO THAT IMMINENT HAWKEYE LIFE-THREATENING SCENARIO TIME,
BUT ABOUT A MINUTE BEFORE THAT--

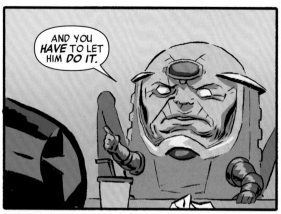

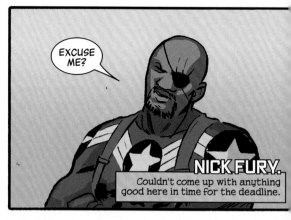

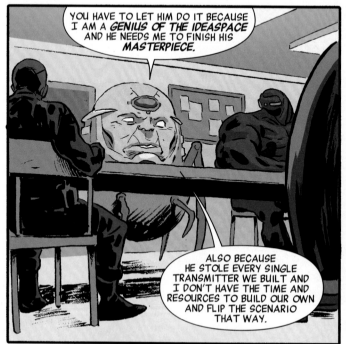

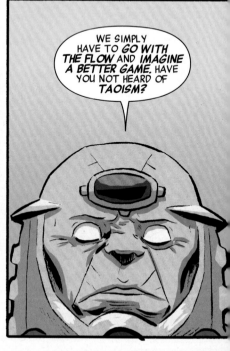

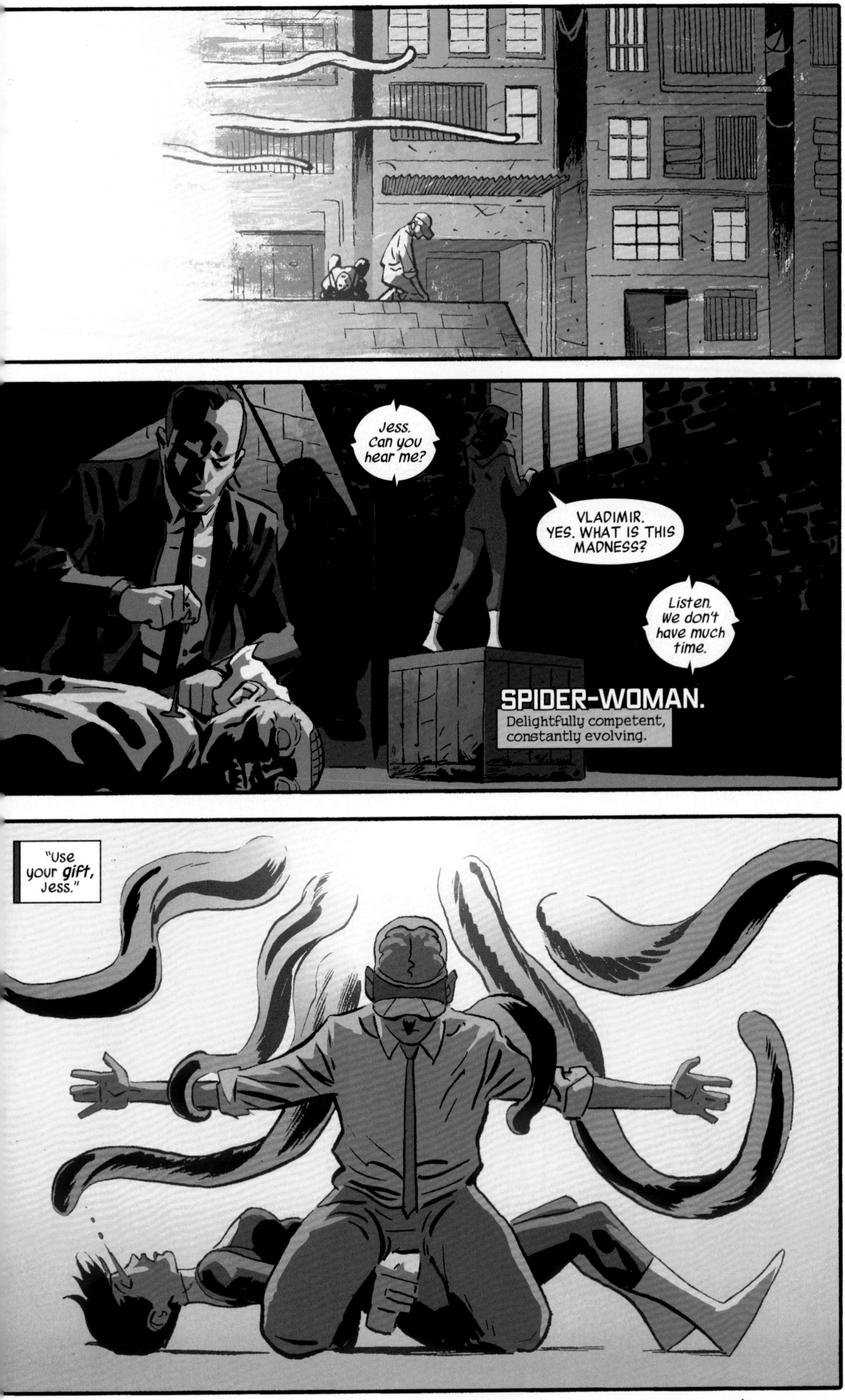
Jess. Can you hear me?
VLADIMIR. YES. WHAT IS THIS MADNESS?
Listen. We don't have much time.
SPIDER-WOMAN.
Delightfully competent, constantly evolving.
"Use your gift, Jess."

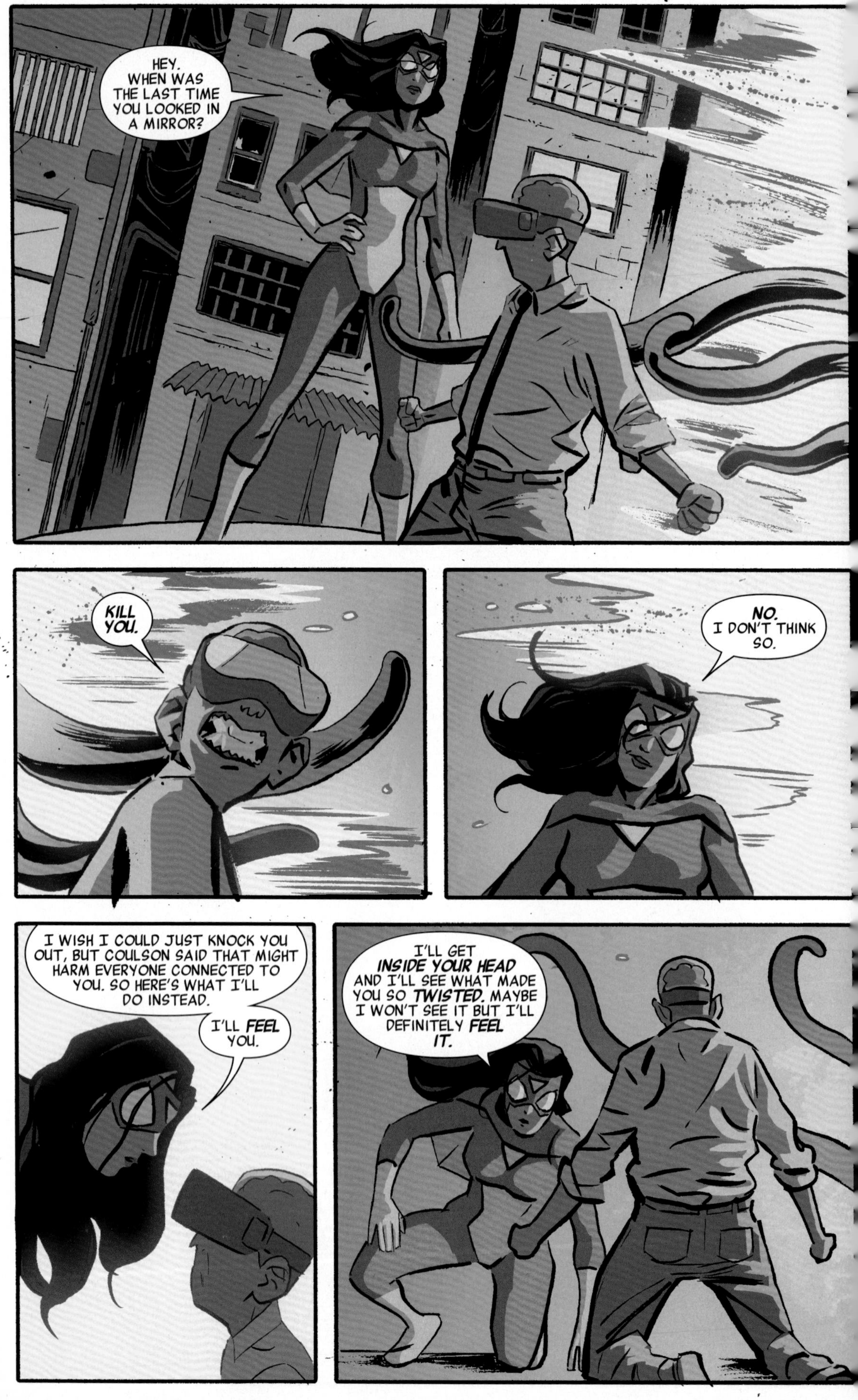
HEY. WHEN WAS THE LAST TIME YOU LOOKED IN A MIRROR?
KILL YOU.
NO. I DON'T THINK SO.
I WISH I COULD JUST KNOCK YOU OUT, BUT COULSON SAID THAT MIGHT HARM EVERYONE CONNECTED TO YOU. SO HERE'S WHAT I'LL DO INSTEAD.
I'LL FEEL YOU.
I'LL GET INSIDE YOUR HEAD AND I'LL SEE WHAT MADE YOU SO TWISTED. MAYBE I WON'T SEE IT BUT I'LL DEFINITELY FEEL IT.

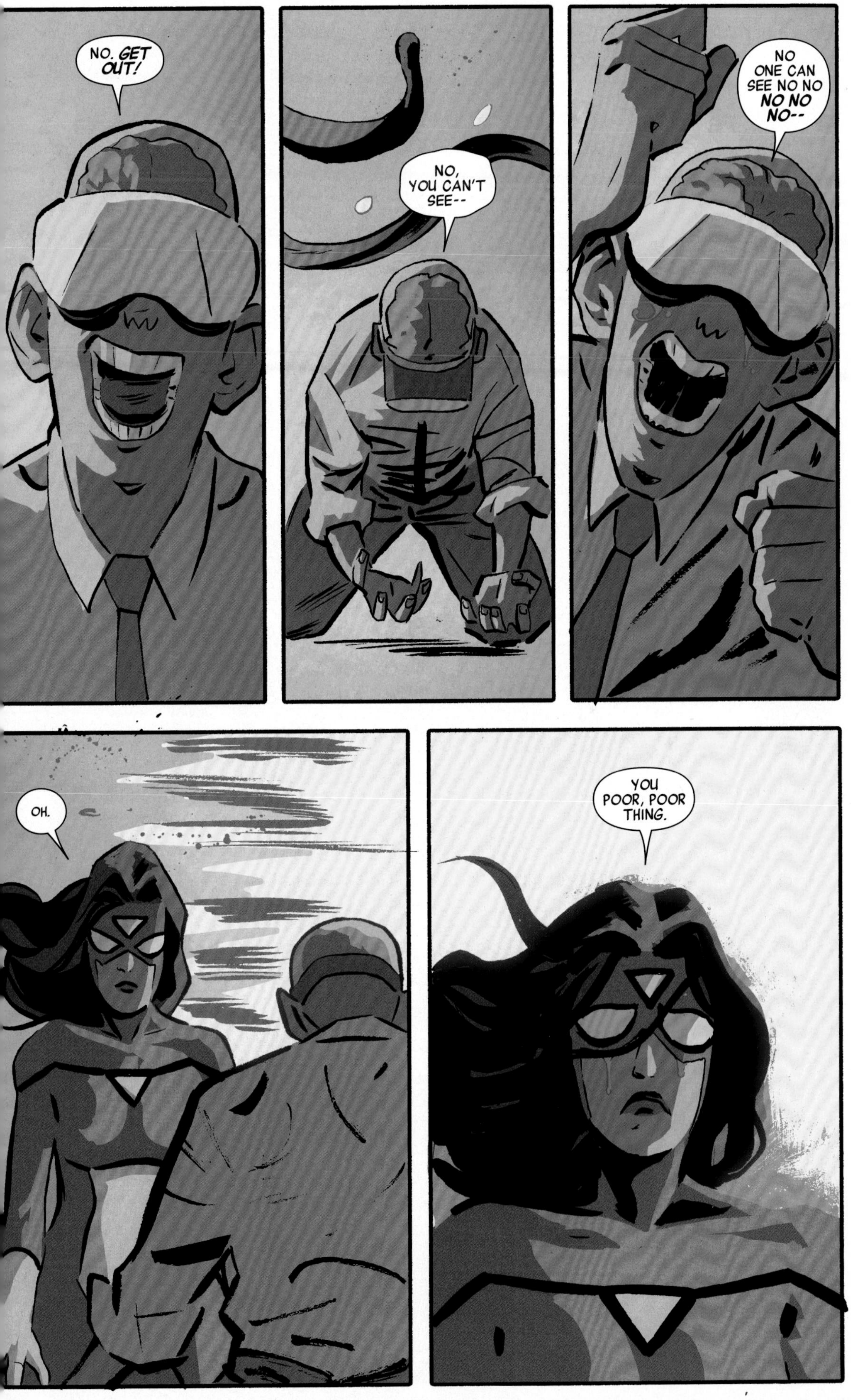
NO. GET OUT!
NO, YOU CAN'T SEE--
NO ONE CAN SEE NO NO NO NO NO--
OH.
YOU POOR, POOR THING.

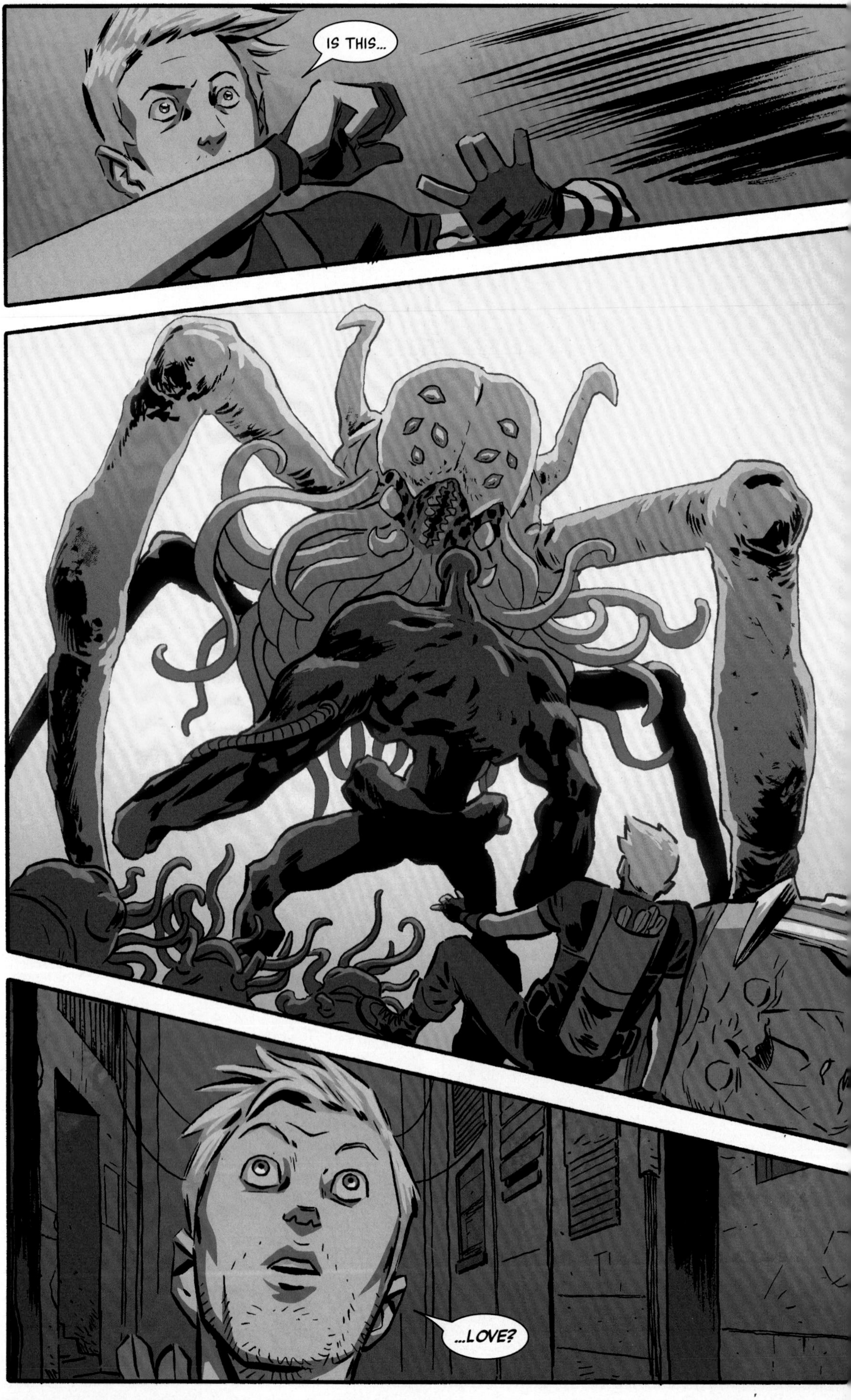
IS THIS...
...LOVE?

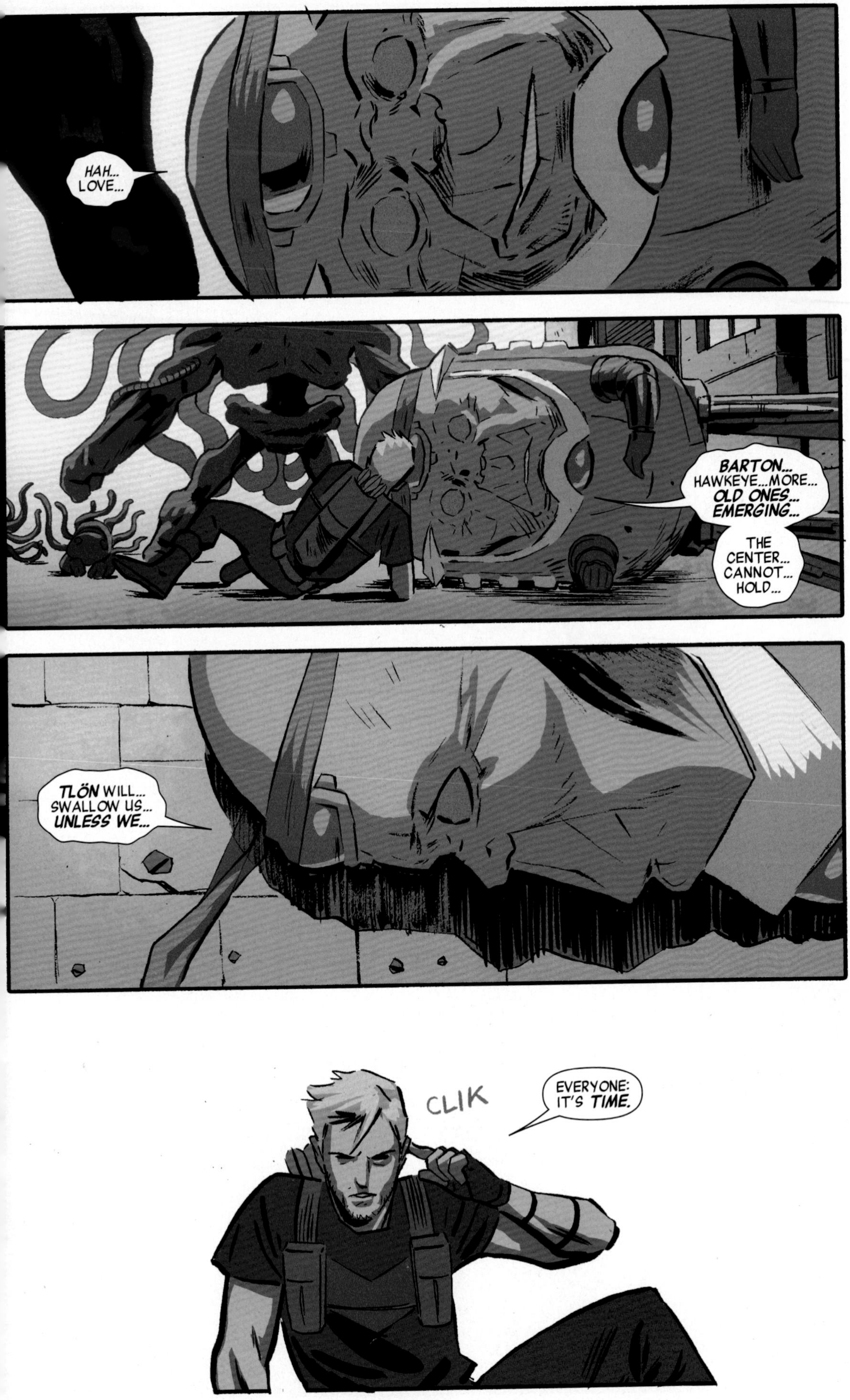
HAH... LOVE...
BARTON... HAWKEYE...MORE... OLD ONES... EMERGING...
THE CENTER... CANNOT... HOLD...
TLÖN WILL... SWALLOW US... UNLESS WE...
CLIK
EVERYONE: IT'S TIME.

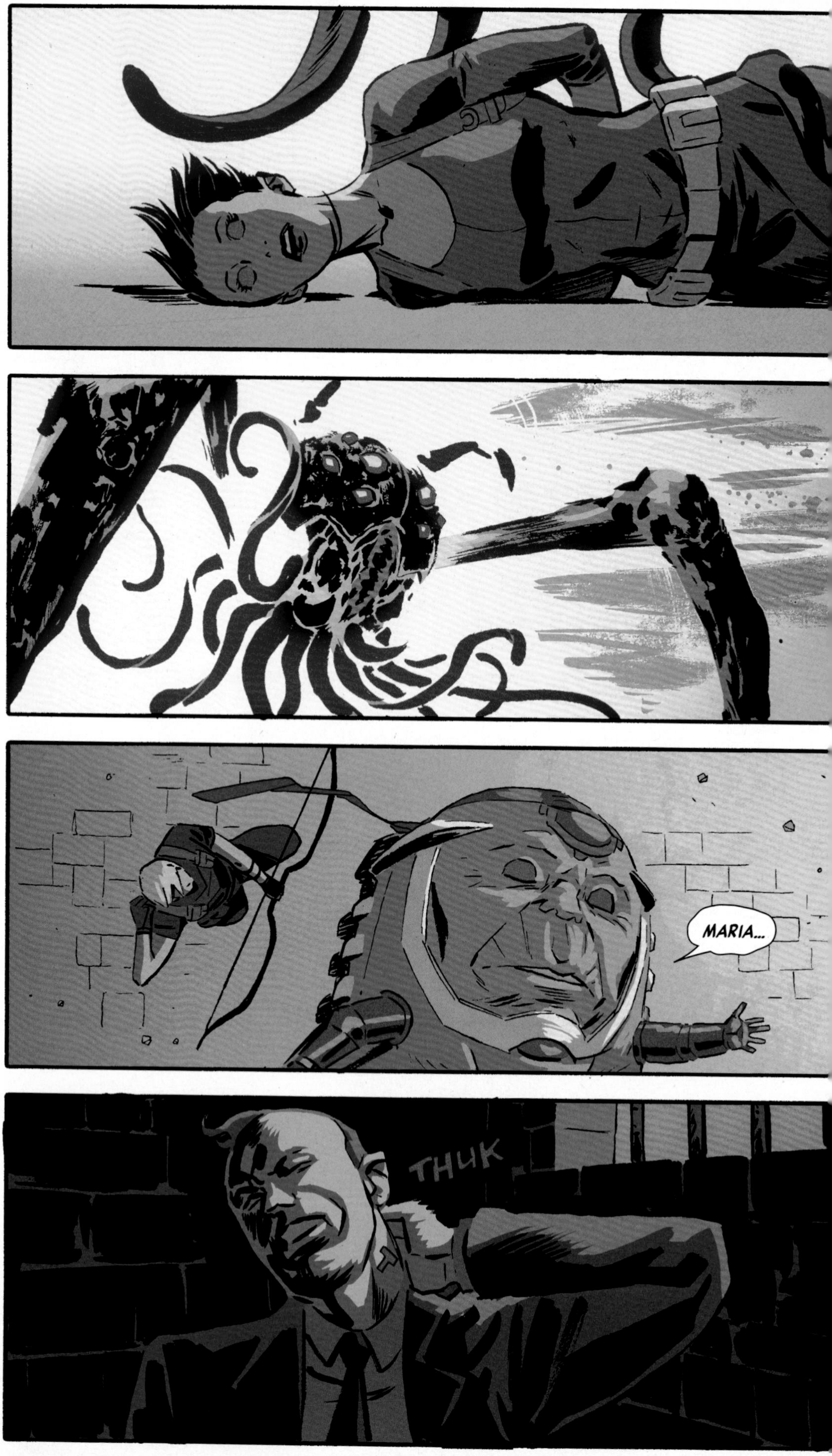
MARIA...
THUK

NICK.

DON'T MOVE.

SHUK

PTOO

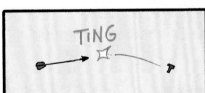

TING

TIK

WHOA.

M.O.D.O.K. VLADIMIR. WE'RE READY.

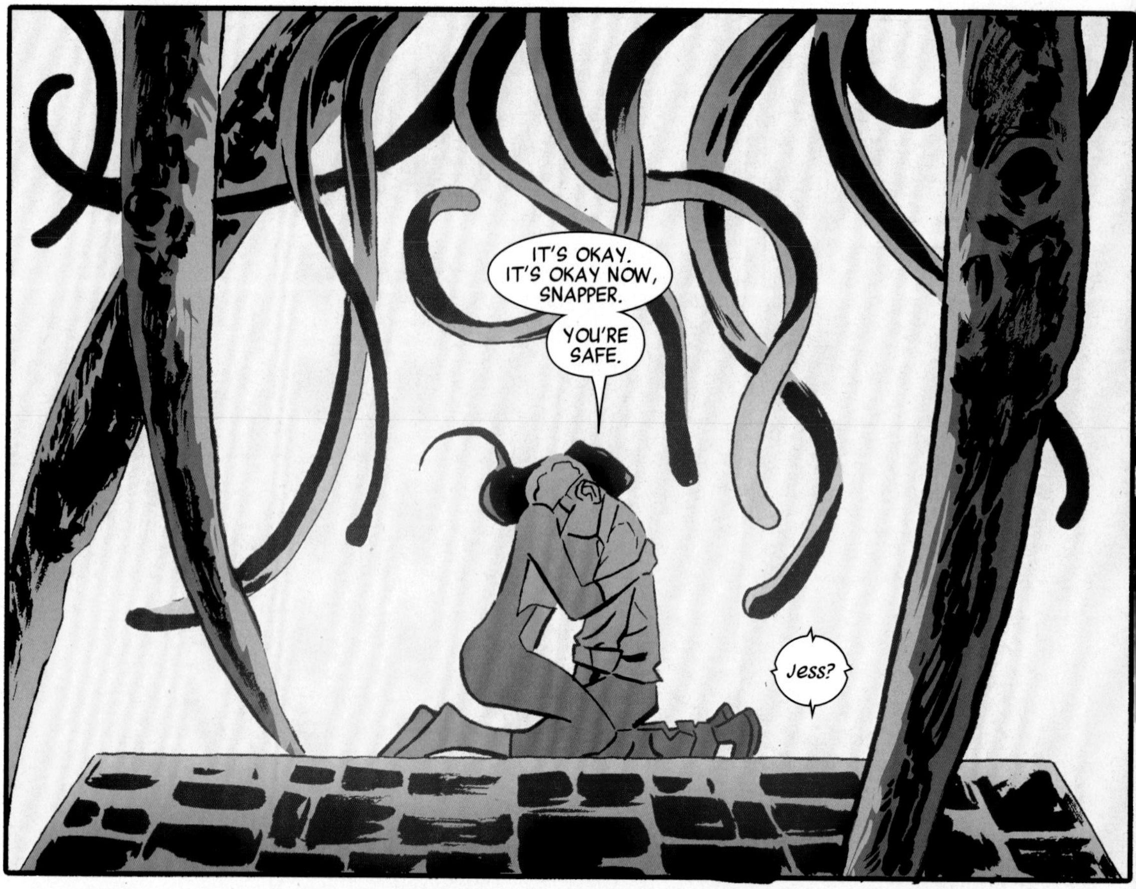
IT'S OKAY. IT'S OKAY NOW, SNAPPER.
YOU'RE SAFE.
Jess?

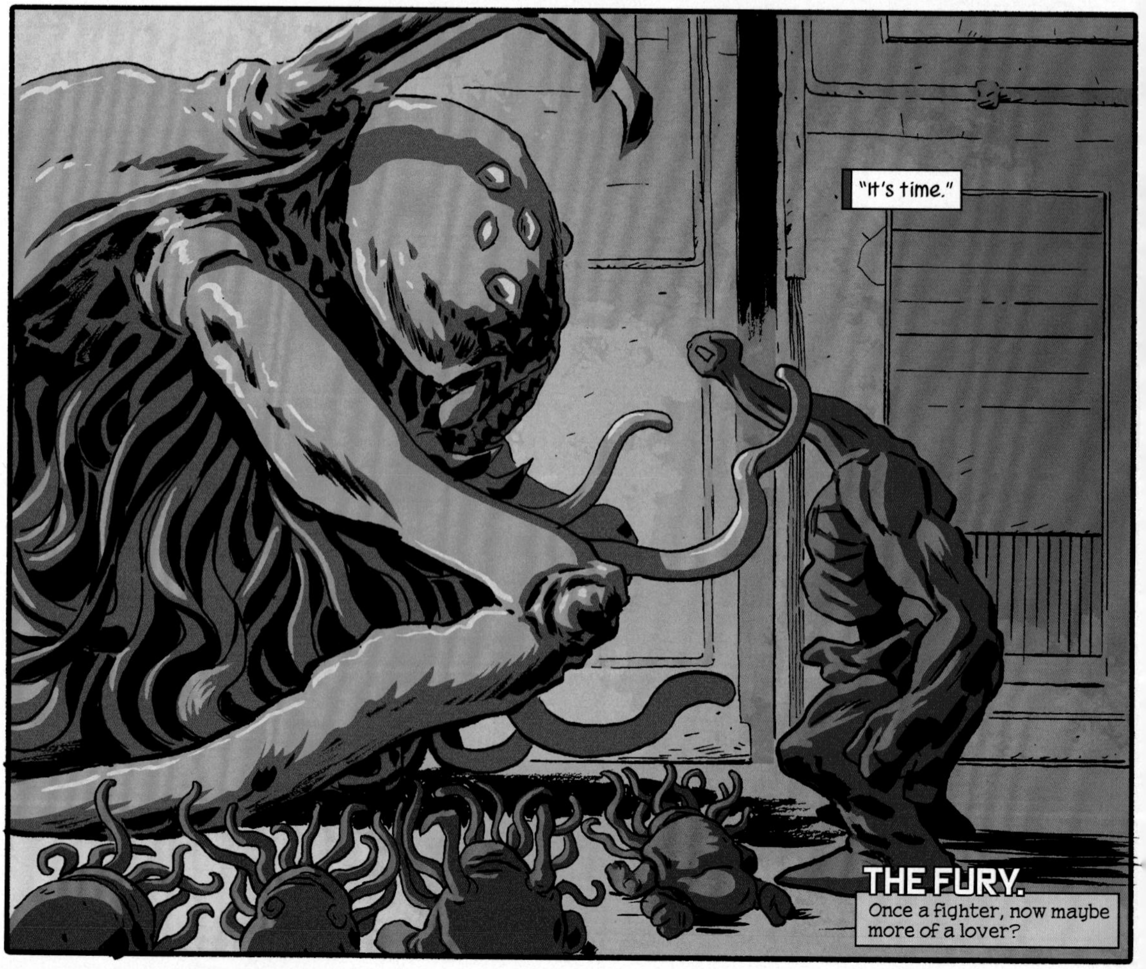
"It's time."
THE FURY.
Once a fighter, now maybe more of a lover?

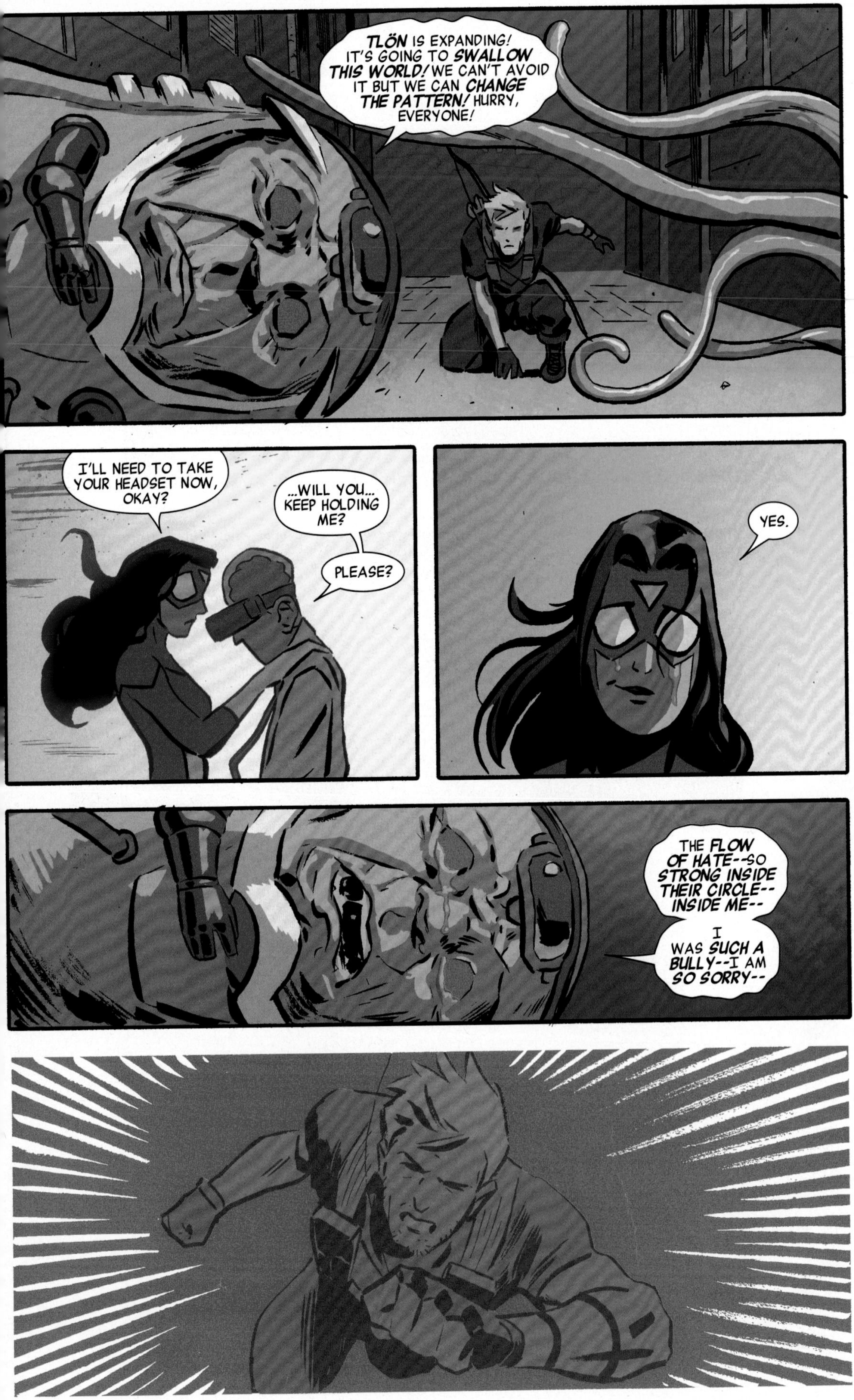

TLÖN IS EXPANDING! IT'S GOING TO SWALLOW THIS WORLD! WE CAN'T AVOID IT BUT WE CAN CHANGE THE PATTERN! HURRY, EVERYONE!
I'LL NEED TO TAKE YOUR HEADSET NOW, OKAY?
...WILL YOU... KEEP HOLDING ME?
PLEASE?
YES.
THE FLOW OF HATE--SO STRONG INSIDE THEIR CIRCLE--INSIDE ME--
I WAS SUCH A BULLY--I AM SO SORRY--

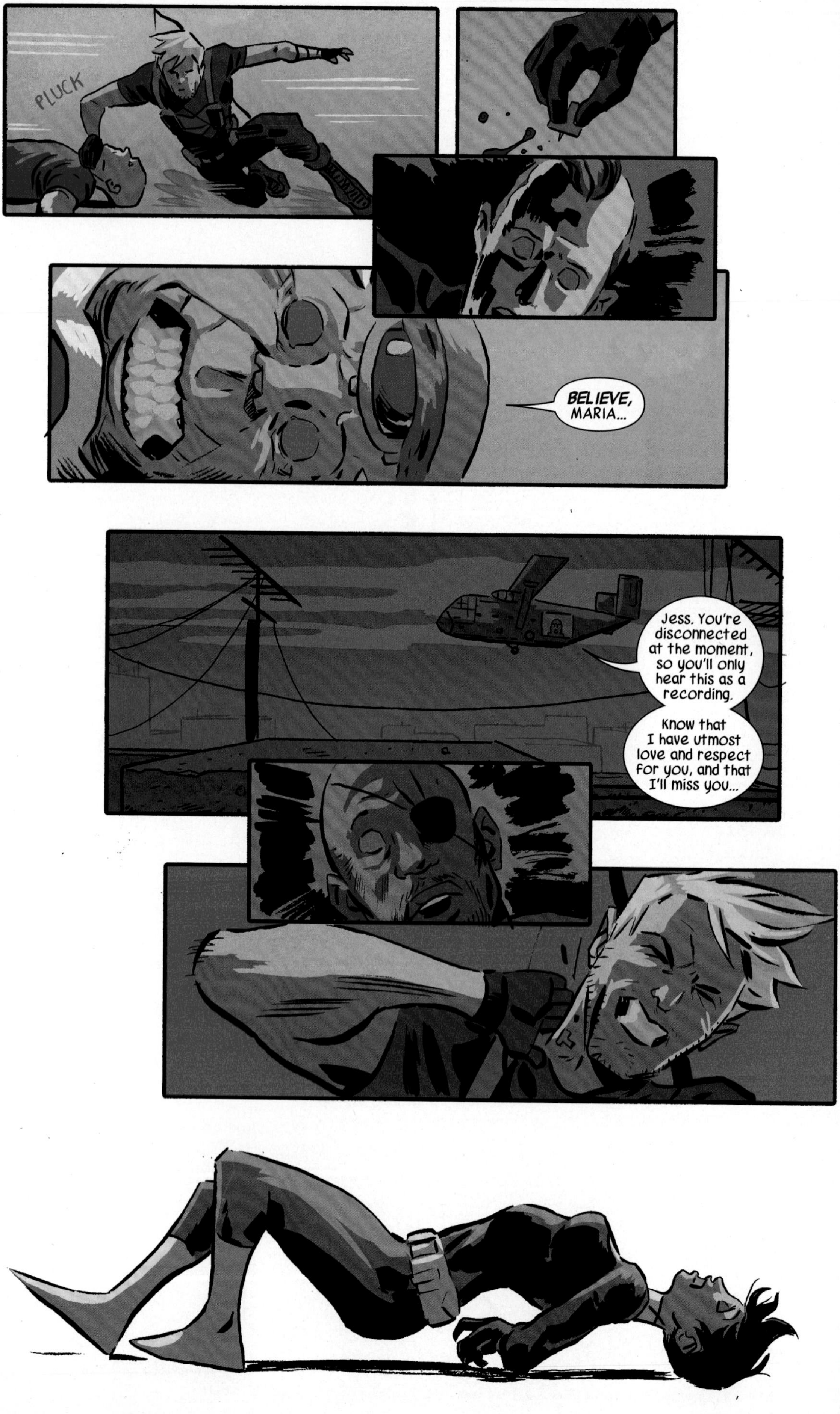
PLUCK
BELIEVE, MARIA...
Jess. You're disconnected at the moment, so you'll only hear this as a recording.
Know that I have utmost love and respect for you, and that I'll miss you...

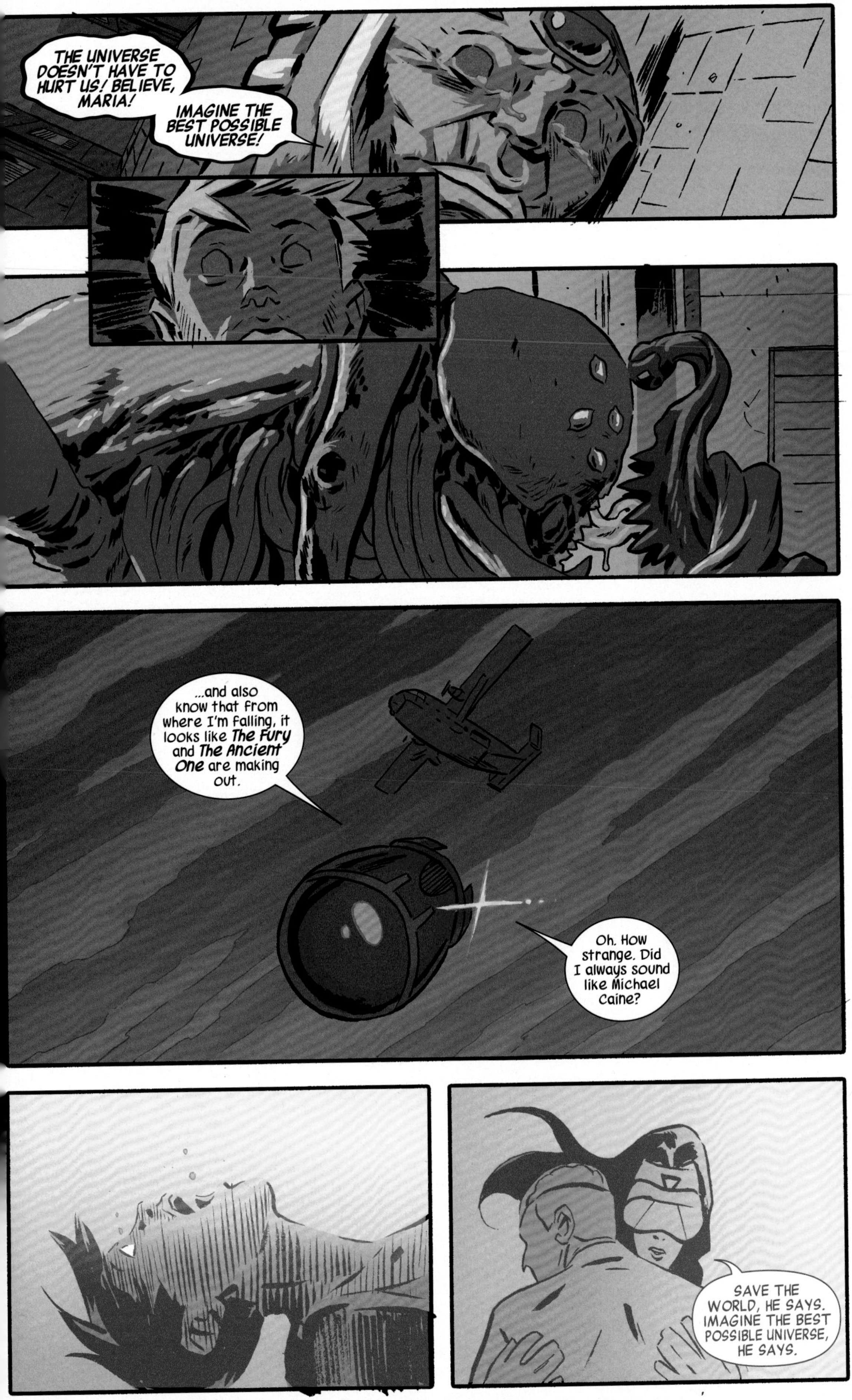

THE UNIVERSE DOESN'T HAVE TO HURT US! BELIEVE, MARIA!
IMAGINE THE BEST POSSIBLE UNIVERSE!
...and also know that from where I'm falling, it looks like The Fury and The Ancient One are making out.
Oh. How strange. Did I always sound like Michael Caine?
SAVE THE WORLD, HE SAYS. IMAGINE THE BEST POSSIBLE UNIVERSE, HE SAYS.

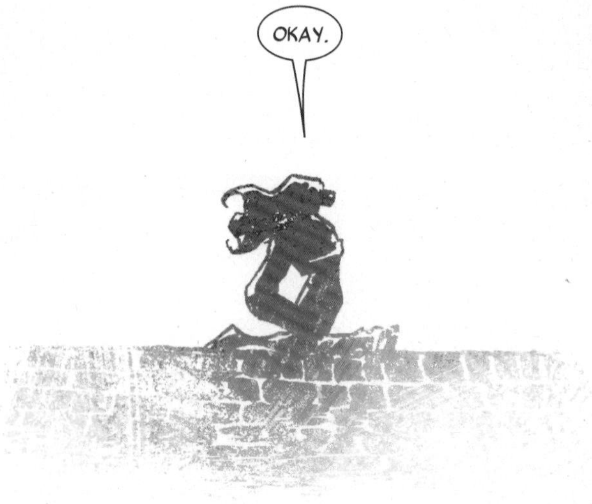
OKAY.

15

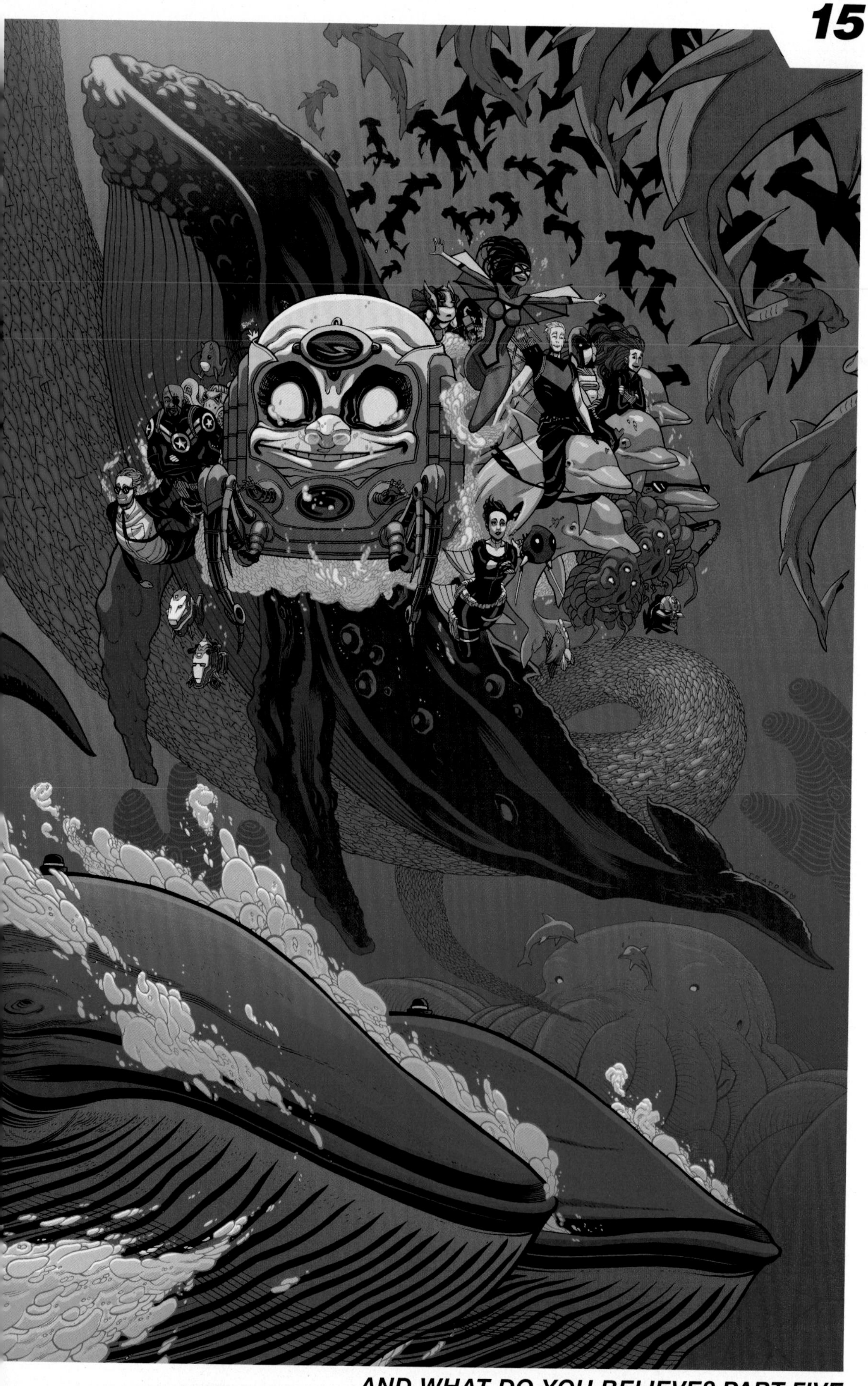

...AND WHAT DO YOU BELIEVE? PART FIVE

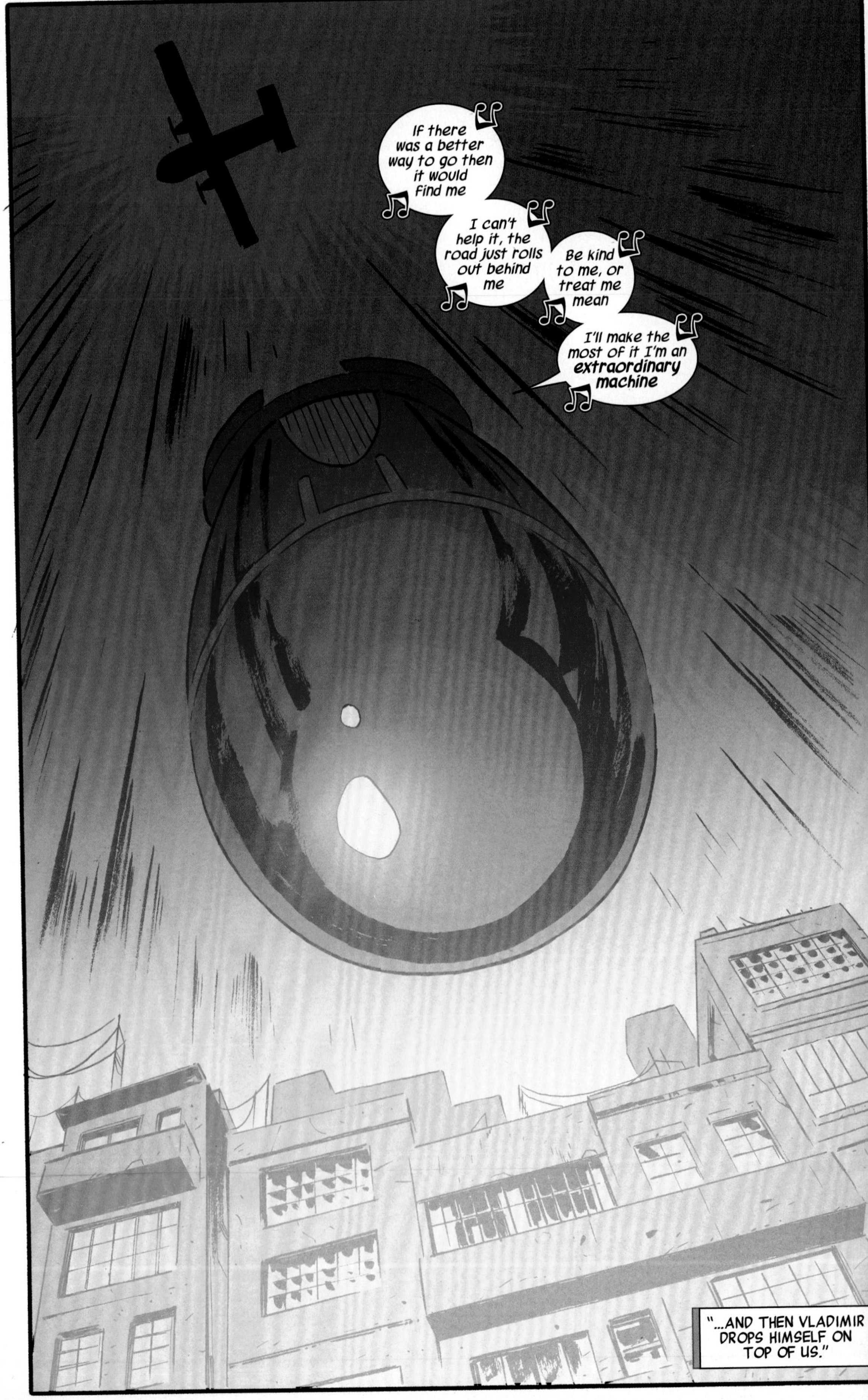
If there was a better way to go then it would find me
I can't help it, the road just rolls out behind me
Be kind to me, or treat me mean
I'll make the most of it I'm an extraordinary machine
"...AND THEN VLADIMIR DROPS HIMSELF ON TOP OF US."

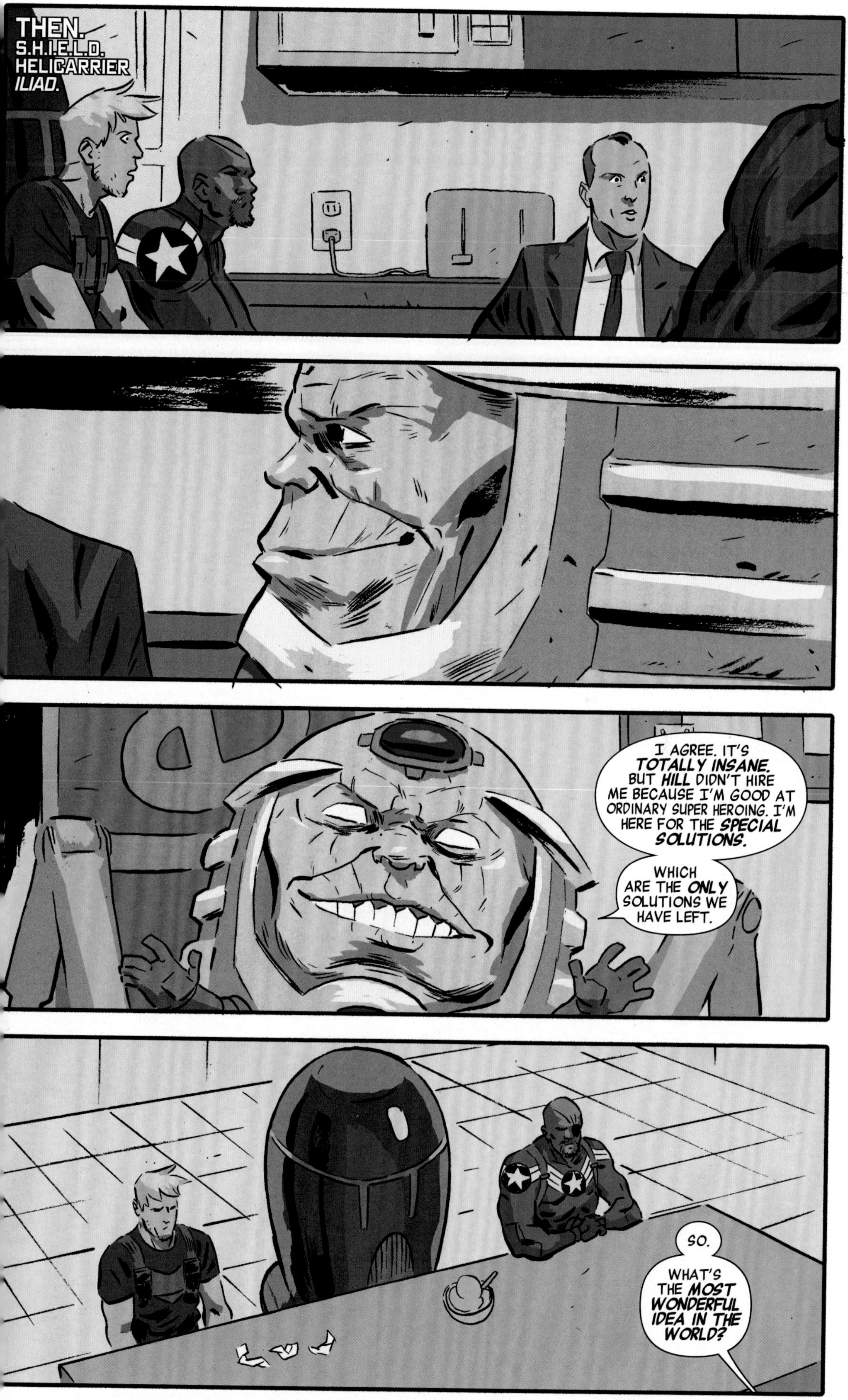
THEN. S.H.I.E.L.D. HELICARRIER ILIAD.
I AGREE. IT'S TOTALLY INSANE. BUT HILL DIDN'T HIRE ME BECAUSE I'M GOOD AT ORDINARY SUPER HEROING. I'M HERE FOR THE SPECIAL SOLUTIONS.
WHICH ARE THE ONLY SOLUTIONS WE HAVE LEFT.
SO.
WHAT'S THE MOST WONDERFUL IDEA IN THE WORLD?

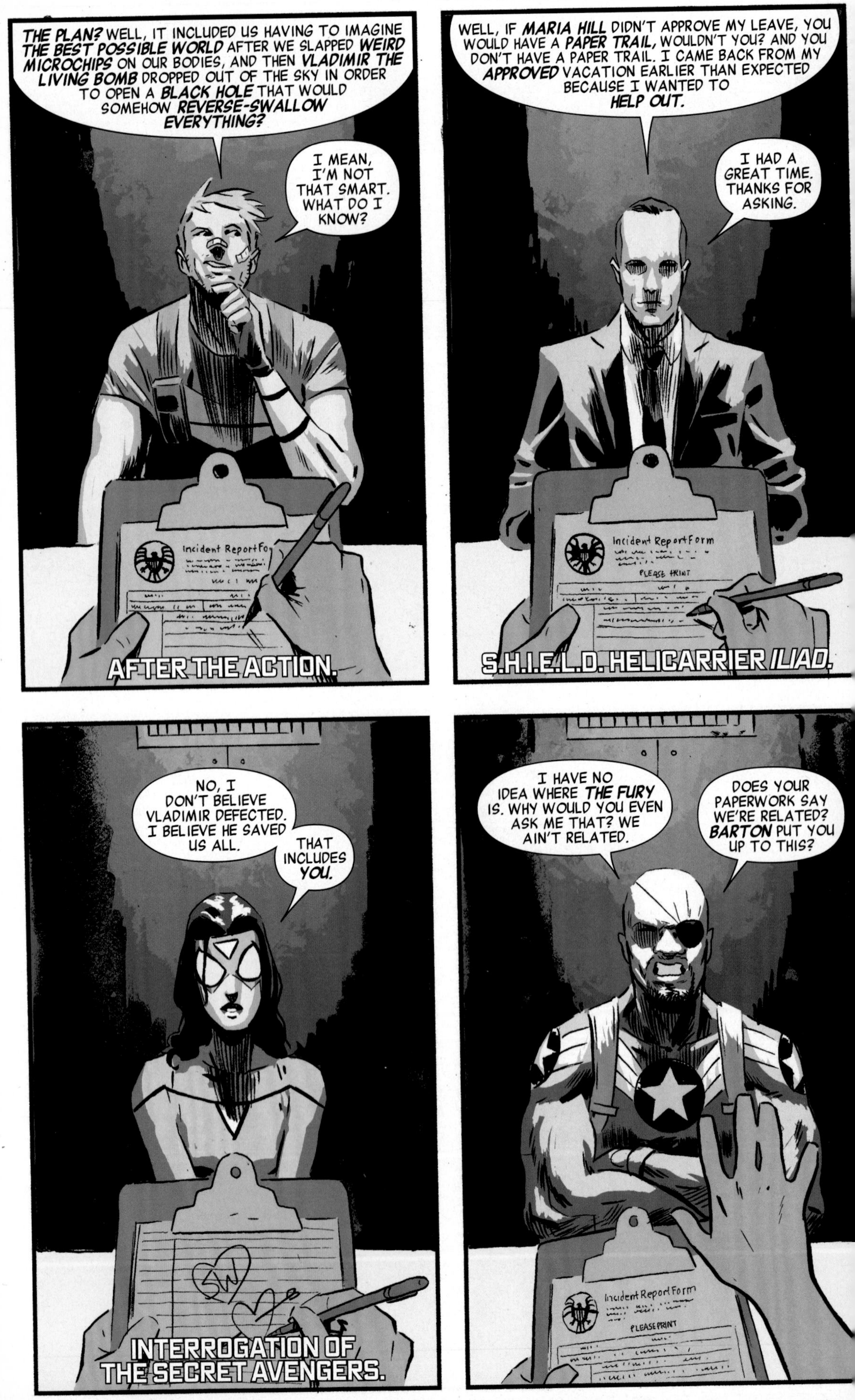
THE PLAN? WELL, IT INCLUDED US HAVING TO IMAGINE THE BEST POSSIBLE WORLD AFTER WE SLAPPED WEIRD MICROCHIPS ON OUR BODIES, AND THEN VLADIMIR THE LIVING BOMB DROPPED OUT OF THE SKY IN ORDER TO OPEN A BLACK HOLE THAT WOULD SOMEHOW REVERSE-SWALLOW EVERYTHING?
I MEAN, I'M NOT THAT SMART. WHAT DO I KNOW?
Incident Report Form
AFTER THE ACTION.
WELL, IF MARIA HILL DIDN'T APPROVE MY LEAVE, YOU WOULD HAVE A PAPER TRAIL, WOULDN'T YOU? AND YOU DON'T HAVE A PAPER TRAIL. I CAME BACK FROM MY APPROVED VACATION EARLIER THAN EXPECTED BECAUSE I WANTED TO HELP OUT.
I HAD A GREAT TIME. THANKS FOR ASKING.
Incident Report Form
PLEASE PRINT
S.H.I.E.L.D. HELICARRIER ILIAD.
NO, I DON'T BELIEVE VLADIMIR DEFECTED. I BELIEVE HE SAVED US ALL.
THAT INCLUDES YOU.
SW
INTERROGATION OF THE SECRET AVENGERS.
I HAVE NO IDEA WHERE THE FURY IS. WHY WOULD YOU EVEN ASK ME THAT? WE AIN'T RELATED.
DOES YOUR PAPERWORK SAY WE'RE RELATED? BARTON PUT YOU UP TO THIS?
Incident Report Form
PLEASE PRINT

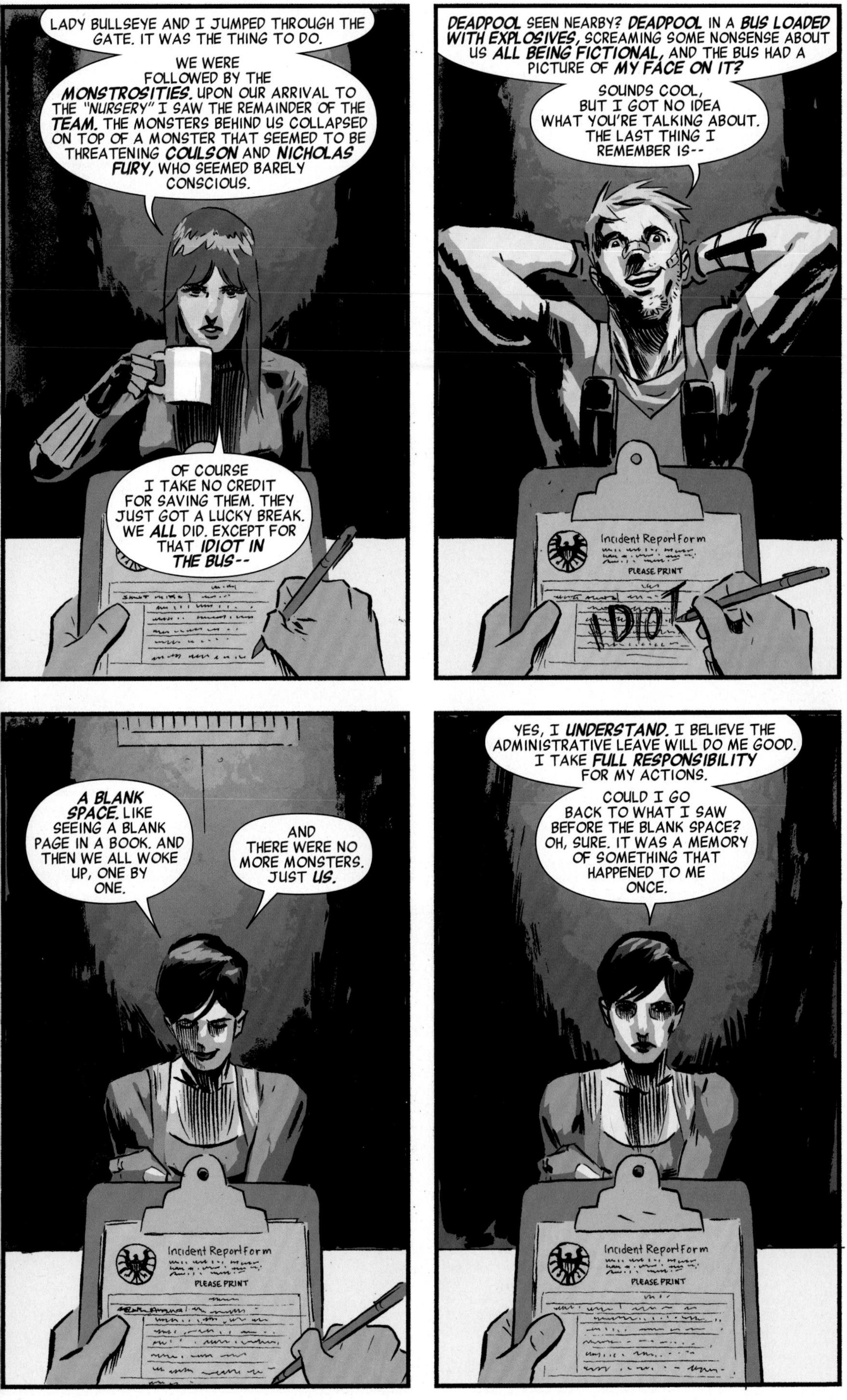
LADY BULLSEYE AND I JUMPED THROUGH THE GATE. IT WAS THE THING TO DO.
WE WERE FOLLOWED BY THE MONSTROSITIES. UPON OUR ARRIVAL TO THE "NURSERY" I SAW THE REMAINDER OF THE TEAM. THE MONSTERS BEHIND US COLLAPSED ON TOP OF A MONSTER THAT SEEMED TO BE THREATENING COULSON AND NICHOLAS FURY, WHO SEEMED BARELY CONSCIOUS.
OF COURSE I TAKE NO CREDIT FOR SAVING THEM. THEY JUST GOT A LUCKY BREAK. WE ALL DID. EXCEPT FOR THAT IDIOT IN THE BUS--
DEADPOOL SEEN NEARBY? DEADPOOL IN A BUS LOADED WITH EXPLOSIVES, SCREAMING SOME NONSENSE ABOUT US ALL BEING FICTIONAL, AND THE BUS HAD A PICTURE OF MY FACE ON IT?
SOUNDS COOL, BUT I GOT NO IDEA WHAT YOU'RE TALKING ABOUT. THE LAST THING I REMEMBER IS--
Incident Report Form
PLEASE PRINT
IDIOT
A BLANK SPACE. LIKE SEEING A BLANK PAGE IN A BOOK. AND THEN WE ALL WOKE UP, ONE BY ONE.
AND THERE WERE NO MORE MONSTERS. JUST US.
Incident Report Form
PLEASE PRINT
YES, I UNDERSTAND. I BELIEVE THE ADMINISTRATIVE LEAVE WILL DO ME GOOD. I TAKE FULL RESPONSIBILITY FOR MY ACTIONS.
COULD I GO BACK TO WHAT I SAW BEFORE THE BLANK SPACE? OH, SURE. IT WAS A MEMORY OF SOMETHING THAT HAPPENED TO ME ONCE.
Incident Report Form
PLEASE PRINT

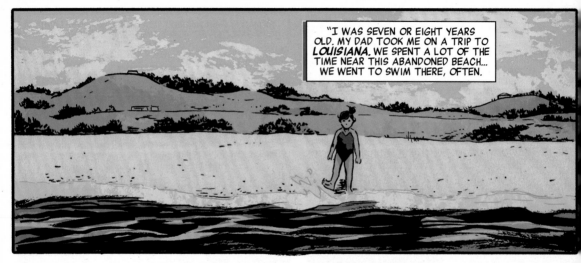

"I WAS SEVEN OR EIGHT YEARS OLD. MY DAD TOOK ME ON A TRIP TO *LOUISIANA.* WE SPENT A LOT OF THE TIME NEAR THIS ABANDONED BEACH... WE WENT TO SWIM THERE, OFTEN.

"I WOKE UP EARLY THAT DAY, EARLIER THAN DAD. SO I SLIPPED OUT AND WENT TO SEE THE BEACH. I LIKED BEING ALONE, YOU KNOW? TIME TO JUST BE. IT WAS SO EASY BACK THEN.

"AND THEN I SEE THEM.

"PORPOISES.

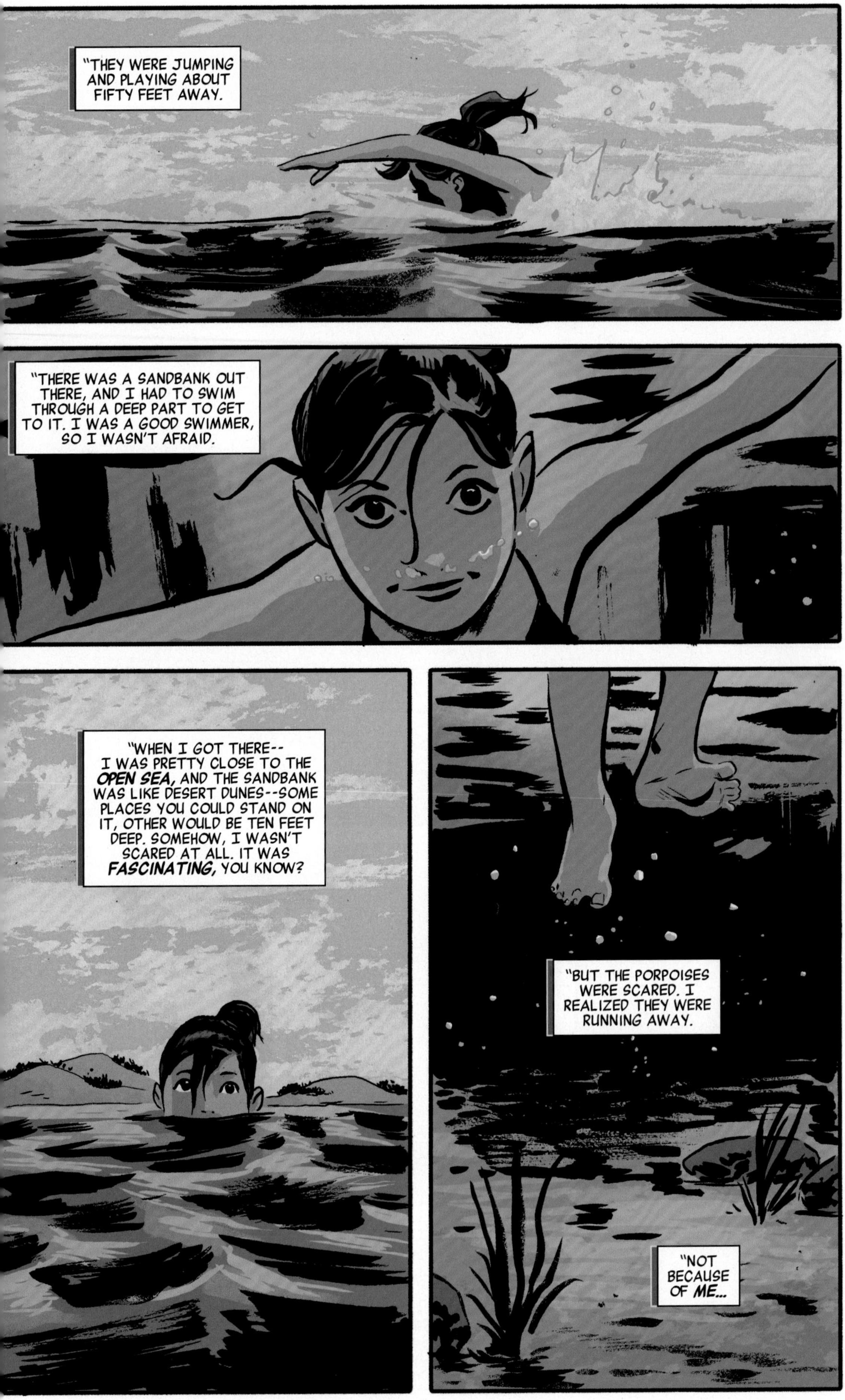
"THEY WERE JUMPING AND PLAYING ABOUT FIFTY FEET AWAY.
"THERE WAS A SANDBANK OUT THERE, AND I HAD TO SWIM THROUGH A DEEP PART TO GET TO IT. I WAS A GOOD SWIMMER, SO I WASN'T AFRAID.
"WHEN I GOT THERE-- I WAS PRETTY CLOSE TO THE OPEN SEA, AND THE SANDBANK WAS LIKE DESERT DUNES--SOME PLACES YOU COULD STAND ON IT, OTHER WOULD BE TEN FEET DEEP. SOMEHOW, I WASN'T SCARED AT ALL. IT WAS FASCINATING, YOU KNOW?
"BUT THE PORPOISES WERE SCARED. I REALIZED THEY WERE RUNNING AWAY.
"NOT BECAUSE OF ME...

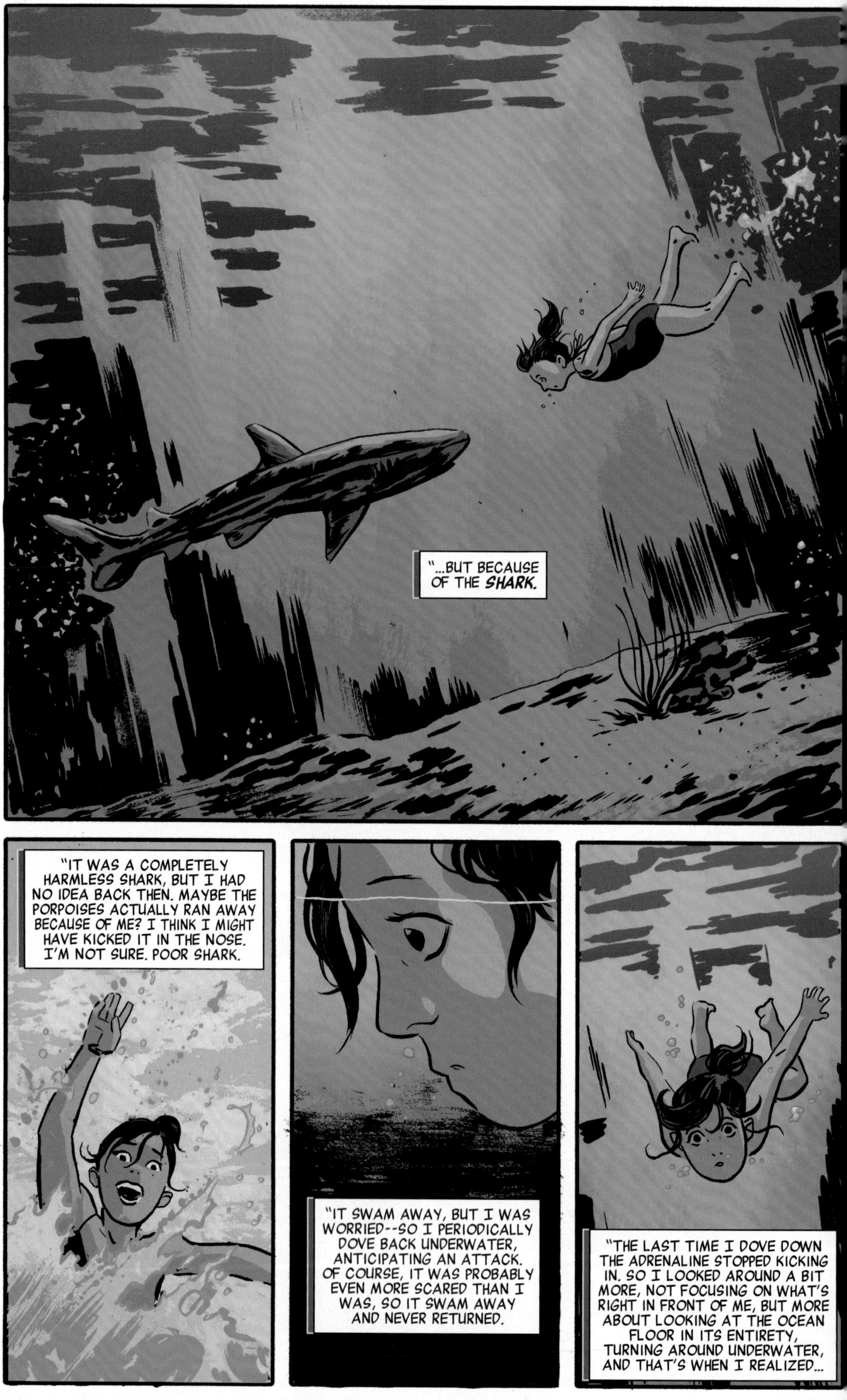
"...BUT BECAUSE OF THE *SHARK.*
"IT WAS A COMPLETELY HARMLESS SHARK, BUT I HAD NO IDEA BACK THEN. MAYBE THE PORPOISES ACTUALLY RAN AWAY BECAUSE OF ME? I THINK I MIGHT HAVE KICKED IT IN THE NOSE. I'M NOT SURE. POOR SHARK.
"IT SWAM AWAY, BUT I WAS WORRIED--SO I PERIODICALLY DOVE BACK UNDERWATER, ANTICIPATING AN ATTACK. OF COURSE, IT WAS PROBABLY EVEN MORE SCARED THAN I WAS, SO IT SWAM AWAY AND NEVER RETURNED.
"THE LAST TIME I DOVE DOWN THE ADRENALINE STOPPED KICKING IN. SO I LOOKED AROUND A BIT MORE, NOT FOCUSING ON WHAT'S RIGHT IN FRONT OF ME, BUT MORE ABOUT LOOKING AT THE OCEAN FLOOR IN ITS ENTIRETY, TURNING AROUND UNDERWATER, AND THAT'S WHEN I REALIZED...

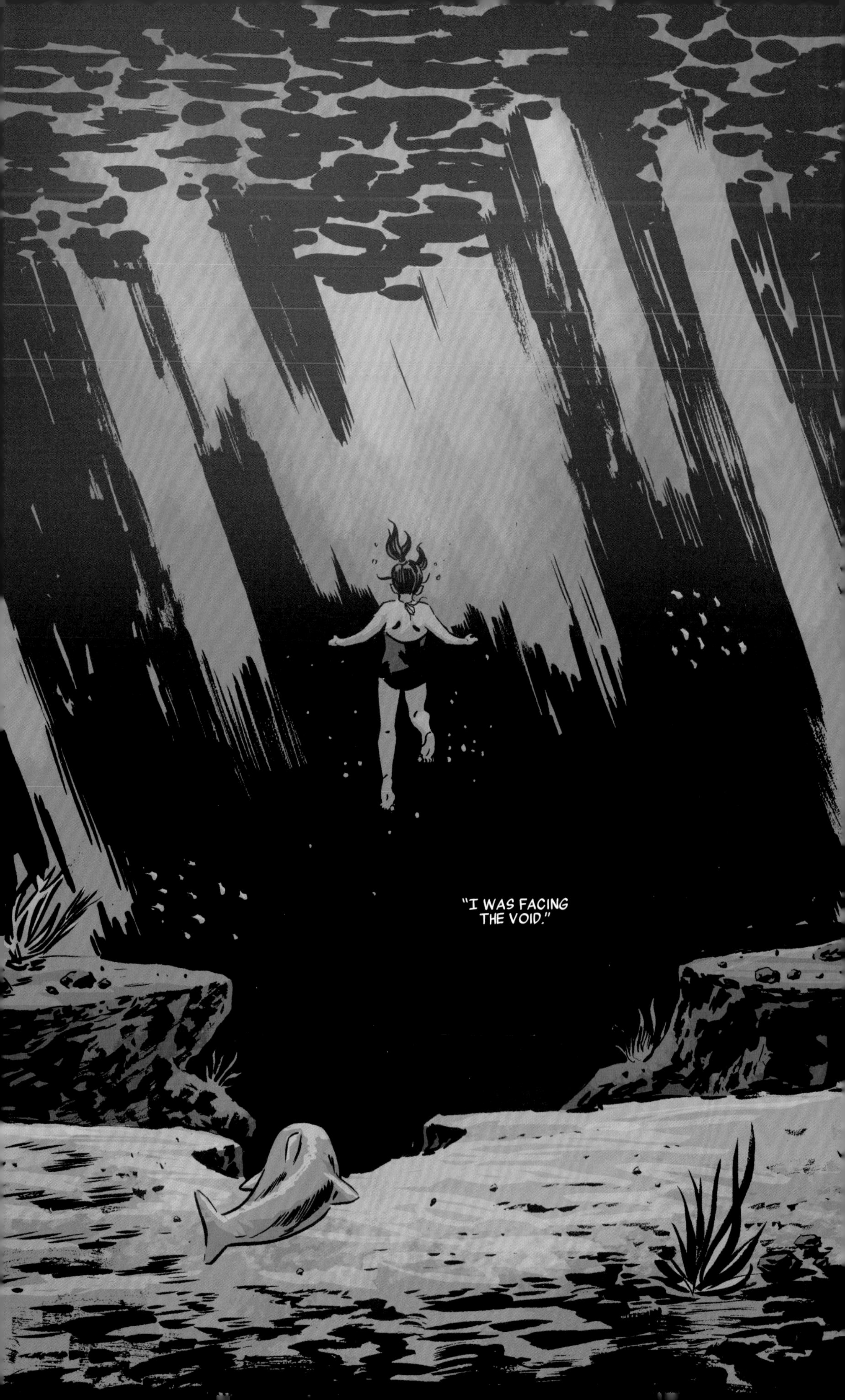
"I WAS FACING THE VOID."

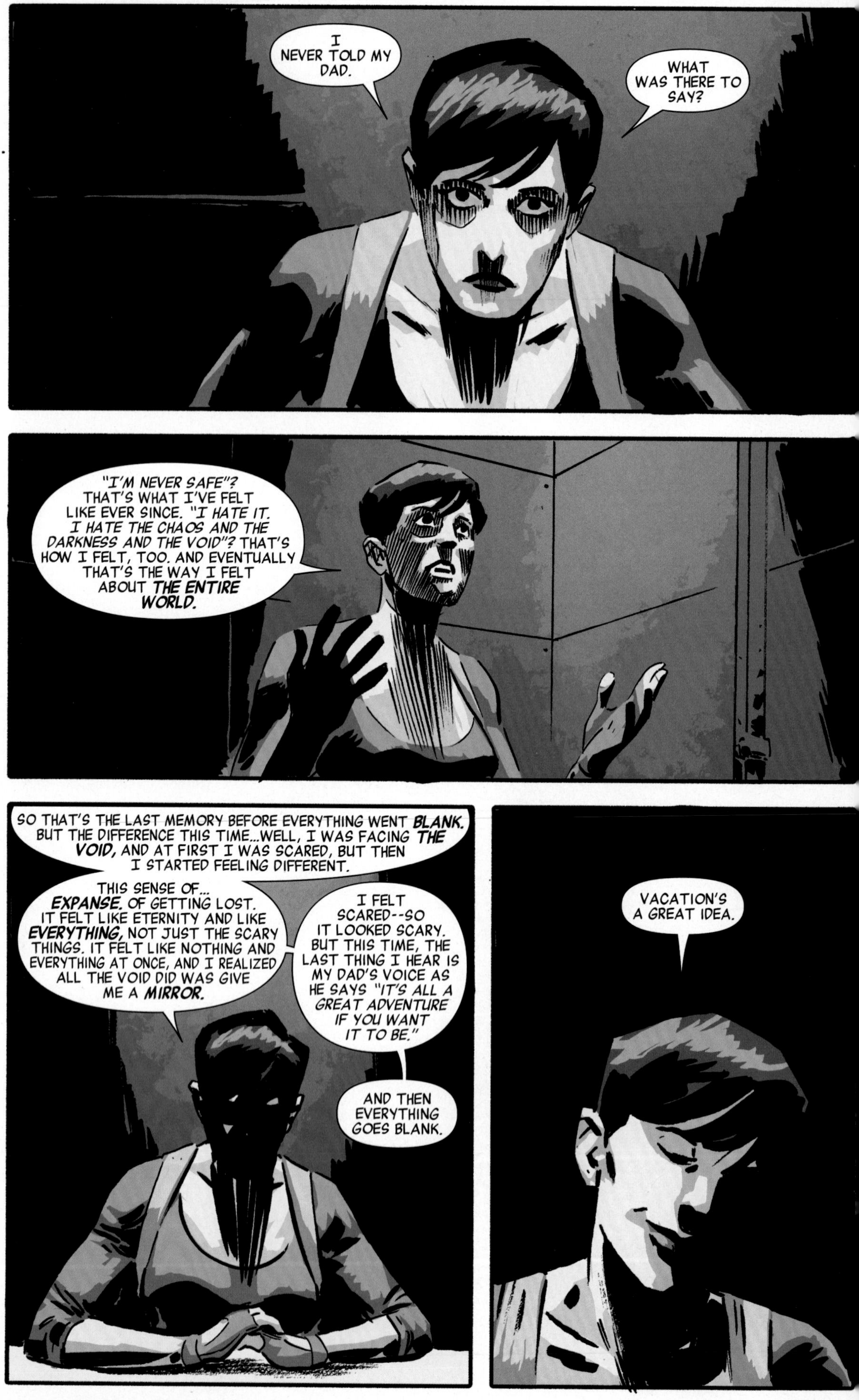
I NEVER TOLD MY DAD.
WHAT WAS THERE TO SAY?
"I'M NEVER SAFE"? THAT'S WHAT I'VE FELT LIKE EVER SINCE. "I HATE IT. I HATE THE CHAOS AND THE DARKNESS AND THE VOID"? THAT'S HOW I FELT, TOO. AND EVENTUALLY THAT'S THE WAY I FELT ABOUT THE ENTIRE WORLD.
SO THAT'S THE LAST MEMORY BEFORE EVERYTHING WENT BLANK. BUT THE DIFFERENCE THIS TIME...WELL, I WAS FACING THE VOID, AND AT FIRST I WAS SCARED, BUT THEN I STARTED FEELING DIFFERENT.
THIS SENSE OF... EXPANSE. OF GETTING LOST. IT FELT LIKE ETERNITY AND LIKE EVERYTHING, NOT JUST THE SCARY THINGS. IT FELT LIKE NOTHING AND EVERYTHING AT ONCE, AND I REALIZED ALL THE VOID DID WAS GIVE ME A MIRROR.
I FELT SCARED--SO IT LOOKED SCARY. BUT THIS TIME, THE LAST THING I HEAR IS MY DAD'S VOICE AS HE SAYS "IT'S ALL A GREAT ADVENTURE IF YOU WANT IT TO BE."
AND THEN EVERYTHING GOES BLANK.
VACATION'S A GREAT IDEA.

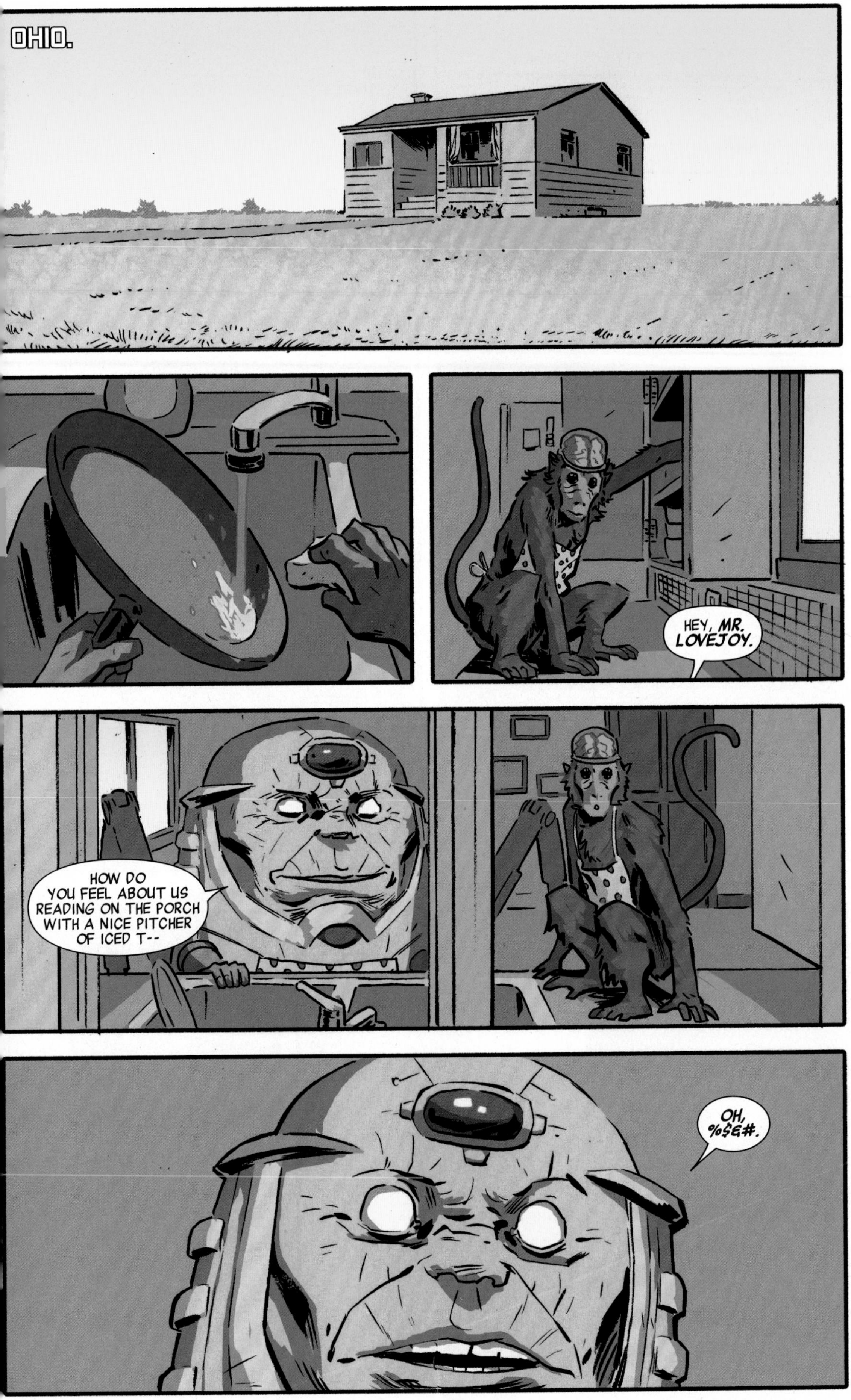
OHIO.
HEY, MR. LOVEJOY.
HOW DO YOU FEEL ABOUT US READING ON THE PORCH WITH A NICE PITCHER OF ICED T--
OH, %$&#.

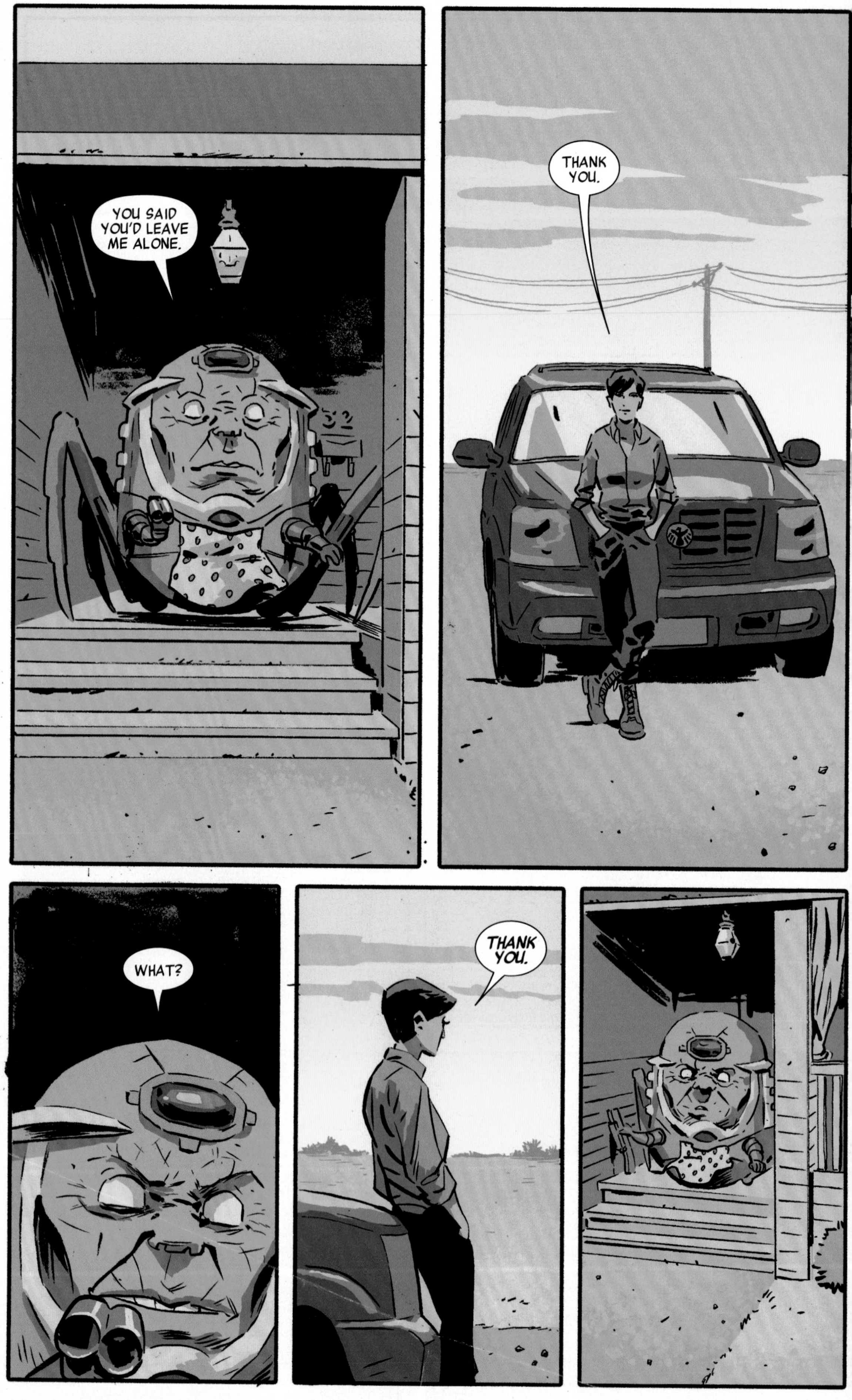
YOU SAID YOU'D LEAVE ME ALONE.
THANK YOU.
WHAT?
THANK YOU.

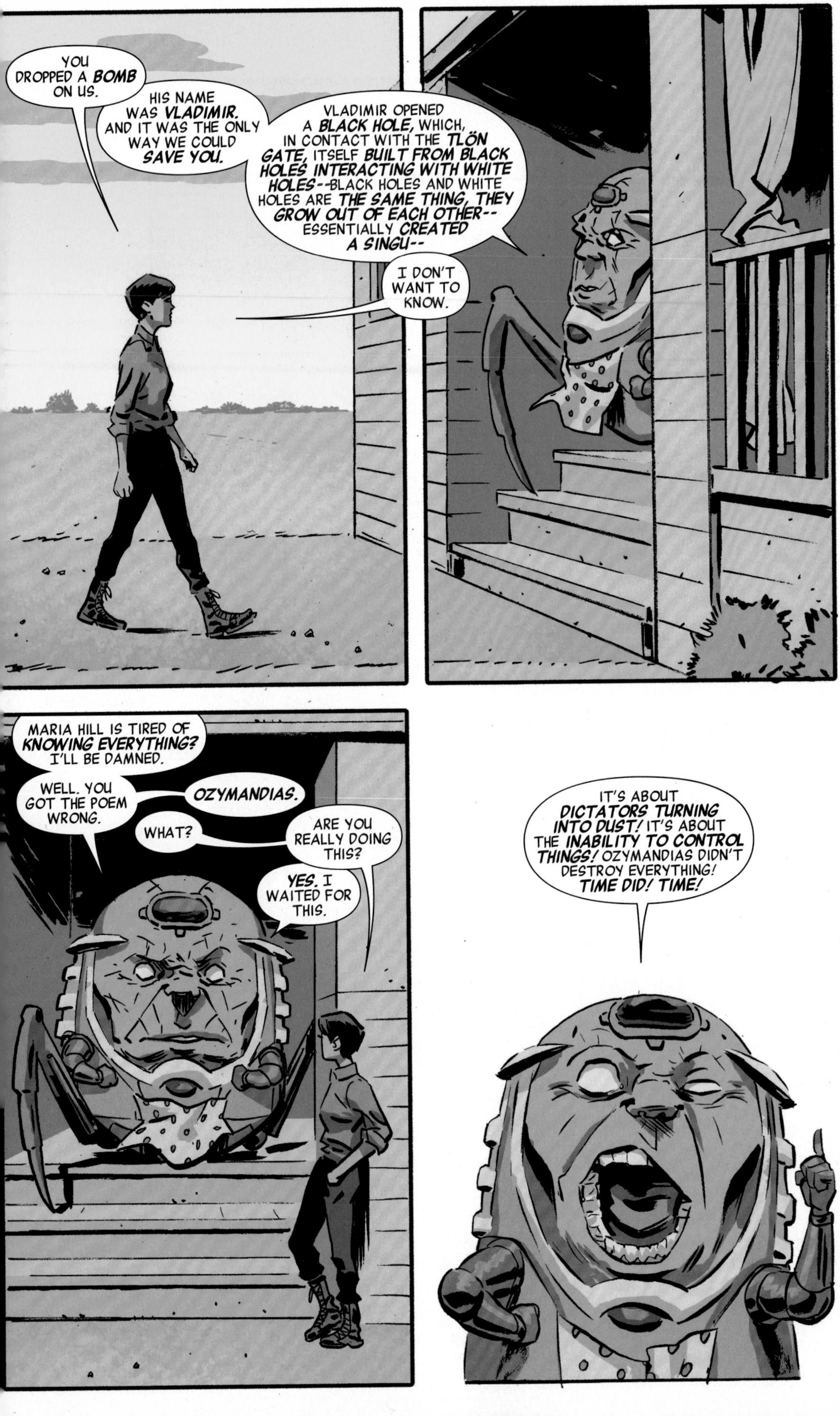

YOU DROPPED A BOMB ON US.
HIS NAME WAS VLADIMIR. AND IT WAS THE ONLY WAY WE COULD SAVE YOU.
VLADIMIR OPENED A BLACK HOLE, WHICH, IN CONTACT WITH THE TLÖN GATE, ITSELF BUILT FROM BLACK HOLES INTERACTING WITH WHITE HOLES--BLACK HOLES AND WHITE HOLES ARE THE SAME THING, THEY GROW OUT OF EACH OTHER--ESSENTIALLY CREATED A SINGU--
I DON'T WANT TO KNOW.
MARIA HILL IS TIRED OF KNOWING EVERYTHING? I'LL BE DAMNED.
WELL, YOU GOT THE POEM WRONG.
OZYMANDIAS.
WHAT?
ARE YOU REALLY DOING THIS?
YES. I WAITED FOR THIS.
IT'S ABOUT DICTATORS TURNING INTO DUST! IT'S ABOUT THE INABILITY TO CONTROL THINGS! OZYMANDIAS DIDN'T DESTROY EVERYTHING! TIME DID! TIME!

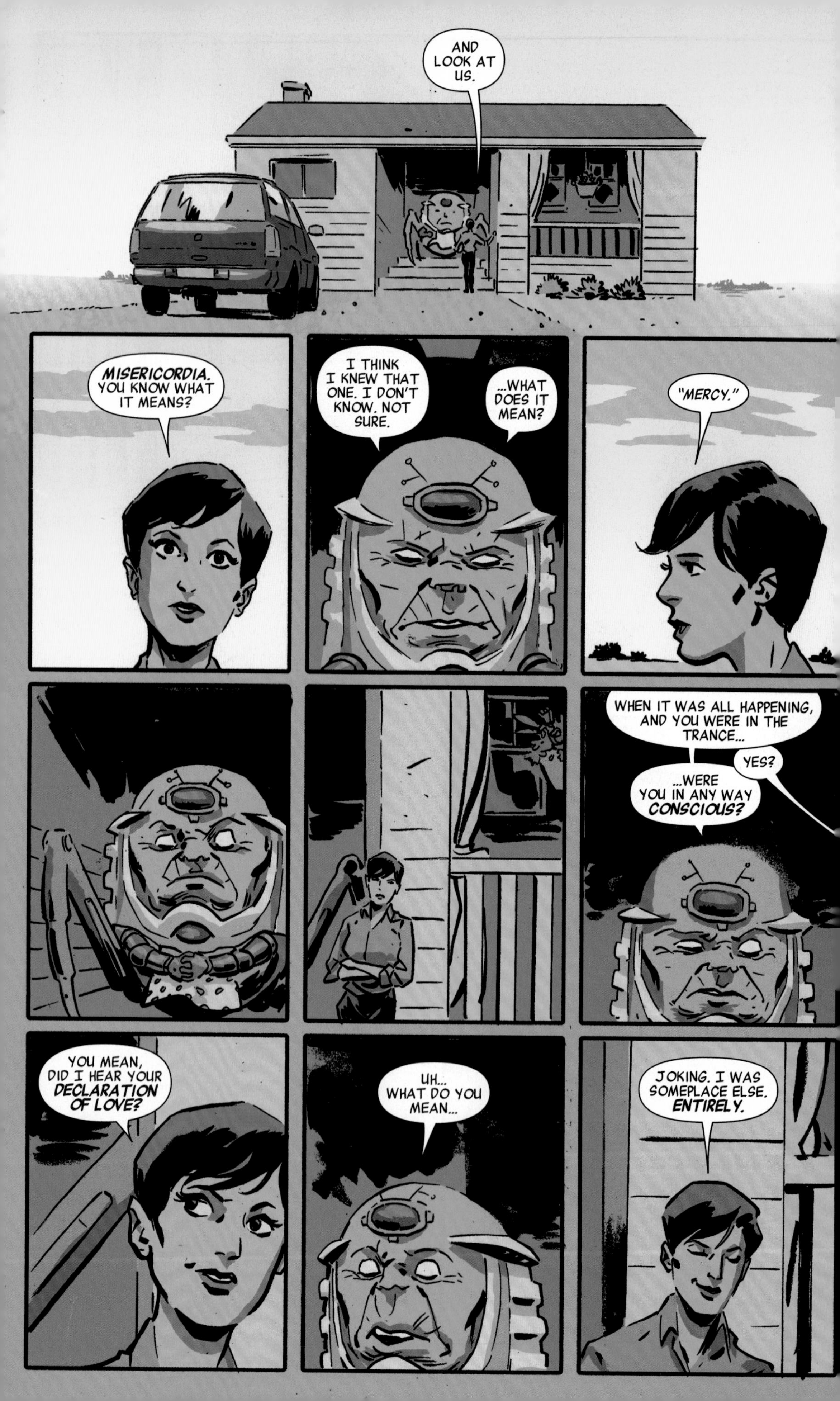
AND LOOK AT US.
MISERICORDIA. YOU KNOW WHAT IT MEANS?
I THINK I KNEW THAT ONE. I DON'T KNOW. NOT SURE.
...WHAT DOES IT MEAN?
"MERCY."
WHEN IT WAS ALL HAPPENING, AND YOU WERE IN THE TRANCE...
YES?
...WERE YOU IN ANY WAY CONSCIOUS?
YOU MEAN, DID I HEAR YOUR DECLARATION OF LOVE?
UH... WHAT DO YOU MEAN...
JOKING. I WAS SOMEPLACE ELSE. ENTIRELY.

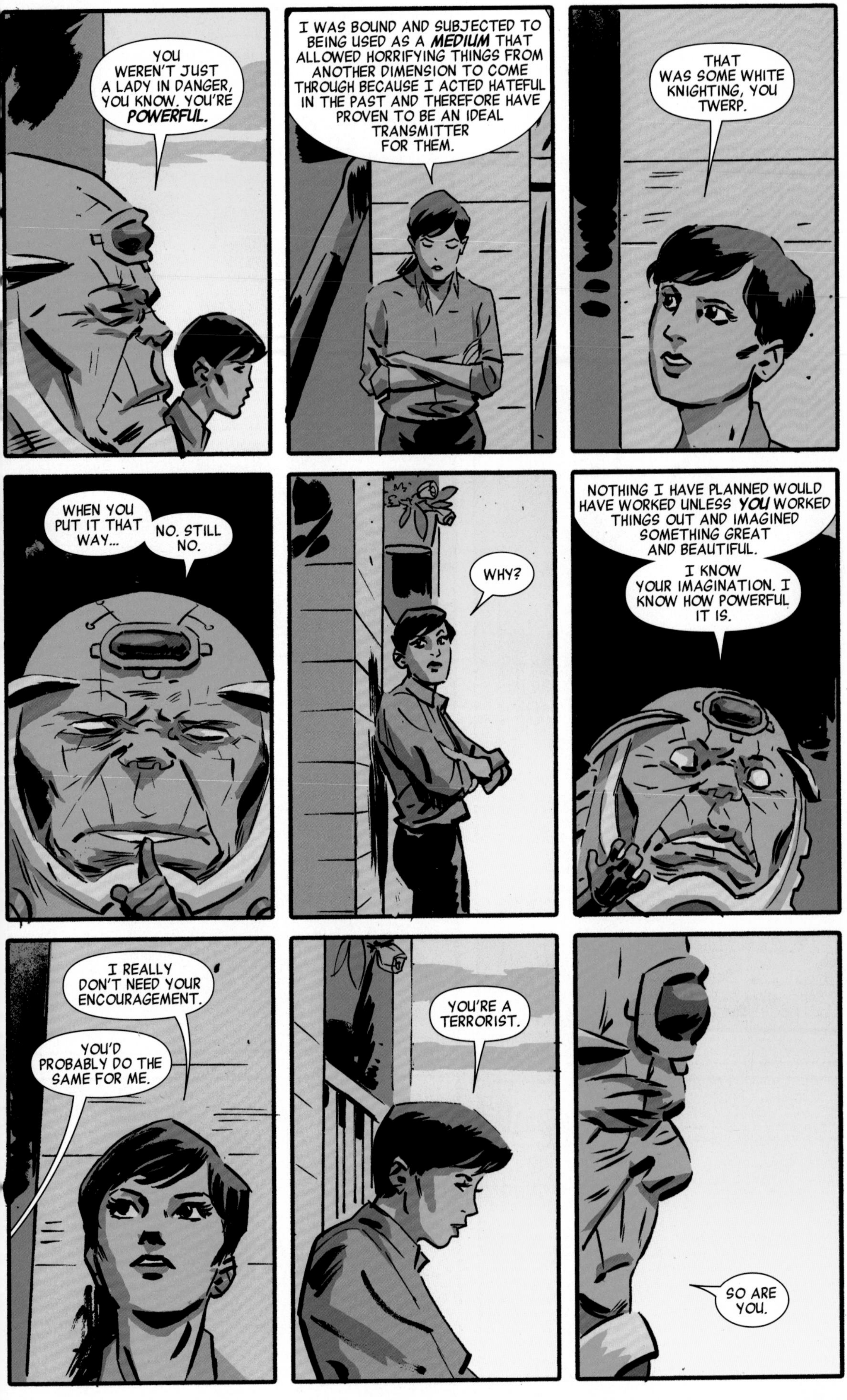
YOU WEREN'T JUST A LADY IN DANGER, YOU KNOW. YOU'RE POWERFUL.
I WAS BOUND AND SUBJECTED TO BEING USED AS A MEDIUM THAT ALLOWED HORRIFYING THINGS FROM ANOTHER DIMENSION TO COME THROUGH BECAUSE I ACTED HATEFUL IN THE PAST AND THEREFORE HAVE PROVEN TO BE AN IDEAL TRANSMITTER FOR THEM.
THAT WAS SOME WHITE KNIGHTING, YOU TWERP.
WHEN YOU PUT IT THAT WAY...
NO. STILL NO.
WHY?
NOTHING I HAVE PLANNED WOULD HAVE WORKED UNLESS YOU WORKED THINGS OUT AND IMAGINED SOMETHING GREAT AND BEAUTIFUL.
I KNOW YOUR IMAGINATION. I KNOW HOW POWERFUL IT IS.
I REALLY DON'T NEED YOUR ENCOURAGEMENT.
YOU'D PROBABLY DO THE SAME FOR ME.
YOU'RE A TERRORIST.
SO ARE YOU.

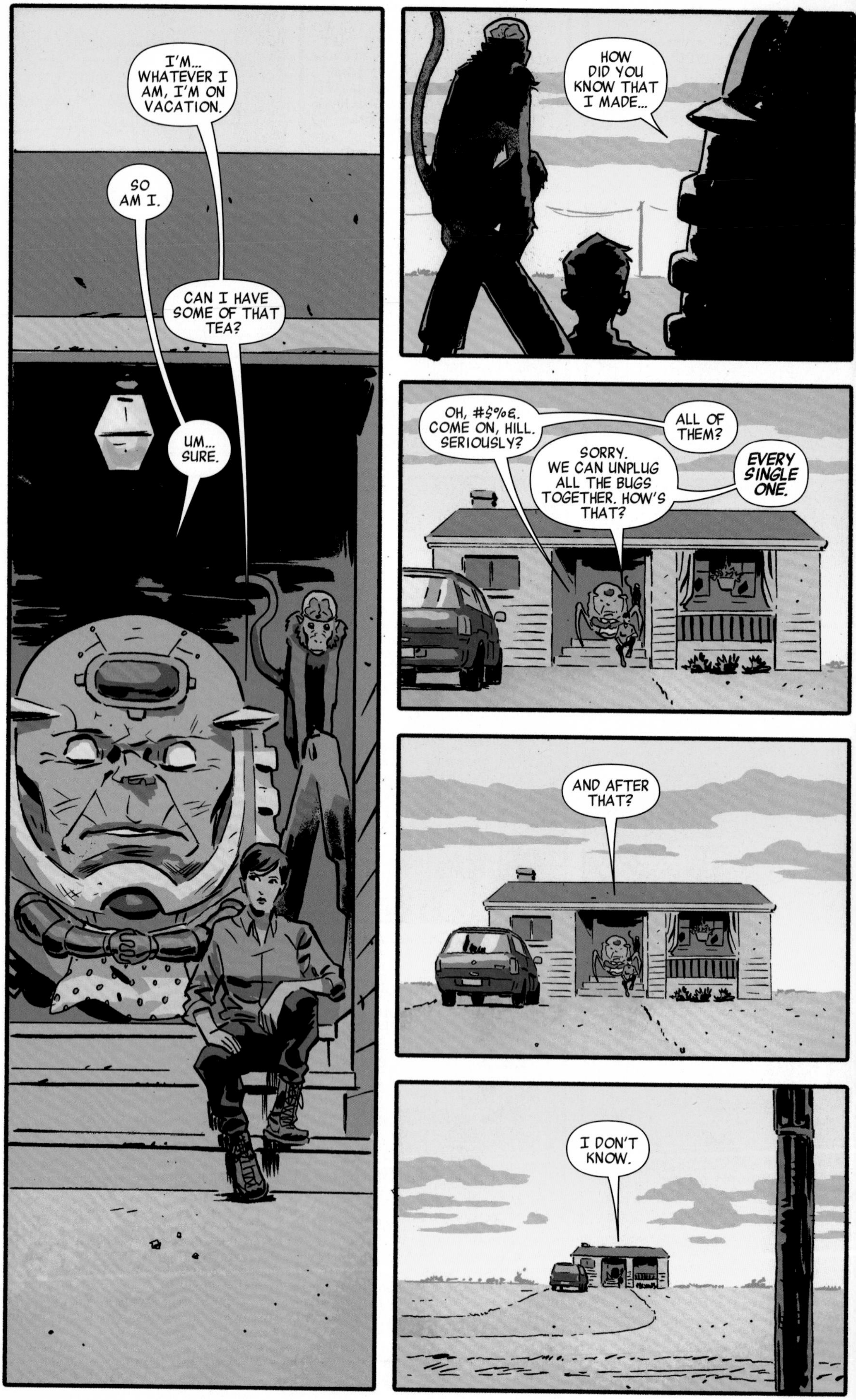
I'M... WHATEVER I AM, I'M ON VACATION.
SO AM I.
CAN I HAVE SOME OF THAT TEA?
UM... SURE.
HOW DID YOU KNOW THAT I MADE...
OH, #$%&. COME ON, HILL. SERIOUSLY?
ALL OF THEM?
SORRY. WE CAN UNPLUG ALL THE BUGS TOGETHER. HOW'S THAT?
EVERY SINGLE ONE.
AND AFTER THAT?
I DON'T KNOW.

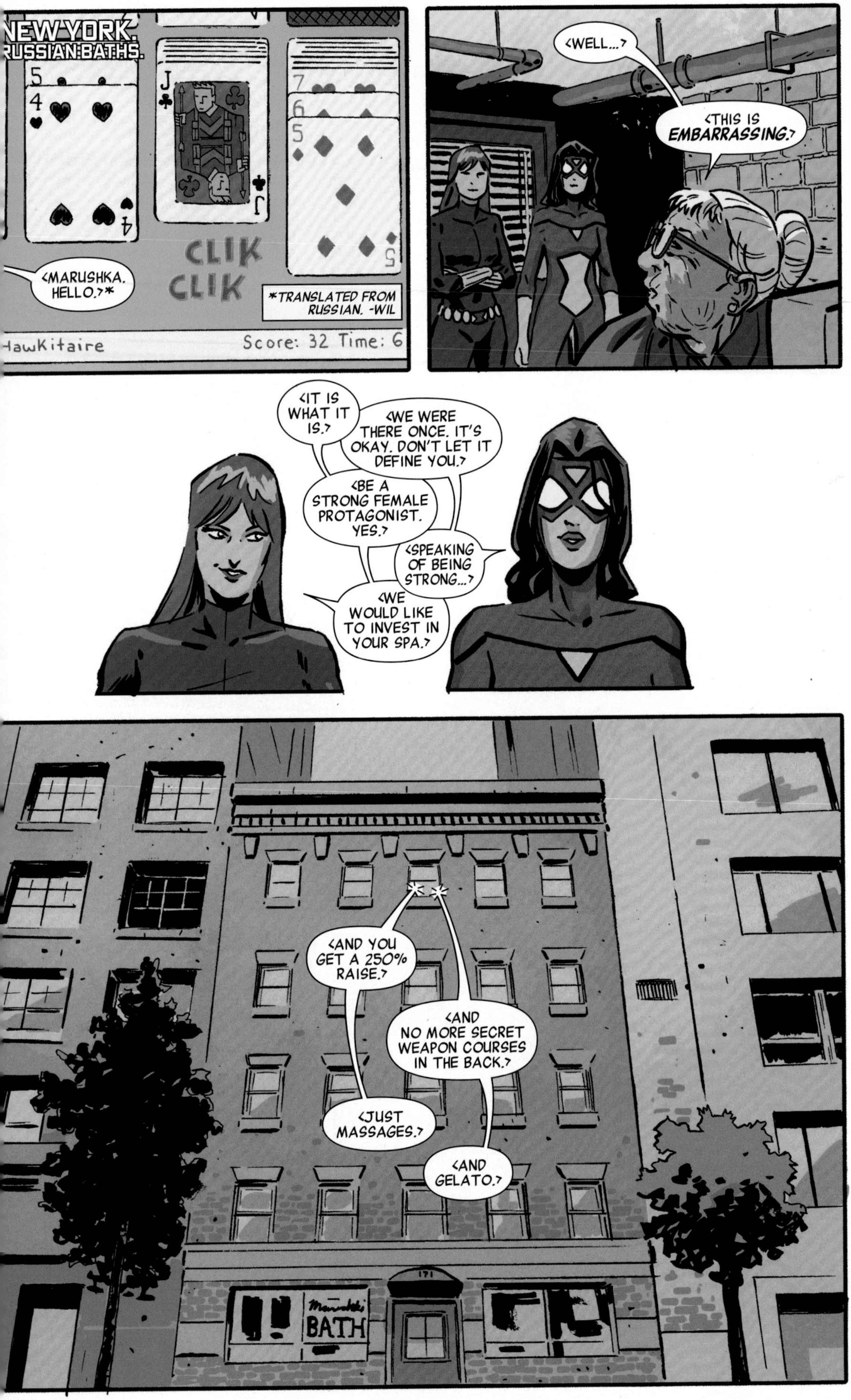
NEW YORK.
RUSSIAN BATHS.
CLIK
CLIK
<MARUSHKA. HELLO.>*
*TRANSLATED FROM RUSSIAN. -WIL
HawKitaire
Score: 32 Time: 6
<WELL...>
<THIS IS EMBARRASSING.>
<IT IS WHAT IT IS.>
<WE WERE THERE ONCE. IT'S OKAY. DON'T LET IT DEFINE YOU.>
<BE A STRONG FEMALE PROTAGONIST. YES.>
<SPEAKING OF BEING STRONG...>
<WE WOULD LIKE TO INVEST IN YOUR SPA.>
<AND YOU GET A 250% RAISE.>
<AND NO MORE SECRET WEAPON COURSES IN THE BACK.>
<JUST MASSAGES.>
<AND GELATO.>
171
BATH

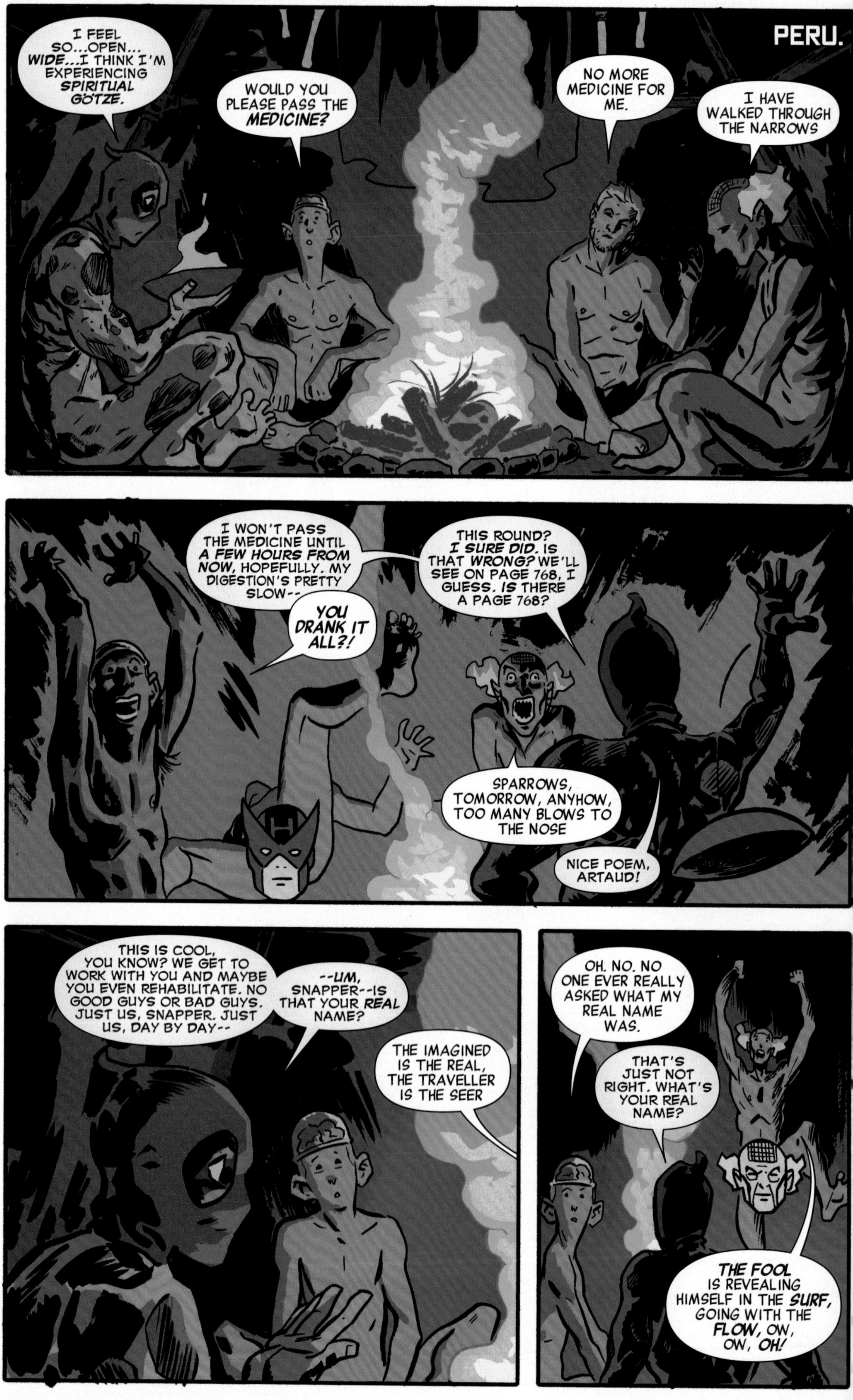
PERU.
I FEEL SO...OPEN... WIDE...I THINK I'M EXPERIENCING SPIRITUAL GÖTZE.
WOULD YOU PLEASE PASS THE MEDICINE?
NO MORE MEDICINE FOR ME.
I HAVE WALKED THROUGH THE NARROWS
I WON'T PASS THE MEDICINE UNTIL A FEW HOURS FROM NOW, HOPEFULLY. MY DIGESTION'S PRETTY SLOW--
YOU DRANK IT ALL?!
THIS ROUND? I SURE DID. IS THAT WRONG? WE'LL SEE ON PAGE 768, I GUESS. IS THERE A PAGE 768?
SPARROWS, TOMORROW, ANYHOW, TOO MANY BLOWS TO THE NOSE
NICE POEM, ARTAUD!
THIS IS COOL, YOU KNOW? WE GET TO WORK WITH YOU AND MAYBE YOU EVEN REHABILITATE. NO GOOD GUYS OR BAD GUYS. JUST US, SNAPPER. JUST US, DAY BY DAY--
--UM, SNAPPER--IS THAT YOUR REAL NAME?
THE IMAGINED IS THE REAL, THE TRAVELLER IS THE SEER
OH. NO. NO ONE EVER REALLY ASKED WHAT MY REAL NAME WAS.
THAT'S JUST NOT RIGHT. WHAT'S YOUR REAL NAME?
THE FOOL IS REVEALING HIMSELF IN THE SURF, GOING WITH THE FLOW, OW, OW, OH!

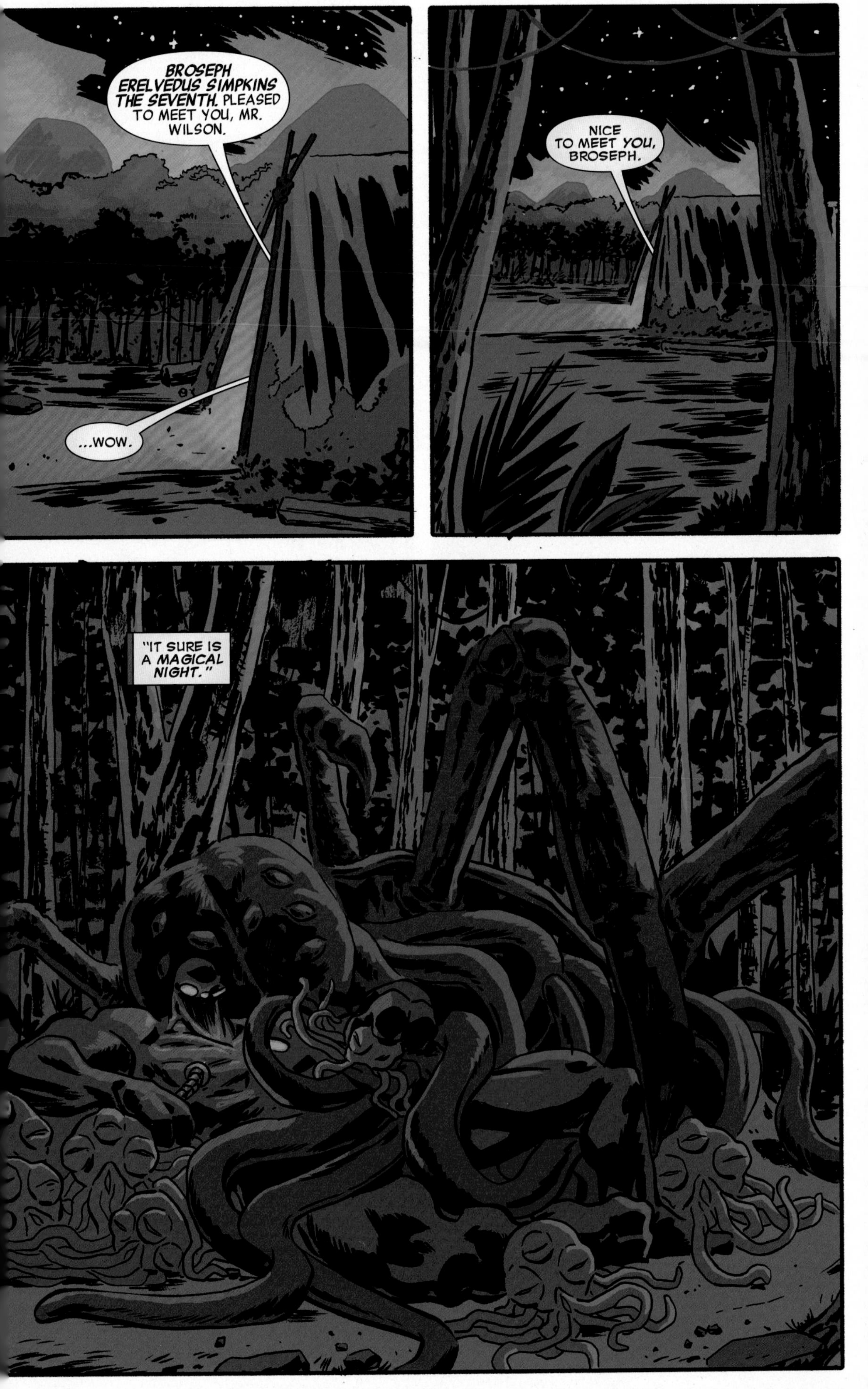
BROSEPH ERELVEDUS SIMPKINS THE SEVENTH. PLEASED TO MEET YOU, MR. WILSON.
...WOW.
NICE TO MEET YOU, BROSEPH.
"IT SURE IS A MAGICAL NIGHT."

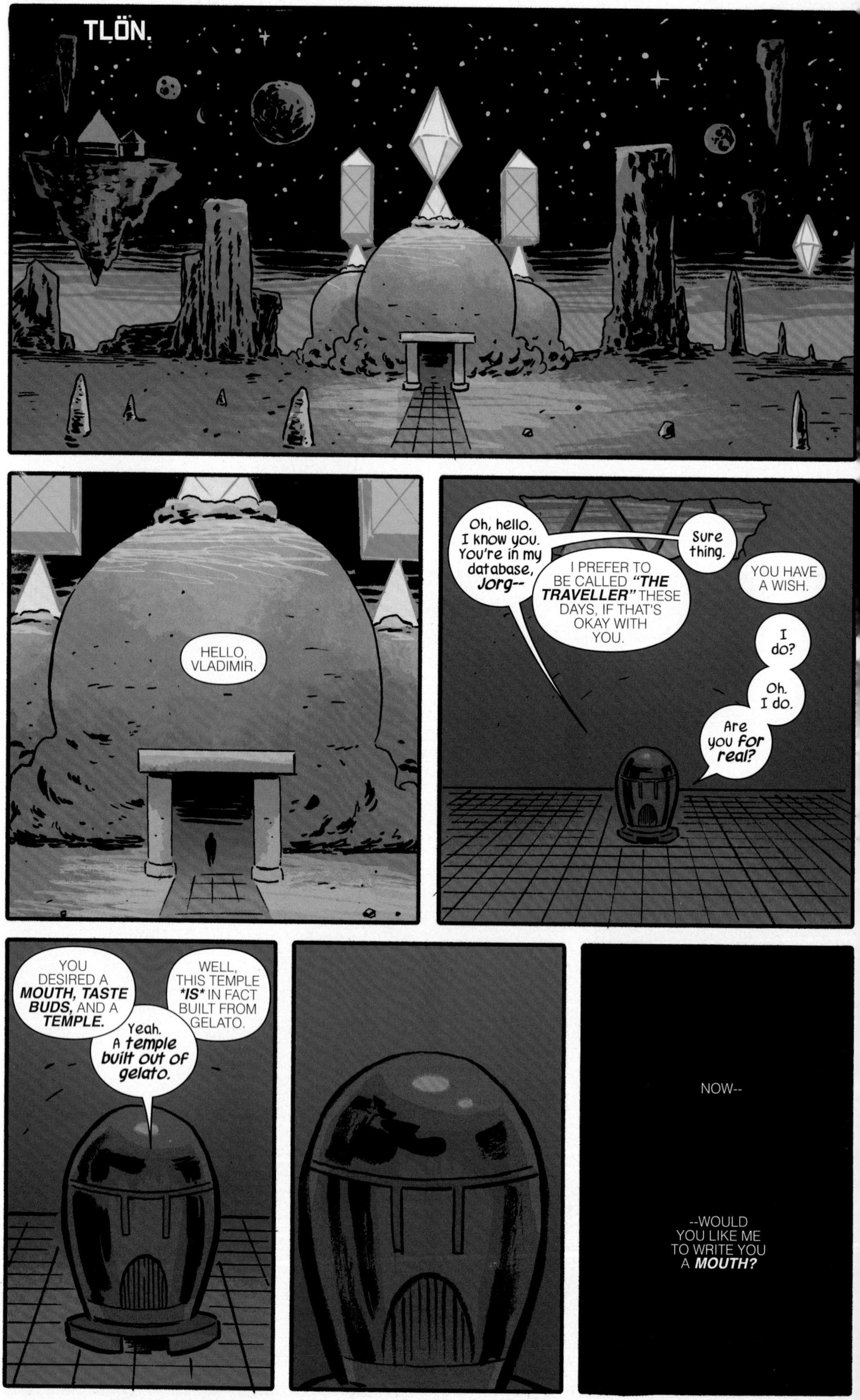
TLÖN.
HELLO, VLADIMIR.
Oh, hello. I know you. You're in my database, Jorg--
Sure thing.
I PREFER TO BE CALLED "THE TRAVELLER" THESE DAYS, IF THAT'S OKAY WITH YOU.
YOU HAVE A WISH.
I do?
Oh. I do.
Are you for real?
YOU DESIRED A MOUTH, TASTE BUDS, AND A TEMPLE.
Yeah. A temple built out of gelato.
WELL, THIS TEMPLE *IS* IN FACT BUILT FROM GELATO.
NOW--
--WOULD YOU LIKE ME TO WRITE YOU A MOUTH?

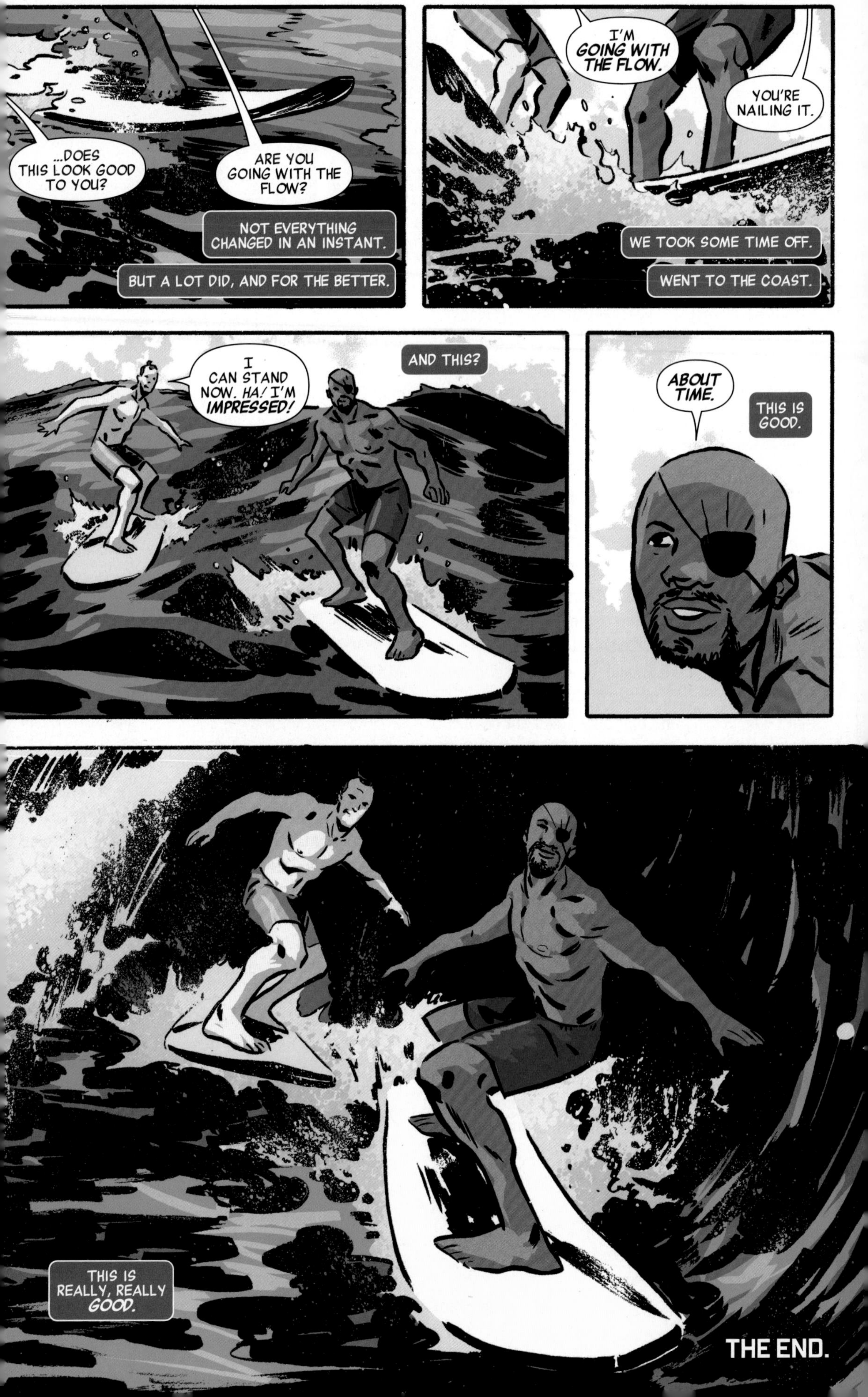
...DOES THIS LOOK GOOD TO YOU?
ARE YOU GOING WITH THE FLOW?
NOT EVERYTHING CHANGED IN AN INSTANT.
BUT A LOT DID, AND FOR THE BETTER.
I'M *GOING WITH THE FLOW.*
YOU'RE NAILING IT.
WE TOOK SOME TIME OFF.
WENT TO THE COAST.
I CAN STAND NOW. HA! I'M *IMPRESSED!*
AND THIS?
ABOUT TIME.
THIS IS GOOD.
THIS IS REALLY, REALLY *GOOD.*
THE END.

TINKER TAILOR
HAWKEYE M.O.D.O.K.

I believe in art that asks questions. In fact, I believe a key purpose of art is an exchange of information. Art is discussion, a way to transfer, empathize, gain insight, experience, re-experience, resolve, find a way deeper into, and more, both for the creators or channelers or whatever they may be called and for the ones receiving -- readers, viewers, adventurers -- and in between us all lies a space where we meet and merge and mingle and something is exchanged and we are never the same.

Thank you for your support. Thank you for your attention, time, energy, love. Thank you for the hate and negative judgment, too -- they helped me grow, helped me see a mirror where I realized I was, in some ways, M.O.D.O.K. and Snapper (and others, too!) all along. Does it reduce the story when I tell you that I was bullied, and that only now I am resolving my wounds, and that writing SECRET AVENGERS helped me with that? I don't believe it does, no. If anything, I believe that knowing can enhance the act of rereading, but you're also welcome to not bother with integrating. Who am I to tell you how to read a story, any story? I just helped channel it.

And so did others. Thank you, my wonderful collaborators, for making this one of the most joyful creative experiences in my life. Thank you for the act of genuinely engaging in a heartfelt conversation that connected with hearts and minds of many people around the world.

I feel grateful. I met a wave that's taking me somewhere new, and I'm finally learning to surf it. Every character in this story is me, because there's no escaping one's subconscious and unconscious. And maybe, just maybe, every character in this story is also you, because why else would you attract it into your life?

I don't know. I could be right. I could be wrong. I could be somewhere in between us all.

...and what do you believe?

-Ales Kot

What a ride it's been. Thanks to all those who were there through it all and those who got in touch through social media or conventions to say how they were enjoying the book. Thanks to family and friends who gave me unending support, most of all my lovely, beautiful, and patient lady. I really learned so much throughout our run and owe a huge debt to my amazing collaborators who made me a better creator and taught me so very much.

-Michael Walsh

I've colored 40-something issues of SECRET AVENGERS over the last few years, and loved working on every issue. Here's a big THANKS to the readers, writers, artists, letterers, and editors that I've shared this ride with. Secret mission accomplished!

-Matthew Wilson

What a bittersweet moment. SECRET AVENGERS was a joy to work on from start to finish. Not only was it artistically satisfying, but every single person on the creative team is someone I consider a friend, which is rare for me (I don't have many friends. I'm cranky and judgmental). I wish to thank Jon and Wil for their endless patience, Michael and Matt for making the visual things pretty and full of life, and Ales Kot for conceiving this weird story about anxious spies and alien killing machines in love. And the readers. I've never met you, but you seem very nice.

-VC's Clayton Cowles

How can I sum up how much I've enjoyed illustrating covers for SECRET AVENGERS? Easily: I drew M.O.D.O.K. wearing a sombrero, a dolphin with nunchucks, a goat with a missile launcher on its back, and Marvel Super Heroes as fish and received nothing but support along the way. This is a special comic where our imaginations were encouraged to run free, and it was an absolute joy to have been a part of. Thanks to the creative team, editorial staff, and readers. It's been fun!

-Tradd Moore

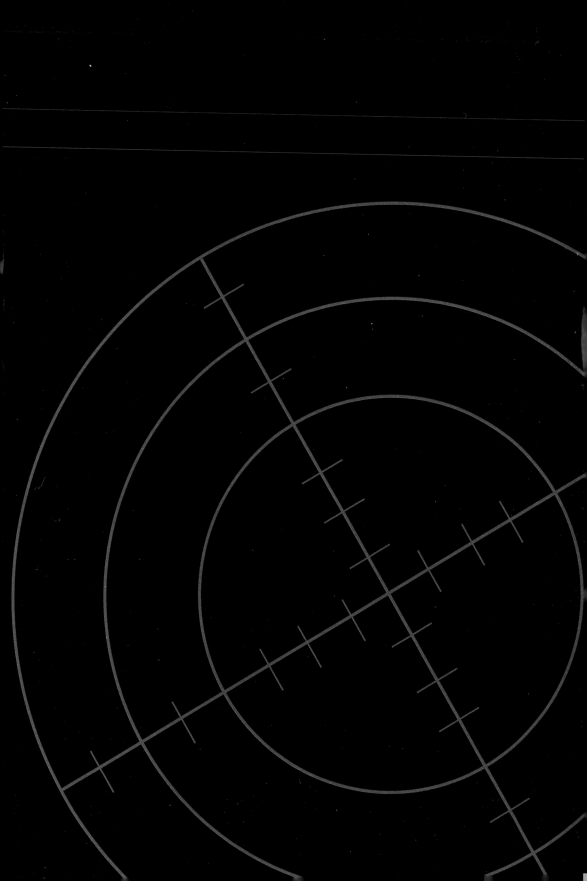

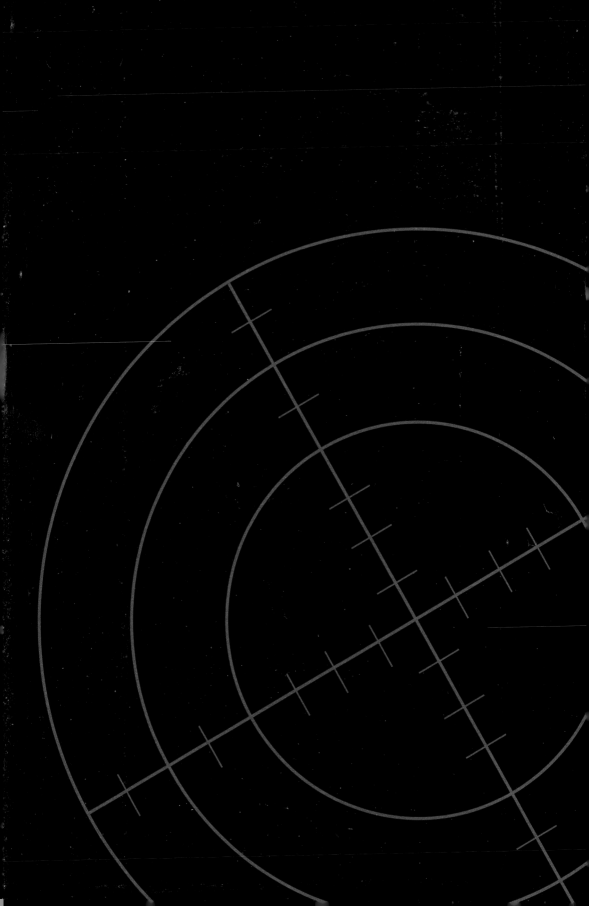